THE *PAST & PRESENT* BOOK SERIES

General Editor
PETER COSS

Body and Tradition
in Nineteenth-Century France

Body and Tradition in Nineteenth-Century France

Félix Arnaudin and the Moorlands of Gascony, 1870–1914

WILLIAM G. POOLEY

OXFORD

UNIVERSITY PRESS

OXFORD
UNIVERSITY PRESS

Great Clarendon Street, Oxford, OX2 6DP,
United Kingdom

Oxford University Press is a department of the University of Oxford.
It furthers the University's objective of excellence in research, scholarship,
and education by publishing worldwide. Oxford is a registered trade mark of
Oxford University Press in the UK and in certain other countries

First Edition published in 2019

Impression: 1

Published in the United States of America by Oxford University Press
198 Madison Avenue, New York, NY 10016, United States of America

British Library Cataloguing in Publication Data
Data available

Library of Congress Control Number: 2019946750

ISBN 978-0-19-884750-2

DOI: 10.1093/oso/9780198847502.001.0001

Printed and bound by
CPI Group (UK) Ltd, Croydon, CR0 4YY

Acknowledgements

My first thanks are to the Archives Départementales des Landes de Gascogne in Mont-de-Marsan, the Musée de Bordeaux, and the Parc Naturel Régional des Landes de Gascogne (PNRLG), who between them hold what remains of Arnaudin's manuscripts and photographs. I owe Hervé Goulaze a debt of gratitude for his help during his time at the PNRLG, and for showing me much of the Landes. Guy Latry of the University of Bordeaux was generous with his time, and I only hope this book does justice to the dedication he has shown to Arnaudin's work.

I would also like to thank the many funding bodies who have funded this research, including the Arts and Humanities Council, the Society for the Study of French History, and the Past and Present Society.

A version of Chapter Three appeared as 'The Singing Postman: The Mobility of Traditional Culture in Nineteenth-Century France', in *Cultural and Social History* 13 (2016), 43–62.

Several people have read parts of this book, or otherwise supported and given critical feedback to the work behind it. I'd like to thank Andrew Berthrong, Paul Cowdell, Julio Decker, James Freeman, Julia Mannherz, Siân Pooley, Nick Stargardt, and Oliver Zimmer. In addition, the following people read full drafts of the whole book, at different stages of development: Robert Bickers, Erika Hanna, Grace Huxford, Gav Jacobson, Josie McLellan, Rob Priest, John Reeks, and Helen Rogers. The insights, questions, and criticisms of my PhD examiners Ruth Harris and Colin Jones shaped this project in ways that I hope they recognize.

The book would not be what it is without the #twitterstorians, and especially many of the ones that I know in real life, including Mark Hailwood, Matt Houlbrook, Laura Sangha, Andrew Smith, and Alison Twells, and also many others involved in blogging and discussing new approaches to history under the #storypast hashtag.

The intellectual influence of David Hopkin on this book will be obvious to anyone familiar with his work. It was David who first suggested folklore as an area of research to me when I was a master's student, and without his supervision, I would never have been able to attempt the doctoral dissertation out of which this book has grown. I am immensely grateful for his support and encouragement during and after the PhD.

Cat Rutter Pooley has had to put up with this research almost as long as she has known me. I hope at least it brings back some good memories of meals and wine shared in southern France. I could not have written it without you.

Contents

List of Illustrations   ix
List of Abbreviations   xi

1. Introduction   1
   The History of the Body   3
   Why the Moorlands?   7
   Folklore Sources and Methods   17
   Structure of the Book   23

2. Arnaudin and the Moorlands   27
   'The Invisible Félix Arnaudin'   29
   Forestation and Folklore   32
   Crafting a Terrain   38
   Fieldwork Methods   42
   Conclusion   47

3. Singers and Storytellers   49
   'My Rustic Collaborators'   50
   Networks   58
   Conclusion   63

4. Body Talk   64
   'From the Mouth of the People'   66
   Body Parts and Fluids   70
   The Unbridled Body   74
   'The Earth Calls to Them'   78
   Language Change   84
   Conclusion   87

5. Monstrous Bodies   89
   Changing Places   90
   The Werewolf Tradition   93
   The Poverty of Horror   97
   Religion, Gender, and Family   101
   Conclusion   106

6. Singing Love   107
   The Shared Culture of Love   109
   'They Eat the Jam, and Blame the Rats'   111
   The Rise of Gossip   117
   Conclusion   123

7. Silence and Chastity   125
   Catherine's Silences   126
   Catholicism   133
   Sewing and Limping   138
   Conclusion   141

8. Exploited Bodies   143
   Foxes and Sharecroppers   144
   The Loyalty of Donkeys   147
   Henri and the Fox   151
   Conclusion   159

9. Conclusion   161
   Stars and Exemplars   162
   Changing Cultures of the Body   164
   The Moorlands and Beyond   166

Bibliography   169
Index   183

List of Illustrations

2.1. Self-portrait of Arnaudin as a young man   30

3.1. Shepherds on stilts watching their flocks   55

4.1. A pine plantation   83

5.1. A typical traditional house in the moorlands   104

6.1. Portrait of three women, most likely singers. The physical resemblance
suggests they might represent three generations of the same family   112

8.1. Babé Plantié and Jean Saubesty, with their son, daughter-in-law,
and grandchildren   149

List of Abbreviations

ADL Archives départementales des Landes de Gascogne

ATU Tale type as catalogued in the Aarne-Thompson-Uther tale type catalogue. See Hans-Jörg Uther, *The Types of International Folktales: A Classification and Bibliography, Based on the System of Antti Aarne and Stith Thompson* (3 vols, Helsinki, 2004)

CPF Paul Delarue, Marie-Louise Tenèze, and Josiane Bru, *Le Conte populaire français: catalogue raisonné des versions de France et des pays de langue française d'outre-mer* (4 vols, Paris, 1957–2000)

ESI *Enquête sur les incendies de forêts dans la region des Landes de Gascogne*, ed. Henri Faré (Paris, 1873)

NFA 'Notes de Félix Arnaudin', Archives départementales des Landes de Gascogne, 2 MI 29

OC Félix Arnaudin, *Oeuvres complètes*, ed. J. Boisgontier, J.-Y. Boutet, B. Fénié, J.-J. Fénié, F. Lalanne, G. Latry, L. Mabru, J.-B. Marquette, and J. Miró (9 vols, Bordeaux, 1994–2007)

RCFTO Patrice Coirault, Georges Delarue, Yvette Fédoroff, and Simone Wallon, *Répertoire des chansons françaises de tradition orale* (3 vols, Paris, 1996–2006)

1

Introduction

In 1893, the American folklorist Alexander Francis Chamberlain declared:

> there is scarcely a spot of the human anatomy to which does not cling some myth
> or legend of the people. No peculiarity has been allowed to go by unnoticed.
> From the hair of his head to the soles of his feet he has been scrutinized, and a
> whole library of books would scarcely contain the lore of the 'folk' regarding
> his every characteristic. From the dimple in his chin to the little white spots
> on his toe-nail, all have been noticed, thought over, and accounted for, not in
> exactly the same way, to be sure, all over the world, but in a manner as ingenious
> as it is characteristic of the 'folk'.[1]

Many French folklorists have echoed his point. Two of the most important
accounts of rural life in France, Philippe Richard and Françoise Loux's *Wisdom
of the Body* and Yvonne Verdier's *Ways of Speaking, Ways of Doing*, put the body
at the centre of their analysis, and the great synthesizer of French folklore, Arnold
van Gennep focused his own research into popular traditions around sexuality,
bodies, and 'rites of passage'.[2]

Historians, too, have taken a bodily turn. In the second half of the twentieth
century, research began to document how the human body itself is historical.
Historians such as Roy Porter argued that not only have ideas about flesh, and
representations of bodies changed over time, but the experiences, and even size
and shape of bodies have transformed in the recent past.[3] The histories of cultures
of embodiment are more than accounts of perception, and as bodily cultures
change, bodies themselves undergo material transformations. The body is not
just the linguistic construction that a generation of historians influenced by

---

[1] A.F. Chamberlain, 'Human Physiognomy and Physical Characteristics in Folk-Lore and Folk-Speech', *Journal of American Folklore*, vi (1893), 13.
[2] Françoise Loux and Philippe Richard, *Sagesses du corps: La Santé et la maladie dans les proverbes* (Paris, 1978).
[3] For a call to arms, see: Roy Porter, 'The History of the Body', in *New Perspectives on Historical Writing*, ed. Peter Burke (London, 1991), 206–32; for examples that have particularly influenced me, see: Ruth Harris, *Lourdes: Body and Spirit in the Secular Age* (New York, 1999); Lyndal Roper, *Oedipus and the Devil: Witchcraft, Sexuality, and Religion in Early Modern Europe* (London, 1994). The point that bodies are physically constructed from food, and that historical nutritional conditions affect the sizes and shapes of bodies is fundamental to historical anthropometrics. See, for instance: Laurent Heyberger, *Santé et développement économique en France au XIXe siècle: essai d'histoire anthropométrique* (Paris, 2003).

Body and Tradition in Nineteenth-Century France: Félix Arnaudin and the Moorlands of Gascony, 1870–1914.
William G. Pooley, Oxford University Press (2019). © William G. Pooley.
DOI: 10.1093/oso/9780198847502.001.0001

post-structuralism explored: it is also a material construction, built out of specific objects, clothes, and food, made through gesture and repeated habit.[4] In this tradition, historians interested in food, clothing, gender, sexuality, health, death, and religion have all contributed to understanding the 'epoch-specific' bodies of our ancestors.[5] For many of these writers, the point of departure is just how different the 'very fleshiness' of past populations was from our own.[6] Although the history of the body is well enough established as a topic for a group of French academics to organize a comprehensive survey entitled simply the *Histoire du Corps*, rural labourers remain absent from the general picture for the nineteenth century.[7] Most of the working population of France was rural until at least 1870, and even in 1900 the balance had only just tipped towards the cities.[8] For most French workers the nineteenth century happened in the countryside, yet historians have had surprisingly little to say about how change happened within rural culture, rather than just to it. My interest is in taking questions and methods about bodies that modern historians have applied to innovators and trend setters, such as urban populations, medical sources, art and literature, and instead turning them to populations and sources that historians too often imagine trapped in an immobile past.[9]

In order to historicize the bodily cultures of the nineteenth-century rural population in France, the focus of this book is on a set of sources that is often considered to provide the best evidence for the stasis of rural culture: folklore. At first glance it might be hard to imagine a source more retrograde than the folklore collections, whose instigators—the folklorists—were often self-consciously anti-modernist. The folklorist at the heart of this research is no exception. Félix Arnaudin

---

[4] Paul Connerton suggests that 'the body is seen to be socially constituted in the sense that it is constructed as an object of knowledge or discourse; but the body is not seen equally clearly to be socially constituted in the sense that it is culturally shaped in its actual practices and behaviour'. Paul Connerton, *How Societies Remember* (Cambridge, 1989), 104; for studies of gesture, see for instance: David Efron, *Gesture, Race, and Culture; a Tentative Study of the Spatio-Temporal and 'Linguistic' Aspects of the Gestural Behavior of Eastern Jews and Southern Italians in New York City, Living under Similar as Well as Different Environmental Conditions* (The Hague, 1972); Yvonne Verdier, *Façons de dire, façons de faire* (Paris, 1979); Polhemus draws attention to the way that 'not only complicated, formalised and ritualised expressions, gestures, postures, etc., but also "simple" bodily activities such as the rate of eye-blinking are culturally learned'. Ted Polhemus, in *The Body as a Medium of Expression: Essays Based on a Course of Lectures given at the Institute of Contemporary Arts, London*, eds. Jonathan Benthall and Ted Polhemus (London, 1975), 17.

[5] Ivan Illich, 'A Plea for Body History (Twelve Years after Medical Nemesis)', *Bulletin of Science, Technology and Society*, vi (1986), 20.

[6] The phrase is from: Annemarie Mol, *The Body Multiple: Ontology in Medical Practice* (Durham, NC, 2003), 25; see, for example: Jan Goldstein, *Hysteria Complicated by Ecstasy: The Case of Nanette Leroux* (Princeton, 2011).

[7] Alain Corbin, Jean-Jacques Courtine, and Georges Vigarello, eds, *Histoire du corps* (3 vols, Paris, 2005–6).

[8] Eugen Weber, *Peasants into Frenchmen: The Modernization of Rural France, 1870–1914* (Stanford, 1976), 8.

[9] Good examples of the work that has been done on nineteenth-century literature and medicine can be found, for instance, in: Catherine Gallagher and Thomas Laqueur, eds, *The Making of the Modern Body: Sexuality and Society in the Nineteenth Century* (Berkeley, 1987).

(1844–1921) could fairly be described as a very late romantic and a conservative. He devoted much of his published work to lamenting the disappearance of what he believed was a simpler way of life that had existed in his own childhood, on his own doorstep, in the moorlands of Gascony. Historians have long recognized the importance of folklore collections of the late nineteenth and early twentieth centuries. Most, however, have shared the folklorists' own opinions, seeing folk traditions as a window into a disappearing and unchanging world, on the brink of being swept away by modern transport, education, and urbanization.[10] But scholarship by folklorists since the 1970s has emphasized the flexibility and adaptability of folklore, showing how individuals and communities make novel uses of tradition. This book is a contribution to a growing field of historians who have adopted the insights of recent folklore research to explore changing folk traditions. This folklore is the high road to an understanding of changing bodily cultures in the nineteenth-century countryside.

The History of the Body

Perhaps the greatest challenge facing historians of bodily experience is finding relevant evidence. This is especially true of writing about the illiterate and the poor, but there are also specific problems with writing about bodies as a topic. The philosopher Drew Leder has pointed out that the body is an 'absent presence'. As the means by which we experience the world, the body itself tends not to be the focus of our attention, unless it is hungry, sick, tired, or aroused.[11] This problem has also been noticed by historians, such as Colin Heywood, who has remarked that French people 'in the nineteenth and even twentieth centuries... [were] generally reticent when it came to discussing their bodies', and this is particularly challenging when dealing with parts of the population who did not write about their own lives.[12] There are very few 'peasants' in the volume of the *Histoire du Corps* that covers the nineteenth century, and little consideration of rural life, or even the differences between town and country, despite the fact that historians have long known that France remained predominantly rural until after 1900.[13]

The accounts written by outsiders about rural life are little help. Travellers during the eighteenth and nineteenth centuries who wrote about the moorlands where Arnaudin collected folklore saw them as a foreign land within the borders of France, whose population were different at the level of their very bodies. Tourists, administrators, and novelists described a feeling of 'affliction' at the

---

[10] The classic study is: Weber, *Peasants into Frenchmen*.
[11] Drew Leder, *The Absent Body* (Chicago, 1990).
[12] Colin Heywood, *Growing up in France: From the Ancien Régime to the Third Republic* (Cambridge, 2007), 269.
[13] Weber, *Peasants into Frenchmen*.

sight of the flat, desolate plains that made up the landscape, going so far as to call it
'the most disgraceful part' of France.[14] They wrote of how this strange landscape
was populated by a race that seemed somehow foreign. The locals were not just
'primitive', 'savage', and uneducated, they were 'small', 'weak', and 'brown'.[15] They
suffered from malnutrition, malaria, and a skin condition known as pellagra, and
their living conditions suggested they were more like beasts than citizens of a
modern nation state.[16] Jacques Sargos has written that in these sources 'the
peasant [of the Landes de Gascogne] is a negative mirror image of a modern
citizen'.[17] Their sexual habits were as heathen as their religious beliefs.[18] In short,
what made the inhabitants of the moorlands different from Frenchmen was not
just their culture or the fact that they spoke a different language: like the 'savage'
'peasants' Eugen Weber described across all of nineteenth-century France, the
rural population of the moors embodied difference. But, as Guy Latry has pointed
out, these sources are deeply problematic. Travellers' accounts often plagiarized
earlier writers without bothering to check their claims, and many of these writers
saw what they wanted to.[19] Their pseudo-colonial accounts may tell historians
more about the outsiders' worldview than what the nineteenth-century moorlands
were really like.[20] Sources written after the moorlands had been transformed into
an industrial forest reinforce a straightforward teleology of reformed landscapes
and reformed bodies. By the end of the century, tourists were more likely to
marvel at the quaintness of the culture of the moorlands than to despair of the
future of their inhabitants.[21] At some point between the middle of the nineteenth
and the start of the twentieth centuries, the 'peasants' of the moorlands had
become modern and 'French', not simply in a cultural sense, but in their flesh.

Lyndal Roper has warned against the dangers of such universalizing teleologies,
which make the history of the body a story of the uneven but steady emergence of

[14] Joseph Lavallée, 'Voyage dans le Département des Landes', in *Les Landes de Bordeaux: moeurs et usages de leurs habitants, suivi de Voyage dans le Département des Landes*, ed. Guy Latry (Pau, 2004), 71; Victor Gaillard, 'L'habitant des Landes', in *Les Français peints par eux-mêmes: encyclopédie morale du 19e siècle* (Paris, 1841), ii, 413.
[15] Gaillard, 'L'habitant des Landes', 414; Edmond About, *Maître Pierre* (4th edn, Bordeaux, 1862), 27; Jean-Pierre Lescarret, *La Vie dans la Grande-Lande au temps des bergers et des loups* (Pau, 2008), 82.
[16] On pellagra, see: Lescarret, *La Vie dans la Grande-Lande au temps des bergers et des loups*, 85–7.
[17] See: Jacques Sargos, *Histoire de la forêt landaise: du désert à l'âge d'or* (Bordeaux, 1997), 60, 81.
[18] On loose sexual morals, see, for instance: M. de Caila, 'Recherches sur les moeurs des habitants des Landes de Bordeaux, dans la contrée connue ci-devant sous le nom du Captalat de Buch', in *Mémoires de l'Académie Celtique*, iv (1809), 70–82; on the religious question, see: E. Mangin, La Situation religieuse des Landes au milieu du IIème Empire', *Bulletin de la Société de Borda* (1950), 68–73.
[19] Guy Latry, 'Deux voyageurs de l'an VI dans les Landes de Gascogne', in *Les Landes de Bordeaux: Moeurs et usages de leurs habitants, suivi de Voyage dans le département des Landes*, ed. Guy Latry (Pau, 2004), 7–27.
[20] This is not to say that this is the same thing as colonialism, simply that the logics were similar. For a comparison, see: Michael Taussig, 'Culture of Terror—Space of Death: Roger Casement's Putumayo Report and the Explanation of Torture', *Comparative Studies in Society and History*, xxvi (1984), 467–97.
[21] The narrative is not unchallenged by historians such as: Lescarret, *La Vie dans la Grande-Lande*; Sargos, *Histoire de la forêt landaise*.

'modern' attitudes to flesh.[22] According to this account, from an 'old regime', where the body was both more open to its environment and less individualized, European societies have slowly moved to a closed and individualized body. The anthropologist David le Breton, for instance, has written that:

> The modern body is a different kind of thing [from the bodies of other times and places]. It is based on severing the subject from others (an individualist social structure), from the cosmos (the physical components of the body are no longer related to other cosmic bodies), and from itself (having a body rather than being the body). The Western body is a site of isolation, the objective enclosure of the sovereign Ego.[23]

This developmental view of the history of the body sees 'modernity' as a set of complex and connected social and cultural changes. But this breadth and imprecision is the weakness of understanding the changes to bodies as a progression towards modernity.

The medical profession stands at the centre of these accounts. For Michel Foucault, psychiatry, sexology, and medicine endowed sex 'with an inexhaustible and polymorphous causal power'.

> [S]ex gradually became an object of great suspicion; the general and disquieting meaning that pervades our conduct and our existence, in spite of ourselves; the point of weakness where evil portents reach through to us; the fragment of darkness that we each carry within us: a general signification, a universal secret, an omnipresent cause, a fear that never ends.[24]

Where before there had been sexual practices, people now came to understand their own identities in sexual terms. Before the triumph of sexuality, rural communities seem to have tolerated experimentation such as fellatio and masturbation among heterosexual youths, and even allowed young men and women to share beds. Increasingly, sexuality was associated with risk, as syphilis and other venereal diseases began to play more prominent roles as cultural fears.[25] In the place of an older pluralism and permissiveness when it came to sexuality, a binary vision of heterosexual bodily complementarity triumphed.[26]

---

[22] Roper, *Oedipus and the Devil*, 1–16.
[23] David Le Breton, *Anthropologie du corps et modernité* (6th edn, Paris, 2011), 11.
[24] Michel Foucault, *The History of Sexuality*, trans. Robert Hurley (3 vols, 1998), i, 65, 69.
[25] Alain Corbin, 'La Rencontre des corps', in *Histoire du corps*, eds. Jean-Jacques Courtine, Georges Vigarello, and Alain Corbin (3 vols, Paris, 2005–6), ii, 187–9, 210–4.
[26] Thomas Laqueur, *Making Sex: Body and Gender from the Greeks to Freud* (Cambridge, MA, 1990); Sara Matthews-Grieco, 'Corps et sexualité dans l'Europe d'ancien régime', in *Histoire du Corps*, eds. Alain Corbin, Jean-Jacques Courtine, and Georges Vigarello (3 vols, Paris, 2005–6), i, 234.

Other historians have emphasized the benefits of the advent of the modern body. Before the twentieth century, for most workers, life was gruelling. The body was, in the words of Roy Porter, 'rank, foul and dysfunctional; for all of medicine's best efforts, it was frequently racked with pain, disability and disease; and death might well be nigh'.[27] Disease 'was man's common condition', a condition probably worsened by the complete disregard of the general population for any sort of hygienic practices.[28] Before the 'Pasteurian Revolution', the popular classes washed very infrequently.[29] According to Guy Thuillier, this reluctance to wash the hair or body, which was characteristic of 'the old regime of hygiene', continued much later than historians might expect. Despite the efforts of the Third Republic, or 'the Republic of Hygiene', very few people had access to or much apparent interest in dental care, regularly changed linen, or washing at the start of the twentieth century.[30]

Poor nutrition was coupled with this poor hygiene. Most of the population depended on the 'necessary evil' of grain.[31] Until the end of the nineteenth century, hunger was general. As Eugen Weber wrote, 'everywhere [hunger] shaped behaviour, attitudes, and decisions'.[32] Nutrition was so poor that it stunted the growth of army conscripts up until the First World War.[33] Such shortages encouraged a cultural belief in 'limited good'. According to the anthropologist George Foster, rural cultures do not simply believe that food is scarce; they extend this belief in scarcity into all domains of life. Honour, affection, health, and luck are also perceived to be limited, leading to a situation where the success of any individual is necessarily perceived to come at a cost to all of that individual's neighbours.[34]

This material hardship translated into harsh attitudes. For historians such as Jean Flandrin, Lawrence Stone, and Philippe Ariès, pre-modern people were less loving, and quicker to anger.[35] In the rural Finnish case studied by Laura Stark, it seems that anger was not so much an individual emotion as an involuntary social

[27] Roy Porter, *Flesh in the Age of Reason* (London, 2004), 25.
[28] William Coleman, 'The People's Health: Medical Themes in Eighteenth-Century French Popular Literature', *Bulletin of the History of Medicine*, li (1977), 72–3.
[29] Olivier Faure, 'Le Regard des médecins', in *Histoire du corps*, eds. Jean-Jacques Courtine, Georges Vigarello, and Alain Corbin (3 vols, Paris, 2005–6), ii, 47; Nicole Pellegrin, 'Corps du commun, usages communs du corps', in *Histoire du Corps*, eds. Alain Corbin, Jean-Jacques Courtine, and Georges Vigarello (3 vols, Paris, 2005–6), i, 145.
[30] Guy Thuillier, 'Pour une histoire de l'hygiène corporelle: Un exemple régional: le Nivernais', *Revue d'Histoire Économique et Sociale*, xlvi (1968), 232–53.
[31] Jacques Mulliez, 'Du Blé, 'mal nécessaire'. Réflexions sur les progrès de l'agriculture de 1750 à 1850', *Revue d'Histoire Moderne et Contemporaine*, xxvi (1979), 3–47.
[32] Weber, *Peasants into Frenchmen*, 17.
[33] Heyberger, *Santé et développement*; Jean-Paul Aron, Paul Dumont, and Emmanuel Le Roy Ladurie, *Anthropologie du conscrit français d'après les comptes numériques et sommaires du recrutement de l'armée, 1819–1826* (Paris, 1972).
[34] George Foster, 'Peasant Society and the Image of Limited Good', *American Anthropologist*, lxvii (1965), 293–315.
[35] Philippe Ariès, *Centuries of Childhood: A Social History of Family Life* (London, 1965); Jean Louis Flandrin, *Familles: Parenté, maison, sexualité dans l'ancienne société* (Paris, 1976); Lawrence Stone, *The Family, Sex and Marriage in England, 1500–1800* (New York, 1977).

response that suggested strength.[36] Eugen Weber argued that 'violence was a fact of everyday life, and that it receded only slowly and then selectively'. The inter-village fights described in autobiographies and horrified administrative sources from the nineteenth century seem to confirm his judgement.[37] In this rough bodily culture, there was a widespread distrust of the disabled, which extended into neglect from carers or outright abuse.[38] These accounts suggest that before modernity, the body was above all a burden, a cage, a wound.

But the straightforward chronology of the emergence of the modern body should give historians pause, not least in light of the large body of work by historians of religion and medicine who have called into question 'secularization' and 'medicalization'.[39] These processes were more uneven and slower than historians once assumed, and there is considerable disagreement over how useful they are for understanding the crucible of the nineteenth century, when the modern body is supposed to have emerged.[40] The particular challenge that this teleology poses to rural historians is that it risks making 'peasants' embody the 'tradition' against which modern bodies were progressively defined.[41] It is true that some aspects of nineteenth-century rural bodily culture are opaque to twenty-first century researchers. Witchcraft and werewolves make little sense to audiences accustomed to thinking of these phenomena as Hollywood entertainment. The grind of agricultural labour was central to the worldview of men and women in the moorlands, yet it is distant from my everyday life. Alain Corbin has warned historians that even basic experiences such as 'light and darkness, hot and cold' held different meanings for our recent ancestors.[42] Historians know that the basic feelings of the body may have changed in the last two centuries, but have only recently begun to address the questions of how and why.

Why the Moorlands?

There are two reasons why the moorlands of Gascony make a particularly compelling example for exploring changing rural cultures of the body. The first

[36] Laura Stark, *The Magical Self: Body, Society and the Supernatural in Early-Modern Finland* (Helsinki, 2006), 57, 221.
[37] Weber, *Peasants into Frenchmen*, 54, 56–7, 385.   [38] Ibid., 150, 175.
[39] For example, see: Harris, *Lourdes*; Faure, 'Le Regard des médecins'.
[40] The idea of the nineteenth century as the crucial turning point appears in, for instance: Jacques Le Goff and Nicolas Truong, *Une Histoire du corps au moyen âge* (Paris, 2009), 203; it is also key to Michel Foucault's many works, including: Michel Foucault, *Discipline and Punish: The Birth of the Prison*, trans. Alan Sheridan (new edn, London, 1991).
[41] For the same point, see Hull's sensitive critique of Barbara Duden: Isabel V. Hull, 'Review: The Body as Historical Experience: Review of Recent Works by Barbara Duden', *Central European History*, xxiix (1995), 76–7.
[42] Alain Corbin, *The Life of an Unknown: The Rediscovered World of a Clog Maker in Nineteenth-Century France*, trans. Arthur Goldhammer (New York, 2001), 24.

is the extensive ethnographic research undertaken there by Félix Arnaudin between around 1873 and 1914. Arnaudin himself came to regret the ambition of his own project, and increasingly felt that his life's work had been a failure.[43] Having spent more than four decades and most of his money trying to document the culture and traditions of his native moorlands in Gascony, he had little to show for his efforts. Before his death in 1921, he had published only a tiny selection of the songs, stories, proverbs, and local dialect notes that he had amassed. While he was known to specialists at the time and was the subject of an obituary by the folklorist Césaire Daugé, his published works do not compare to the most important folklore publications of the period, such as Paul Sébillot's *Le Folk-lore de France*, which appeared between 1904 and 1906, and Arnold van Gennep's *Les Rites de passage*, first published in 1908.[44] But the value of Arnaudin's folklore collecting partly comes from his failure to publish most of his research. It is the uncertainties, contradictions, and downright mess of Arnaudin's notes—only recently, and still partially, edited into a complete works—that makes them of such value to historians. Rather than the polished, tidied, and edited versions of the songs, stories, proverbs, and everyday speech he heard, his notes are as close as we can get to an attempt to faithfully record speech as it was spoken. They include thousands of song texts, as well as stories, proverbs, and direct speech noted down from over 700 people who lived in the area within walking and cycling distance of Arnaudin's house, and represent a huge source for a cultural historian, filled with materials exploring changing experiences of embodiment.

The second reason why the moorlands make such an interesting example is that they can be considered an exaggerated example of similar changes that happened elsewhere in France, and Europe. The moorlands had long been seen by reformers as a sterile desert that required benevolent outside intervention. Many outsider accounts from the eighteenth and nineteenth centuries exoticized and caricatured the agro-pastoralist population, presenting them as 'Hottentots' or 'Arabs' living within the modern nation, or even beasts and savages.[45] Guided by ideas about the formative influence of landscape over bodies, novelists and utopian schemers from the early nineteenth century onwards dreamt of saving these unfortunate and unhappy men and women from the wretched swamps and deserted moors they inhabited.[46] The simplest solution was the one that was eventually adopted: a national law was passed ordering the moorlands to be auctioned, drained, and

---

[43] Throughout the book, I call Arnaudin by his surname, but use the names he himself used to refer to his informants, which were often first names or nicknames. For an explanation of this choice, see p. C3.P8.

[44] He merited, for instance, an obituary by the folklorist Césaire Daugé: Césaire Daugé, 'Félix Arnaudin: 1844–1921', *Bulletin de La Société de Borda* (1922), 1–5. He also corresponded with many of the better-known folklorists of his generation, including Sébillot. See *OC*, v.

[45] Sargos, *Histoire de la forêt landaise*, 57–61; Weber, *Peasants into Frenchmen*, 3–22.

[46] For examples of the utopian novelists, see: Jean-Baptiste Lescarret, *Le Dernier pasteur des Landes: Étude de moeurs* (Bordeaux, 1858); About, *Maître Pierre*.

planted with maritime pine trees, at the expense of the sheep that had been central to local ways of life.[47] At the same time as these broad environmental changes were imposed from above, the moorlands underwent pronounced demographic and social transitions that saw both family life and work transform dramatically. Similar changes to landscape, family, and work can be identified in many rural regions, but their speed and scale in the moorlands make the region a useful case study for thinking about changing cultures of the body from below, and the Arnaudin manuscripts are an ideal source base.[48]

The department of the Landes de Gascogne was one of the original eighty-three departments created in 1790. Although it was named after the moorlands, the department did not include all of them. The northern tip of moors stretches into the department of the Gironde, and their eastern reaches fall within the Lot-et-Garonne. The heart of the moorlands was the area that Arnaudin referred to as the Grande-Lande, a vast open plain, with only a very few pine trees at the start of the nineteenth century, unlike the heavily planted coastal region of the Marensin.[49] It was this area of open moorland that underwent a set of environmental reforms in the nineteenth century which involved draining the landscape and creating the largest man-made forest in Europe.[50] This environmental change depended on a revolution in landholding, as vast areas that had previously belonged to local communities were sold to private investors, first during the French Revolution, and then much more widely following a national law passed in 1857. In turn, this privatization of the commons encouraged the survival, and even extension, of a system of sharecropping that historians have argued perpetuated neo-feudal social and economic relations in the countryside.[51] Yet, at the same time, the forest created a new industry of resin farming, and along with it a new working class. Having been a region of relative political moderation in the mid-nineteenth century, the moorlands hosted a passionate syndicalist movement by the start of the twentieth century.[52]

These cross-cutting, and sometimes contradictory changes to the environment, landholding, work, and class practices cannot be reduced to the binaries such as

[47] Samuel Temple, 'The Natures of Nation: Negotiating Modernity in the Landes de Gascogne', *French Historical Studies*, xxxii (2009), 419–46.

[48] For an example of an author who has argued that the moorlands were perhaps the most dramatic example, see: Graham Robb, *The Discovery of France: A Historical Geography from the Revolution to the First World War* (New York: Norton, 2007), 268.

[49] See the maps Jean Thore produced at the start of the nineteenth century: *Promenade sur les côtes du Golfe de Gascogne ou aperçu topographique, physique et médical des côtes occidentales de ce même Golfe* (Bordeaux, 1810), 6–7, 177–8.

[50] Roger Sargos, *Contribution à l'histoire du boisement des Landes de Gascogne* (Bordeaux, 1949); Sargos, *Histoire de la forêt landaise*.

[51] Pierre Massé, 'Survivances des droits féodaux dans l'ouest (1793–1902)', *Annales Historiques de La Révolution Française* (1965), 270–98; Albert Soboul, 'Survivances "féodales" dans la société rurale du XIXe siècle', *Annales* 23, no. 5 (1968), 965–86.

[52] Robert Desbordes, *Les Syndicats résiniers dans les Landes* (Bordeaux, 1908).

'modernity' and 'tradition'. Sharecropping, for instance, was a traditional, and often informal practice that could take the form of an oral agreement or customary understanding. Yet sharecropping also expanded with the project of industrial forestation and the growth of a divide between employers and employees. In a similar way, although forestation has often been perceived as an innovation, evidence for resin farming in the region dates back to the fourth century.[53] Nor does an opposition between the 'state' and 'peasants' make good sense. Evidence for widespread resistance from below to state-led environmental reforms is surprisingly rare. Individual sharecroppers, pastoralists, landowners, and labourers played multiple roles in the complex processes that transformed the moors into the industrial forest. Understanding these environmental changes and the social transformation that accompanied them is an important context for interpreting Arnaudin's folklore collections, but these traditions have surprisingly little to tell historians about how ordinary workers felt about forestation, perhaps because these feelings were muted, or perhaps because they were complex and contradictory.

In fact, regional specialists have questioned the dramatic narratives of a barren desert instantly transformed—against the will of locals—into a pine forest by the 1857 law. As both Jacques Sargos and Jean-Pierre Lescarret have pointed out, there is no question that pines were already being farmed for resin in the region during the early-modern period, even if the majority of the region remained open moorland. Towards the end of the eighteenth century, however, plantation gathered pace, as innovators realized that the pine tree provided a solution to the problem of the migratory dunes of the Atlantic coast. Powered by the wind, these dunes clogged useful watercourses, or even marched inland across the open plains.[54] In this way, planting the dunes with pines served two purposes: it fixed the landscape into place, and provided both resin and wood. But the main impediment to further forestation during this period remained transport. Without direct access to a watercourse, neither resin farming nor the production of wood was economically viable, so there was little reason for the pine trees to spread much further than the coast and along the rivers of the moorlands.[55] For this geographical reason, the Revolutionary assault on the commons that has been so important to the historiography of the rural environment only had a limited impact in the moorlands.[56] Unlike regions of established forests, where the peasantry was blamed for their 'misguided greed' in devastating existing communal woodlands during the Revolution and its aftermath, the common lands of the south-west were not forests, but moorland. If investors had been interested in

[53] Sargos, *Histoire de la forêt landaise*, 109.
[54] Sargos, *Histoire de la forêt landaise*, 261–84.
[55] Lescarret, *La Vie dans la Grande-Lande*, 154–5.
[56] Kieko Matteson, *Forests in Revolutionary France: Conservation, Community, and Conflict, 1669–1848* (Cambridge, 2015).

privatizing them during the Revolution, it would have been in order to plant them with trees. They were not, and the communal moors were relatively untouched by the Revolutionary reforms.[57]

At the start of the nineteenth century, the region was among the most sparsely populated in France, with an average of under fourteen people per square kilometre, compared to the national average of fifty. This reflected the continuing predominance of moorland, which covered 60 per cent of the region, even after the Revolutionaries' attempts to privatize the common lands. Only 18 per cent of the area was planted with pine trees, and just 8 per cent was under the plough.[58] This division of the landscape was the basis for an agricultural system that only just exceeded subsistence, and actively depended on using the common moorlands for pastoralism. While sheep and goats were not very profitable in terms of wool or meat, they provided the manure that farmers needed to grow crops. Most families would have supplemented this diet with the fish and game that were abundant in the moorlands, and many men would also have worked as resin farmers. This system of agro-sylvo-pastoralism depended on all three elements— pines, sheep, and farming. It was a way of life that constantly struggled against the sandy soil of the moorlands, which flooded in winters, dried out in the summers, and contained little organic matter to fertilize crops. Just how difficult that life was can be glimpsed through the subsistence statistics available for the moorlands. Jean Cailluyer has calculated that the wages in the village of Sore in the early nineteenth century would have left the average family with an annual deficit of 62.50 francs, meaning that survival depended on foraging and farming to supplement this income.[59] Edmond About's 1858 novel *Maître Pierre*, which reads more like an agricultural manual than a fictional adventure, summed up the situation: 'It's a bad deal for everyone, for the State, for the landowners, for the farmers, and for the sheep!'[60]

From the eighteenth century onwards, the moorlands, like other 'barren' regions, became an increasingly important concern for reformers. The Physiocrats objected to marshlands and moors that they considered unproductive and useless, sheep notwithstanding. Their intellectual heirs in the nineteenth century combined this with ideas drawn from German forestry science to advocate for direct state intervention to create uniform forests, consisting of regimented plantations

---

[57]   Peter McPhee, '"The Misguided Greed of Peasants"? Popular Attitudes to the Environment in the Revolution of 1789', *French Historical Studies*, 24, no. 2 (20 March 2001), 247–69; Lescarret, *La Vie dans la Grande-Lande*, 106, 187; Noelle L. Plack, 'Agrarian Individualism, Collective Practices and the French Revolution: The Law of 10 June 1793 and the Partition of Common Land in the Department of the Gard', *European History Quarterly*, 35, no. 1 (1 January 2005), 45; Noelle Plack, 'Environmental Issues during the French Revolution: Peasants, Politics and Village Common Land', *Australian Journal of French Studies*, 47, no. 3 (2010), 294.

[58]   Lescarret, *La Vie dans la Grande-Lande*, 18–19, 20.

[59]   Jean Cailluyer, *Regards sur l'histoire sociale des Landes* (Toulouse, 1983), 20–2.

[60]   About, *Maître Pierre*, 38–9.

of individual species. These forests should, the reformers believed, be created in areas such as the moorlands, where the soil was too poor for agriculture.[61] These ideas combined with the mid-nineteenth-century drive for internal colonization to produce the 1857 law.[62] The law was designed to encourage local communities to sell their moorlands to private investors, who would then drain and plant the land with pine trees. Measures intended to overcome previous obstacles to plantation included plans for new roads and railway lines that would make the forest more accessible. The investors would reap huge profits, the communities would receive a large windfall which they could put towards schools, churches, and the new roads, and the local population would be saved from themselves.

Reformers not only envisaged reforming a barren territory, but also sought to improve the bodily health of notoriously tiny and malnourished locals.[63] The novelist Jean-Baptiste Lescarret described the horror outsiders felt on encountering these throwbacks: 'The girls begin losing their teeth at fifteen. The whole population is rotting where it stands, like a tree with its roots in water.'[64] In this way of thinking, improving the health and vigour of the local population was the same thing as environmental reform. Lescarret's novel dramatized this through the utopian vision of a young engineer named Henri, who was probably modelled on the real-life reformer Henri Crouzet (1817–80). Draining the moorlands and planting pine trees, Lescarret's hero believed, was a solution to the malnutrition, disease, and weakness of the local population. Similarly, in About's novel *Maître Pierre*, the reformers go so far as to declare that technological innovations such as canals would 'get rid of diseases such as pellagra, fevers, and all other known illnesses, except old age'. 'This poor landscape, which has long been neglected like an incurable patient, has finally found its doctors.'[65] The solitary shepherds perched on their stilts would be replaced by 'a robust and joyous population', and from the 1870s onwards, even some doctors were cautiously optimistic that this change really had come about, and that reform of the landscape really had benefited local health.[66]

The changes to the local economy and landscape are easier to measure. Between them, the three departments of the moorlands had around 184,000 hectares of forest before 1853. Between 1853 and 1873, the area under forest more than

---

[61] See: Tamara L. Whited, *Forests and Peasant Politics in Modern France* (New Haven, 2001), 2–3, 27–59 for the summary of the development of the ideas of the Physiocrats and German forestry science.

[62] Hugh D. Clout, *The Land of France, 1815–1914* (London, 1983), 48, 52–5; Sargos, *Histoire de la forêt landaise*, 59–60.

[63] The other obvious motivation would be nationalism. See: Julien Aldhuy, 'Imaginaire géographique, idéologie territoriale et production régionale: Réflexions autour des Landes de Gascogne (XVIIIème–XIXème)', *Hegoa* (2006), http://halshs.archives-ouvertes.fr/halshs-00080645/.

[64] Lescarret, *Le Dernier pasteur des Landes*, 71. There was clearly some truth in this. Jean Cailluyer found that an incredible 73.5 per cent of conscripts in Parentis in 1859 had cavities. Cailluyer, *Regards sur l'histoire sociale des Landes*, 24.

[65] About, *Maître Pierre*, 250, 13.

[66] Lescarret, *Le Dernier pasteur des Landes*, 52; *ESI*, xli; Urbain Guérin, 'Paysan-résinier de Lévignacq (Landes)', in *Les Ouvriers des deux mondes*, v (1884), 52.

tripled, to 604,000 hectares.[67] This massive expansion in the pine plantations came at the expense of pastoralism. In 1789 there were 319,000 sheep as well as 13,900 goats in the moorlands. By 1832, this had risen to 440,000 sheep, and in 1852, the numbers peaked at 540,000 sheep and 34,000 goats. The decline triggered by the 1857 law was rapid: by 1892 there were just 300,000 sheep left.[68] With fewer sheep, the local population would lack the manure to fertilize the crops they needed to survive.[69] The reformers did not understand the local cultural attitudes to the landscape, grounded in the most basic bodily needs of the population.[70] Mass forestation did not just threaten the food supply, but brought greater risks of fire, drought, and other ecological imbalances.

The expanding system of sharecropping worked to mask, but not alleviate, the growing conflicts between pines and sheep, and sharecroppers and landlords. Under sharecropping contracts, landowners normally leased land to a family group. Sometimes the landowner might also provide some tools, seed, or animals, as well. Rather than a monetary rent, the sharecropper would give the landowner a proportion—normally half—of their crop. Sharecropping had proved a difficult issue for the revolutionaries in the 1790s. Although it was widely recognized to be exploitative, the revolutionaries settled on the view that it was a private contract between individuals.[71] Yet, within these private contracts survived some of the most hated elements of the feudal system. The feudal charge called the *dîme*, for instance, was officially abolished in 1789, but some landlords simply wrote a *néo-dîme* into sharecropping contracts. References to this *néo-dîme* can be found in sharecropping agreements up until the twentieth century.[72] The sources that historians have suggest that the endurance of sharecropping was deeply resented in many parts of France. One of the semi-fictionalized 'peasant' characters in Émile Guillaumin's *La Vie d'un simple* bitterly exclaims 'we are just as much slaves now as we were in the old days'.[73] By the close of the nineteenth century, the moorlands had the highest density in France of shareholdings. In 1882, 46 per cent of farmers in the department of the Landes were sharecroppers, a proportion that was double that of any other department.[74] Far from being in decline, Jacques

[67] *ESI*, vi.
[68] These numbers are a combination of the statistics in: Sargos, *Histoire de la forêt landaise*, 418 and Sargos, *Contribution à l'histoire du boisement des Landes de Gascogne*, 437.
[69] As some of the more perceptive respondents to the Faré inquiry noted. *ESI*, 111–2, 198.
[70] On the failure of the reformers to understand local uses of space, see: Alice Garner, *A Shifting Shore: Locals, Outsiders, and the Transformation of a French Fishing Town, 1823–2000* (Ithaca, 2005), especially 17; Marie-Dominique Ribéreau-Gayon, 'Perceptions sensorielles et représentations des Landes de Gascogne', in *Le Littoral gascon et son arrière-pays* (Arcachon, 1993), especially 153.
[71] Peter Jones, *Liberty and Locality in Revolutionary France: Six Villages Compared, 1760–1820* (Cambridge, 2003), 251.
[72] Soboul, 'Survivances "féodales" dans la société rurale du XIXe siècle', 975.
[73] Émile Guillaumin, *La Vie d'un simple* (new edn, Paris, 1977 [1904]), 126.
[74] Annie Moulin, *Peasantry and Society in France since 1789* (Cambridge, 1991), 113; Clout, *The Land of France, 1815–1914*, 37–8.

Sargos has described sharecropping in the region as being 'the instrument of a conquering modernity'.[75]

It was an ambivalent instrument, both heightening and repressing conflicts between landowners and workers. It repressed direct confrontations by encouraging clientelism, as the sharecropper's interests should align with the landlord's interests in terms of the profitability of the farm. The sharecropper was also under pressure to curry favour with the landlord, due to the wide-ranging powers landlords had over the buildings, tools, and even family life of the tenants. And this clientelism continued down the economic hierarchy below the sharecropper, who had to manage the labour of his own family, as well as any hired hands they needed during the year. The voting patterns of the moorlands in the nineteenth century suggest that this clientelism was relatively well ingrained, with most communities opting for conservative candidates in the crucial period of the establishment of the Second Republic and then Second Empire. While some aspects of the sharecropping system therefore worked to repress conflict, others also heightened hidden resentments. There were examples of communities in the moorlands who tended to vote for secular, republican candidates, and the village of Sore even voted against the plebiscite that established Louis-Napoleon as emperor in 1852.[76] But rather than democratic politics, it was a quirk in the application of sharecropping that would eventually bring these grievances into the open: most sharecropping agreements covered the agricultural production of the farm, but not the pine resin, which was paid by the barrel. The element of piece work within the sharecropping system meant that fluctuations in the value of pine resin could create a situation in which workers as a whole found their interests were in conflict with landowners. The first time this happened was in the 1860s. The American Civil War removed the largest competing source of pine resin from the European markets, leading to rapid rises in the price of resin. Few landowners passed this price rise onto their workers, instead attempting to reduce the percentage they received per barrel of resin. The result was civil unrest, and things were only destined to get worse.[77] With the end of the Civil War, American pine resin flooded back onto the European market, and resin prices collapsed.[78] Unwilling to share the profits in the good times, the landowners were no more likely to protect their workers from the fall in prices.

This was the context for a series of devastating forest fires between 1869 and 1872. Between 1869 and 1872 over 24,000 hectares burned down in the department of the Landes alone, and the damage was even more catastrophic in the parts

---

[75] Sargos, *Histoire de la forêt landaise*, 212; Lescarret, *La Vie dans la Grande-Lande*, 110.

[76] These details on voting patterns can be found in: Lescarret, *La Vie dans la Grande-Lande*, 257.

[77] For a first-hand account, see Pierre Toulgouat, 'La vie d'autrefois d'après les souvenirs du "Bielhot de Sabres", dernier tisserand des Landes', *Bulletin de la Société de Borda* (1986), 183–220.

[78] Sargos, *Histoire de la forêt landaise*, 492–8.

of the moorlands in the Gironde, which had also been affected by the 1857 law.[79] Many of the local landowners and experts who gave evidence to the inquiry into the fires published in 1873 by the *conseiller d'état* Henri Faré were in agreement about their cause: dramatically dispossessed of their pastures by the 1857 law encouraging the forestation of the moorlands, the shepherds were seeking to take the land back by fire. There is some evidence that disgruntled locals were responsible for some of the fires, and this has meant that the most important historians of the region have accepted—with reservations—the idea of a battle between pastoralism and the pine.[80] Some arsonists were caught, many incendiary devices supposedly discovered, and shepherds had an obvious motive: in burning the forests they would regain the pastures they needed for their sheep.[81]

By the end of the nineteenth century, reformers hardly seemed to have gained a better understanding of the challenges of sharecropping and the agro-sylvo-pastoralism of the moorlands. The fires continued, as did the utopian schemes, such as a plan to flood the region with water from the Pyrenees in order to bring nutrients into the soil.[82] This disconnect between reformers and the struggles of the working population helps to explain the surprise that greeted the emergence of a syndicalist movement in the moorlands. Much like the 1860s, the steep rise in resin prices of the start of the twentieth century was not always passed on to resin collectors. But since the 1860s the rural syndicalist movement had provided templates for workers to organize. In the event, the first syndicate came about by accident, when a local judge from Sabres embarked on a fact-finding mission among the resin workers in the first years of the twentieth century. In Luglon, his enquiries encouraged the local sharecroppers to draw up a petition aimed at addressing their grievances. The judge responded that he was not acting in an official capacity and could do nothing about them, and it seemed the matter was closed. But rumours began to circulate that the sharecroppers of Luglon had formed a syndicate, on the suggestion of the judge. When the sharecroppers in nearby Arjuzanx heard about this, they decided to follow suit. Although they did not carry their plan through, the sharecroppers in Lit-et-Mixte did, founding the first syndicate in January 1906 and immediately launching a strike against the landowners. By December of the same year, there were thirty-two

---

[79] *ESI*, viii, 347.

[80] Most importantly: Sargos, *Histoire de la forêt landaise*, 499–500.

[81] It is worth noting, however, that when one specialist studied arson in the Grande Lande, out of thirteen fires between 1880 and 1935, they could only identify two arsons. E. Lafon, discussed in: Bernard Traimond, 'Le Feu est dans la lande, ou l'incendie comme fait social', *Revue Forestière Française*, 32 (1980), 335. I have not systematically researched criminal arson cases in the incomplete criminal trial records in the ADL.

[82] 'Les Incendies dans les forêts de pin maritime', *Revue des Eaux et Forêts* (1900), 340–1; E. Blanc, 'Les Landes, leur passé et leur avenir', *Revue des Eaux et Forêts* (1893), 401–27.

syndicates representing resin collectors in the moorlands.[83] The sharecroppers had found a voice.

Before the syndicalist movement was established, what did the sharecroppers think of these changes as they were unfolding, in the second half of the nineteenth century? In a recent book advocating using folklore as a historical source, David Hopkin has warned historians to allow 'historical actors...to voice judgements about what mattered in their own lives'.[84] Key historians of environmental change and rural politics in France have argued that culture provides the key to under-standing reform of the landscape and the spread of democratic politics in the nineteenth century.[85] But that is not the approach this book takes. Folk traditions were not silent on the question of environmental change, and sometimes even addressed questions of contemporary politics directly. But neither topic accounts for a great deal of local folklore. Rather than using culture to help understand something else, why not study it for its own sake?

This is not an argument about the importance of politics and environmental change to people in the region. Both could be deeply important, as the historians who have drawn on administrative sources from the region have shown.[86] But there are reasons why these issues may not have made good material for folk traditions. The tensions between sharecroppers and landowners were very real, but the environmental reforms did not map easily onto support for forestation, or resistance. As in other regions, such as the Corbières, Lorraine, or the Ariège, different individuals stood to lose or gain by enclosing the commons.[87] Depending on the price of resin, how many sheep they owned, or how many family members they had at their disposal, sharecroppers made different decisions about the desirability of forestation and could change their minds. As for politics, as Peter Jones has pointed out, it should not surprise historians if national politics left rural communities cold.[88] The changes of the nineteenth century were translated into rural culture in different terms. Most importantly, the folklore that Arnaudin collected dealt in the challenges of a changing culture of the body.

---

[83] This is a summary of Desbordes, *Les Syndicats résiniers dans les landes*, 80–2, 5. Desbordes based his account on the recollections of local people, and does not, for instance, provide exact dates for when the judge from Sabres conducted his inquiries.

[84] David M. Hopkin, *Voices of the People in Nineteenth-Century France* (Cambridge, 2012), 253.

[85] Maurice Agulhon, *The Republic in the Village: The People of the Var from the French Revolution to the Second Republic* (Cambridge, 1982); Peter Jones, *Politics and Rural Society: The Southern Massif Central, c. 1750–1880* (Cambridge, 1985); Peter Sahlins, *Forest Rites: The War of the Demoiselles in Nineteenth-Century France* (Cambridge, MA, 1994).

[86] Most obviously: Lescarret, *La Vie dans la Grande-Lande*; Sargos, *Histoire de la forêt landaise*; Bernard Traimond, 'La Sociabilité rurale landaise: Histoire et structure, XVIIIème–XXème siècle' (Doctorat de 3ème Cycle en Anthropologie Sociale et Historique, École des Hautes Études en Sciences Sociales, 1982).

[87] Peter McPhee, *Revolution and Environment in Southern France, 1780–1830: Peasants, Lords, and Murder in the Corbières* (Oxford, 1999), 127; Jones, *Liberty and Locality in Revolutionary France*, 243; Whited, *Forests and Peasant Politics in Modern France*, 76–7.

[88] Jones, *Politics and Rural Society*, 220–1.

Folklore Sources and Methods

Folklore provides both an important set of sources for understanding rural cultural change in this period, and a set of methods. Historians have drawn on a range of different sources to understand the countryside during the period often called the 'apogee and crisis' of French rural civilization, from 1870 to 1914.[89] Many of these sources raise more questions than answers. For all of their talk of how the 'peasants' lived, for instance, real people are strangely absent from the official sources written by administrators and reformers.[90] Even when they were sympathetic, studies and reports written by outsiders present changing practices of work and social life as abstractions, rather than everyday struggles, defeats, and triumphs played out in personal experiences. Although the level of detail that state archives provide about the everyday lives of rural workers in this period can be impressive, for instance when an individual committed a crime, the lives of most men and women are hardly captured by the official archive. When Alain Corbin tried to reconstruct the life of an illiterate nineteenth-century clog maker, chosen at random in a regional archive, he was forced to admit that writing this man's story was essentially 'impossible'.[91] Administrative sources gave Corbin too little to produce anything more than an absence where his protagonist should have been. While the first surviving autobiographies written by rural workers also date to this period, there are serious problems with treating these as in any way typical of workers' experiences.[92] Writers such as Jean-Marie Déguignet or Pierre-Jakez Hélias produced vivid accounts of their humble origins, but historians have pointed out that such individuals marked themselves out by embracing literacy, and often sought to transcend their own humble origins through writing.[93] The criminal trial records used by other historians suffer from analogous problems.[94] Men predominate in cases of violent crime, and the general picture of rural society from criminal sources is one of conflict, between social groups, and over resources.[95]

[89] This is the title of the third volume of: Georges Duby and Gabriel Wallon, eds, *Histoire de la France rurale* (new edn., 4 vols, Paris, 1992).

[90] This is one reason why, despite its commitment to comprehensive vision of the history of the moorlands, Roger Sargos' history of the forestation of the Landes de Gascogne remains so top down. Sargos, *Contribution à l'histoire du boisement des Landes de Gascogne,*.

[91] Corbin, *The Life of an Unknown*, 212.

[92] Mary Jo Maynes, *Taking the Hard Road: Life Course in French and German Workers' Autobiographies in the Era of Industrialization* (Chapel Hill, 1995); the exceptional autobiographical graffiti of Joachim Martin is a slightly different matter: Jacques-Olivier Boudon, *Le Plancher de Joachim: L'histoire Retrouvée d'un Village Français* (Paris, 2017).

[93] Hopkin, *Voices of the People*, 9–10.

[94] Elisabeth Claverie and Pierre Lamaison, *L'Impossible mariage: Violence et parenté en Gévaudan, XVIIe, XVIIIe et XIXe siècles* (Paris, 1982); Sylvie Lapalus, *La Mort du vieux: Une histoire du parricide au XIXe siècle* (Paris, 2004).

[95] Octave Festy, *Les Délits ruraux et leur répression sous la révolution et le consulat. Étude d'histoire économique* (Paris, 1956); Matteson, *Forests in Revolutionary France*; McPhee, *Revolution and Environment*.

In response to these source problems, David Hopkin has recently argued for a 'folkloric turn'. The tales, legends, songs, and other materials collected by men— and some women—like Arnaudin provide a broader range of sources for the cultural history of rural workers, both male and female, in conflict, but also in calmer times.[96] Folklore sources such as Arnaudin's collection provide one of the few ways historians can gain insight into these experiences. But these sources must be handled carefully, using the appropriate specialist methods developed by anthropologists and folklorists. In his recent book arguing for a 'folklore turn' David Hopkin addresses several misconceptions about what folklore is, arguing that historians should not assume it is old, oral, unchanging, and communal.[97] The interest folklorists have recently shown in the internet demonstrates just how unhelpful these assumptions are, but there is also a longer history of unhelpful boundary disputes among specialists concerning literate and oral cultures. For the purposes of a folklorist, it is not enough to know whether a song or story was orally transmitted, written, or sent by email. What matters are what Barre Toelken has called the twin laws of dynamic variation: folklore is both traditional, in the sense of belonging to a recognized tradition, and informal, meaning that every transmission of the tradition is free to make it up a little differently. Lynne McNeill summarizes this definition of folklore succinctly as 'informal, traditional culture'.[98]

From this point of view, what would make the songs Arnaudin collected, for instance, folklore? Some he noted from the mouths of his singers, but some he included based on notes that correspondents sent to him. The fact that they may have read the songs before they sang them, or that they passed them on in writing tells us little about whether they are informal or traditional. If the singer made a song up from scratch, without reference to how this song is normally sung, there would be little about it that is traditional. Equally, if the singer simply copied a song from a book and did not sing it or write it in a way that was meaningful to them and to their community, it would not be informal. What makes these sources interesting, then, is not that they are orally transmitted, although the vast majority were. What makes them interesting are the twin laws. Because they are traditional, folklore sources often speak in the voice of a community, and a shared history. But because they are informal, this shared voice is inflected by individual expression. This interplay between the individual and the community is why folklore collections such as Arnaudin's offer unrivalled insights into cultural change from below.

It is this balancing act between shared culture and individual improvisation that was absent in much of the work of the generation of early-modern historians who

---

[96] Hopkin, *Voices of the People*.   [97] Ibid., 23.
[98] Lynne S. McNeill, *Folklore Rules: A Fun, Quick, and Useful Introduction to the Field of Academic Folklore Studies* (Colorado, 2013). Barre Toelken, *The Dynamics of Folklore* (new edn, Logan, 1996), 33, 39.

used folklore as a route to understand popular culture.[99] But the more recent 'folkloric turn' evident in work by Hopkin, Guy Beiner, and Peter Sahlins on the eighteenth and nineteenth centuries, for instance, is distinguished from this earlier scholarship by a closer engagement with folklore theory as it developed from the 1970s onwards.[100] Along with oral culture and comparative methods, this more recent work has also tended to emphasize the cultural creativity of traditional singers and storytellers, paying greater attention to individual performances and skill. This 'folkloric turn' is characterized by six different principles: culture is an active process of making meaning; folklore must be understood as a performance; folklore is not static, but changing; folklore gives special insight into the extraordinary nature of everyday life; the traceability of cultural traditions is a more meaningful question than their 'authenticity'; folklore is best understood comparatively.

Culture is an active process of making meaning. The most fundamental definitions that historians have offered for 'culture' agree that it is the domain of symbolism or semiotics. Anything that humans do can be understood symbolically.[101] This simple starting point has two important consequences: it invites historians to decode or decipher the meanings found in this culture and it draws attention to agency, creativity, and even art in surprising places. The importance of 'decoding' past cultures has been central to cultural history since the popularization of anthropological methods, especially among early-modern historians.[102] As Robert Darnton has put it: 'When we cannot get a proverb, a joke, or a ritual, or a poem, we know we are on to something. By picking at the document where it is most opaque, we may be able to unravel an alien system of meaning.'[103] This work to interpret symbolic meanings has often required the kinds of fine-grained, micro-historical research championed by early-modernists. And it has also widened historians' attention from words, to actions, and even silence. The same kinds of tools of contextualization and deconstruction that historians use to understand texts and images can also be turned to silence. The reaction against linguistic constructionism has taught historians not that language is unimportant, but that it is not enough.[104] This is a view of culture that

---

[99] Natalie Zemon Davis, 'Proverbial Wisdom and Popular Error', in *Society and Culture in Early Modern France* (new edn, London, 1988), 227–67; Carlo Ginzburg, *The Night Battles: Witchcraft and Agrarian Cults in the Sixteenth and Seventeenth Centuries*, trans. John A Tedeschi and Anne Tedeschi (London, 1983); Robert Darnton, *The Great Cat Massacre and Other Episodes in French Cultural History* (New York, 1985); Peter Burke, *Popular Culture in Early Modern Europe* (London, 1978).

[100] Guy Beiner, *Remembering the Year of the French: Irish Folk History and Social Memory* (Madison, 2009); Sahlins, *Forest Rites*.

[101] Peter Burke, *What Is Cultural History?* (2nd edn, Cambridge, 2008), 3; William Sewell, 'The Concept(s) of Culture', in *Beyond the Cultural Turn*, eds. Richard Biernacki, Victoria Bonnell, and Lynn Hunt (Berkeley, 1999), 48–9.

[102] William G. Pooley, 'Native to the Past: History, Anthropology, and Folklore in Past and Present', *Past and Present*, 239, no. 1 (May 2018), e1–e15.

[103] Darnton, *The Great Cat Massacre*, 5.

[104] This point is explored evocatively in: Ruth Harris, 'Possession on the Borders: The "Mal de Morzine" in Nineteenth-Century France', *Journal of Modern History*, 69, no. 3 (September 1997), 451–78.

emphasizes creativity from below. As David Hopkin has pointed out, the emphasis that folklorists have placed on cultural agency is quite different to the dominant ways of understanding culture that have been influential among modern histor- ians since the 1980s. Rather than the 'invention of traditions', and the top-down model of social change it implies, folklorists do not see culture 'as something that impinges on people from the outside, but as something that people do: the stories they themselves tell, the songs they themselves sing, the tools they themselves make, the rituals they themselves enact'.[105] This is not to say that folklore is an area where people were free to express themselves as they wished. As an embodied performance, folklore can be described in the same terms Judith Butler has used to describe gender: 'a practice of improvisation within a scene of constraint'.[106]

It is in this sense that folklore must be understood as a performance. To understand the meanings of a song or a story or a proverb, folklorists turn first to the context where it was performed, as well as the identities of the performer(s) and audience.[107] Barre Toelken, for instance, discusses how a sexually suggestive song sung by young people in courting situations in the area around Salzburg could be sung by a very polite older woman in the same region as if it was really about mowing.[108] Robert Darnton has expressed a similar idea in a study of eighteenth-century singing, pointing out that performers used well-known tunes, or familiar words, twisting them to change their effect. Without the context, the meanings of these performances would be lost. This insight is central to how historians such as David Hopkin have understood folklore as a way for both groups and individual performers to express coded messages.[109] The skilled traditional storyteller does not tell just any story, but the ones that best suit their own life, and the way they tell the story is individual, as well as trad- itional.[110] Divorced from performance, transcribed, and reproduced in folklore collections, these texts lose their meaning.[111] This is why it is so important to recontextualize performances by researching the lives of performers, and the communities they live in.[112] And, although many folk cultures project an image of consensus, they are no exception to the general pattern of cultures suggested by

---

[105] Hopkin, *Voices of the People*, 6; E.J. Hobsbawm and Terence Ranger eds, *The Invention of Tradition* (Cambridge, 1983).

[106] Judith Butler, *Undoing Gender* (New York, 2004), 1.

[107] Richard Bauman, *Verbal Art as Performance* (Prospect Heights, 1977).

[108] Barre Toelken, *Morning Dew and Roses: Nuance, Metaphor, and Meaning in Folksongs* (Illinois, 1995), 88.

[109] Hopkin, *Voices of the People*.

[110] Linda Dégh, *Folktales and Society; Story-Telling in a Hungarian Peasant Community* (Bloomington, 1969), 175.

[111] For another example, see: William G. Pooley, 'Can The "Peasant" Speak? Witchcraft and Silence in Guillaume Cazaux's "The Mass of Saint Sécaire"', *Western Folklore*, 71, no. 2 (2012), 93–118.

[112] This is also why the identities of key performers have been so contentious. See: John Ellis, *One Fairy Story Too Many: The Brothers Grimm and Their Tales* (Chicago, 1983); Chris J. Bearman, 'Cecil Sharp in Somerset: Some Reflections on the Work of David Harker', *Folklore*, 113, no. 1 (2002), 11–34.

William Sewell.[113] Cultural coherence, Sewell argues, is always 'variable, contested, ever-changing, and incomplete'.[114] It is, in other words, historical.

Folk traditions are no exception. Folklorists have long known that traditions are never static, always already changing.[115] The vision of folklore as a 'vanishing subject', always under threat of being swept away by the modern world, has long since been abandoned by contemporary folklorists, who are just as likely to study traditions of graffiti, text messages, and social media as they are to study folk tales or ballads.[116] Folklore does not always provide evidence of the endurance of tradition and the cultural or even political persistence of the 'old regime'.[117] Although it is necessary to describe some of these continuities, my approach here does not follow recent scholarship that has used folklore sources to question established chronologies and explore the endurance of folk memory across centuries.[118] Traditions contain the evidence of their own changeability. Although the Arnaudin materials were not collected over a long enough period to say with certainty how this folk culture was changing, songs, stories, and speech do address their own evolution. When singers or storytellers, or the folklorist himself discuss their own memories of a different past, they highlight the historicity of their culture in the present.

This should not be mistaken for an argument about the 'modernity' of rural culture. As James Lehning has argued, the dichotomy between rural tradition and urban modernity in nineteenth-century France is a false one.[119] Not only did many 'peasants' have a foot in both the world of modern urban wage labour and the traditional life of the village, but the term 'modernity' itself is so broad and complex that it approaches meaninglessness.[120] At its most basic—the idea of a self-conscious rejection of tradition—'modernity' is clearly not the right term to apply to the changing dynamics of folk cultures.[121] The central concern of the

---

[113] Peter Jones has also emphasized the importance of conflict within local culture and local communities. Jones, *Politics and Rural Society*.

[114] Sewell, 'The Concept(s) of Culture', 57.

[115] Richard Handler and Jocelyn Linnekin, 'Tradition, Genuine or Spurious', *Journal of American Folklore*, 97, no. 385 (September 1984), 273–90.

[116] For the older vision: see Barbara Kirshenblatt-Gimblett's reflections on the 'poetics of disappearance': Barbara Kirshenblatt-Gimblett, 'Folklore's Crisis', *Journal of American Folklore*, 111, no. 441 (Summer 1998), 281–327.

[117] For the classic arguments, see: Arno Mayer, *The Persistence of the Old Regime: Europe to the Great War* (New York, 1981); Weber, *Peasants into Frenchmen*.

[118] Hopkin, *Voices of the People*, 256; Guy Beiner, *Remembering the Year of the French*; Éva Guillorel, David M. Hopkin, and William G. Pooley, eds, *Rhythms of Revolt: European Traditions and Memories of Social Conflict in Oral Culture* (London, 2018).

[119] James R. Lehning, *Peasant and French: Cultural Contact in Rural France during the Nineteenth Century* (Cambridge, 1995).

[120] On 'peasants' with a foot in both worlds, see: Jones, *Politics and Rural Society*, 279, 309; Étienne Julliard, *La Vie rurale dans la plaine de Basse-Alsace, Essai de géographie sociale* (Paris, 1953), 277, 402–15; on the problems with the term 'modernity' see the discussion of Frederick Cooper in: Lynn Avery Hunt, *Measuring Time, Making History* (Budapest, 2008), 16.

[121] Hunt, *Measuring Time, Making History*, 1–2, 6.

changes that working men and women worried about, discussed, or embraced was the body, not just in the Bakhtinian sense of a joyous folk culture of bodily fluids, feasting, and copulation, but also in grimmer terms that emphasized exploitation and exhaustion.[122] Although they addressed their concerns in the traditional forms of songs, tales, legends, or proverbs which held an enduring relevance among many rural people, these cultural traditions were not static, but were creatively adapted to reshape the possibilities of the body.

'Traceability' is a more meaningful way to think about these cultural traditions than 'authenticity'. Authenticity has often been used by folklorists and historians as a way to invest cultural traditions with emotional significance, and defend them against perceived pollution.[123] Definitions of the 'authenticity' of traditions often fall back on oral transmission, ethnic or class identities, and linguistic competence. If a storyteller did not learn and perform their story orally, if they do not come from the right ethnic or class group and speak the right language, then their tradition should not be considered 'authentic'. While any of these criteria might help to determine how traditional a given performance is, they are based on a prejudice against cultural contact across classes, languages, and ethnic groups, and between written and oral cultures. The historian Patrick Cabanel has suggested the more useful term of 'traceability'.[124] Where might a performer have learned a song or story? Who else around them knew it, and how popular was it? Few folklorists believe in a dichotomy between authentic 'folklore' and ersatz 'fakelore' any more.[125]

The 'traceability' of traditions depends on the fact that informal traditional cultures are made up of many different, but similar versions of stories, songs, proverbs, or even objects, such as baskets or barns. While folklorists recognize something in common between many different examples, every version is different. This is why a key methodology of folklore is comparison, a methodology that has been underpinned by the compilation of catalogues documenting available examples of cultural traditions.[126] The story of *Little Red Riding Hood*, for instance, has been told in many slightly different forms in many rural European cultures, and is included in the catalogue of tale 'types' launched by Anti Aarne and Stith Thompson, and recently updated by Hans-Jörg Uther.[127] This allows folklorists to compare the different versions of this tale type (ATU 333) that have

[122] Mikhail Bakhtin, *Rabelais and His World* (Cambridge, MA, 1965).

[123] Regina Bendix, *In Search of Authenticity: The Formation of Folklore Studies* (Madison, 1997).

[124] Patrick Cabanel, 'La guerre des camisards centre histoire et mémoire: la perpétuelle réinvention du témoignage', *Dix-huitième siècle*, 39, no. 1 (1 July 2007), 211–27. This is an important concept for the regressive methods employed in: Guillorel et al., *Rhythms of Revolt*.

[125] The distinction was popularized by: Richard Mercer Dorson, *Folklore and Fakelore: Essays Toward a Discipline of Folk Studies* (Cambridge, MA, 1976).

[126] Dégh, *Folktales and Society*, 179; Tom Cheesman, *The Shocking Ballad Picture Show: German Popular Literature and Cultural History* (Oxford, 1994), 42.

[127] Hans-Jörg Uther, *The Types of International Folktales: A Classification and Bibliography, Based on the System of Antti Aarne and Stith Thompson*, 3 vols (Helsinki, 2004).

been recorded in different places, using tools such as the French national catalogue of tales compiled by Paul Delarue and Marie-Louise Tenèze.[128] In some
cases, stories turn out to be more popular in certain regions of France. In other
cases, the versions recorded in one region are noticeably different from those from
other regions, suggesting a process of 'ecotypification' where stories adapt to local
cultural contexts.[129] These 'ecotypes' have much to teach historians about the
difference and commonalities of the kinds of local cultures that cannot be found in
official or literary sources.

Catalogues exist not only for tales, but also for songs, and there is even a
comparative works that categorizes 'motifs', the smallest possible units of
a narrative tradition.[130] These tools can help to illuminate not just what made a
region like the moorlands different, but what makes the storytellers and singers
Arnaudin met so extraordinary. Of course, it would be foolish to assume that the
catalogues are complete, or adequate. There have been longstanding debates over
the value and possibility of identifying 'types', which Hans-Jörg Uther carefully
explored when preparing his catalogue of tales.[131] It is also true that the catalogues
are only as good as the available source materials: many of the unpublished stories
Arnaudin himself collected are not mentioned in the French catalogues, as the
compilers did not have the opportunity to read his notes. It is impossible to know
how many more stories and songs simply went unrecorded. What the existing
tools allow historians to do is to situate the specific performances in Arnaudin's
collection in a partially reconstructed vision of a wider shared culture. The sources
and methods of folklore offer one of the few ways to research how a wide range of
rural people experienced and discussed changes that are both intimate, and
fundamental: changing attitudes to the body.

Structure of the Book

The remaining chapters of the book move from an explanation of the context and
genesis of the Arnaudin collection, to an analysis of specific traditions that he
recorded, showing how different folk traditions and performers used songs,
stories, and everyday speech to express and dissect their changing situations.

---

[128] This tale is found in the first volume of *CPF*.
[129] David M. Hopkin, 'The Ecotype, Or a Modest Proposal to Reconnect Cultural and Social History', in *Exploring Cultural History: Essays in Honour of Peter Burke*, eds. Melissa Calaresu, Filippo de Vivo, and Joan Pau Rubiés (London, 2017), 3–54.
[130] See *RCFTO*; Stith Thompson, *Motif-Index of Folk-Literature; a Classification of Narrative Elements in Folktales, Ballads, Myths, Fables, Mediaeval Romances, Exempla, Fabliaux, Jest-Books, and Local Legends*, 5 vols (Copenhagen, 1955).
[131] Hans-Jorg Uther, 'Indexing Folktales: A Critical Survey', *Journal of Folklore Research*, 34, no. 3 (September 1997), 209–20.

Chapters 2 and 3 focus on context. What role did Arnaudin have in shaping the culture he claimed to document? To answer this, Chapter 2 explores his life and ideas, drawing on the extensive letters, diary, and fieldwork notes he left at his death in 1921. The chapter argues that Arnaudin engaged in an unrealizable project to construct an image of a disappearing culture. He himself thought this project a failure, measured by his inability to publish most of his work. But, in one sense, the legacy of his efforts is greater than his print editions could ever have been. Where published folklore collections polished and purified holistic perform-ances into literary narratives, manuscript collections such as the notes from Arnaudin now held by the archives of the department of the Landes de Gascogne in Mont-de-Marsan still include much of the messiness of face-to-face inter-actions. Arnaudin's manuscripts are full of contradictions, crossings-out, snippets of extra information, asides, and misunderstandings. These paratextual details help to reconstruct performances, and allow me to treat the manuscripts as the result of a process of negotiation between the singers and storytellers and the folklorist who recorded them. Arnaudin hovers on the edge of all of the other chapters, as audience, interrogator, and interlocutor, even if the focus of attention is firmly on the women and men he met.

Who were these people? At the beginning of the twentieth century Arnold van Gennep warned that writers on folk culture made a mistake by equating the absence of 'individualism' with anonymity.[132] Arnaudin did provide some bio-graphical details about his storytellers and singers in his notes, but he also deliberately excluded some types of information, and was unsure of the precise identities and backgrounds of some of his informants. Records of births, mar-riages, and deaths, as well as notarial documents, conscription and employment records provide further, scattered clues about the lives of these singers and storytellers. These clues help to make sense of why a singer or storyteller per-formed stories and songs in the way that they did. Chapter 4 presents an overview of this biographical information, and shows that many of the same people who sang folk songs and told legends or tales also worked in new industries, and actively participated in the reform of the landscape.[133] Their traditions belong in this changing world, rather than outside of it.

Arnaudin's collection suggests that the areas of concern to most people in the region should be measured not in the grand sweep of social and environmental transformation, but in more intimate terms. Men and women worried about and discussed their bodies, their families, and their work, and they did so in ways that were historically specific to a changing culture of embodiment. Chapter 4 provides an overview of how people talked in everyday life about their bodies. Using

---

[132] Arnold van Gennep, *Le Folklore français*, 3 vols (Paris, 1998 [1937–58]), 48–50.
[133] William G. Pooley, 'The Singing Postman: The Mobility of Traditional Culture in Nineteenth-Century France', *Cultural and Social History*, 13, no. 1 (January 2016), 1–20.

Arnaudin's notes towards a dictionary of the Gascon dialect, the chapter explores cultural commonplaces about bodies among different groups in the moorlands, arguing that there is little evidence of the emergence of a 'modern' body, centred on the head, and focused on sexual identities. Instead, working men and women worried about physical exhaustion, talked of a body whose centre was the legs and buttocks.

The following chapters draw on these commonplaces to explore individual lives and shared traditions. Folklorists have devoted much attention to how different traditional genres work in different ways, so Chapters 5, 6, 7, and 8 focus on a variety of different genres, using them to understand a thematic issue through the lives of specific storytellers and singers.[134] Chapter 5 explores a werewolf legend told by a woman named Marichoun Bouzats. One of the contexts for understanding this legend is Arnaudin's surprise that his informants had so little to say about the transformation of the moorlands into the industrial forest. Marichoun's story—a recollection of an experience from her own childhood—is set precisely during this period of transition. But rather than environmental change, Marichoun's fears concern the boundaries of households, the family, and the body itself. The chapter draws attention to the pervasive phenomenological sensitivity of rural skin and argues that the werewolf tradition provided Marichoun with a way to talk about the uncertainties of a period of changing boundaries, which were not just experienced as external shifts in physical landscapes or architecture, but as the intimate concerns of real individuals.

Chapter 6 turns to singing traditions. Once again making use of comparative folklore methods, the chapter argues that the songs Arnaudin collected in the moorlands—mostly from women—are more licentious and bawdy than similar songs collected in other parts of France, and documented in Patrice Coirault's index of French traditional song.[135] The chapter explores what these bawdy songs have to do with the demographic revolution that took place in the moorlands. The chapter suggests that the Third Republic was a period of repression of female sexuality in the moorlands, which stands in marked contrast to what historians of sexuality have said about the increasing liberalization of sex in France during this period.[136]

Chapter 7 takes this argument in a different direction by exploring the life of one singer. As the bawdy feminine culture of extra-marital sex increasingly came into conflict with bourgeois and Catholic moral codes, a space was opened for love to be contested by women who did not recognize their own experiences in songs of heartache and desire. This chapter explores how one local seamstress resisted the

---

[134] Trudier Harris-Lopez, 'Genre', in *Eight Words for the Study of Expressive Culture*, ed. Burt Feintuch (Urbana, 2003), 99–120.

[135] *RCFTO*.

[136] Anne-Marie Sohn, *Du Premier baiser à l'alcôve: la sexualité des français au quotidien, 1850–1950* (Paris, 1996).

cultural pressures she faced over her own body, by refusing or forgetting to sing the words to some songs. Her silences were in some way as meaningful as what she chose to sing, and while her life and songs were not typical, the conversation she created with local singing culture is a sideways glance into the bodily pressures that pitted individuals against their families and peers.

Chapter 8 examines a set of tales about foxes told by some of Arnaudin's closest informants, including his friends and the sharecroppers who worked for his family. Unlike the neatened versions of these stories that were published by folklorists at the time, the manuscript versions in Arnaudin's notes, which have so much in common with *Aesop's Fables* or the tales of Reynard the Fox, reveal very personal concerns about exploitation. In particular, comparing these stories to other similar stories found elsewhere suggests a strong link between these stories and the system of sharecropping. Rather than just a reflection of this agricultural system, the chapter explores how the tales were a response, even a strategy on behalf of different individuals who took different stances towards working under this often difficult system.

The conclusion of the book argues that Arnaudin's folklore collections provide evidence both of a resilient and enduring 'peasant' bodily culture, and of changes to this culture in three broad areas: work, sexual relationships, and the household. Historians may be as surprised by what storytellers and singers did not discuss as the things they did, but the traditions of the moorlands do express a changing culture of embodiment that can be compared to broader patterns across the French countryside in this period.

2

Arnaudin and the Moorlands

I listened to a very old shepherd one day, on the still untouched open moor near Labouheyre, towards the road to Pissos, next to the charming lagoon at Bise. He leant back against the lowest part of the sheepfold, wearing his stilts, in the way that the shepherds did, and told me about the old days. I knelt at his feet on the close-cropped grass, with its subtle odour of honey, surrounded by the gentle buzzing of the bees, and eagerly listened to his memories of the old ways, which were often amusing, and sometimes painful. Our encounter was an insight into the hearty race of the shepherds, who lived so strangely and so happily in the moorlands, in the vague dreamscape of unlimited space, with nothing to do.[1]

Félix Arnaudin's published description of his fieldwork cannot be taken at face value. Blended with the verifiable details of visits to listen to his shepherd informants as they watched their flocks is Arnaudin's own nostalgia for a disappearing, strange, yet happy and even carefree existence. In his published works, Arnaudin had the ultimate editorial power. Like other early folklorists, he may be suspected of distorting, or even outright falsifying the identities and words of his informants.[2] The debate over the 'authenticity' of folklore pre-dates even the term itself. In 1760 James MacPherson published the first of the 'Ossian' poems which he claimed were survivals handed down from Scotland's own Homer, an ancient bard named Ossian, whose poems endured in the songs of the Highlands and a few fragmentary manuscripts he had found. Critics were quick to question how much of the material MacPherson published really came from oral tradition and literary archives, and how much came from his own imagination.[3] Within France there were similarly heated discussions over Théodore Claude Henri Hersart de la Villemarqué's Breton songs, first published in 1839, which, like MacPherson's books, presented a similarly epic tradition of singing, supposedly rediscovered by

---

[1] OC, viii, 551.

[2] Ruth B. Bottigheimer, 'Fairy Tales, Folk Narrative Research and History', Social History, xiv (1989), 343–57; David Harker, 'Cecil Sharp in Somerset: Some Conclusions', Folk Music Journal, ii (1972), 220–40.

[3] James MacPherson, Fragments of Ancient Poetry (Edinburgh, 1760); Ian Haywood, The Making of History: A Study of the Literary Forgeries of James Macpherson and Thomas Chatterton in Relation to Eighteenth-Century Ideas of History and Fiction (Rutherford, 1986).

Body and Tradition in Nineteenth-Century France: Félix Arnaudin and the Moorlands of Gascony, 1870–1914.
William G. Pooley, Oxford University Press (2019). © William G. Pooley.
DOI: 10.1093/oso/9780198847502.001.0001

Villemarqué among the rural population on his doorstep.[4] Closer to Arnaudin in both time and space, the folklorist sometimes called the 'Grimm of Gascony', Jean-François Bladé (1827–1900), is still suspected by many specialists of distorting the words of his informants in his published collections.[5] Since very few of Bladé's manuscripts survive, these suspicions are hard to answer.[6]

Fortunately, Arnaudin left much more material to work with. Along with a personal diary, his archive contains a large correspondence, as well as the rough notes and drafts for his published work, and much that remained unpublished until local specialists undertook the daunting task of producing a comprehensive complete works, which appeared between 1994 and 2007. Dealing with his extensive manuscript notes, there is a temptation to read 'against the grain'. Inspired by the work of James C. Scott, historians have taken a special interest in the 'weapons of the weak', such as the codes of silence, inaction, foot dragging, and grumbling.[7] These ideas are important to understanding the agency of a range of actors in Arnaudin's manuscripts, but they are not the only way to read his papers. It is true that Arnaudin's concerns framed the questions that his informants sought to answer. He wielded power in the form of both cultural and financial recognition, and this could sometimes lead to conflicts, which I explore in Chapter 3. But conflict is not the only way to understand this relationship. In a critique of Scott's *Weapons of the Weak*, the anthropologist Lila Abu-Lughod has warned of the 'romance of resistance', which makes conflict the only subject of interest.[8] Before I turn to the tensions between Arnaudin and his informants, I want to explain what Arnaudin himself thought he was doing. Exploring his life and his ideas is a way to practise the opposite of 'reading against the grain', and instead embracing what the colonial historian Ann Laura Stoler has called reading 'along the grain'.[9]

It is Arnaudin's vision of the pre-modern 'dreamscape of unlimited space' that shaped his efforts to record stories and songs from the men and women of the moorlands. To understand their points of view, as the rest of this book does, it is essential to put them back into conversation with Arnaudin. The surviving manuscripts are a record of this ongoing, and unfinished conversation. Arnaudin was so determined to present a complete and perfect account of the culture of the moorlands

---

[4] Théodore Hersart de la Villemarqué, *Barzaz Breiz: Chants Populaires de La Bretagne* (new edn, Paris, 1883); Donatien Laurent, *Aux Sources du Barzaz-Breiz: la mémoire d'un peuple* (Douarnenez, 1989).

[5] Jean Arrouye ed., *Jean-François Bladé, 1827–1900: Actes du Colloque de Lectoure, 20 et 21 octobre 1984* (Béziers, 1985).

[6] The only known surviving manuscripts were recently found by Patricia Heiniger-Casteret: 'Une Collecte chez Jean-François Bladé', in *La Voix occitane* (Bordeaux, 2009), 599–614.

[7] James C. Scott, *Weapons of the Weak: Everyday Forms of Peasant Resistance* (New Haven, 1985).

[8] Lila Abu-Lughod, 'The Romance of Resistance: Tracing Transformations of Power through Bedouin Women', *American Ethnologist*, xvii (1990), 41–55.

[9] Ann Laura Stoler, *Along the Archival Grain: Epistemic Anxieties and Colonial Common Sense* (Princeton, 2008).

that he was unable to finish his life's work. Despite repeatedly announcing the imminent appearance of several volumes of songs and proverbs, he only managed to produce one volume of songs in 1912, some seventeen years after he had told friends it was ready.[10] The majority of his works only appeared after his death.

What did Arnaudin set out to achieve, and why did he do what he did? Who, in fact, was he?

'The Invisible Félix Arnaudin'

Simon Arnaudin, known as Félix, was born to Barthélémy (1816–93) and his wife Marie-Thérèse Bacon (1823–75) in the village of Labouheyre on 30 May 1844. Although Arnaudin's mother came from a solidly bourgeois family of local notaries, his father had a more mixed background. Barthélémy Arnaudin's occupation was recorded as cobbler at his wedding in 1843 and innkeeper at the birth of Arnaudin's brother, Ariste, in 1847. Later in life, he became an agent for the local ironworks in the new railway station in the village. In 1853 he became mayor of Labouheyre, and oversaw the auctions of the village's communal moorlands. Barthélémy and his wife lived in ease, employing a household servant and renting out several properties in Labouheyre, but they were by no means very wealthy. Gascon was the language of everyday life, and his mother's final words—'I am going to die'—were in the dialect.[11] Like many other rural notables, Arnaudin's family were 'half-peasants', neither culturally nor materially that different from the local labourers they employed.[12]

Arnaudin wrote almost nothing about his childhood, beginning his account of his own life for Henri Carnoy's biographical dictionary of folklorists with his departure for school in the *chef-lieu* of the Landes de Gascogne:

> [He spent] three long years in college at Mont-de-Marsan, where he felt out of place, hemmed in, and haunted by the memory of the open horizons of the moorland. He returned to the village with no firm idea of a job or vocation, he took up further study... Once he reached his adulthood, he made a few attempts at business, but lacking both the desire and the aptitude, he soon gave up.[13]

Many of the key elements of Arnaudin's self-image are encapsulated in this account: the passion for his native moorlands, the dedication to learning, and the failure to secure himself a career. It also hints at the character traits that subsequent writers

[10] On this long lead-in, see, for instance, his letter to Jean-Baptiste Lescarret, 15 April 1895: *OC*, v, 144.

[11] *OC*, viii, 107.

[12] Barnett Singer, *Village Notables in Nineteenth-Century France: Priests, Mayors, Schoolmasters* (New York, 1983), 6.

[13] Reproduced in *OC*, v, 169.

Fig. 2.1 Self-portrait of Arnaudin as a young man, courtesy of the Musée d'Aquitaine

would emphasize: romanticism, shyness, and a nostalgia that bordered on paralys-ing depression. His unpublished notes reinforce this self-image of a man out of place: 'Who is the invisible Félix Arnaudin? A melancholic, a dreamer, in short something of a throwback, at whom the upstarts, snobs, and arrivistes sneer'.[14] In his obituary of Arnaudin, the abbé Césaire Daugé remembered him as a shy and melancholy man, so timid that he would not participate in the local learned society.[15] Instead, he preferred solitary walks on the open moorlands, and reading the works of the Pre-Romantics and Romantics, writers such as Alfred de Musset, George Sand, Alphonse de Lamartine, Jean-Jacques Rousseau, François René de Chateaubriand, and Johann-Wolfgang con Goethe.[16]

A series of personal disappointments soured his view of life, and may have encouraged his growing interest in the 'old' ways, drawing him to what one group of historians have called the 'beauty of the dead', a popular culture that was no

---

[14] NFA, 2 MI 29/12, f.68.   [15] Daugé, 'Félix Arnaudin: 1844–1921', 2–4.
[16] Arnaudin was always a wide reader, but it is possible to say these were early favourites, as they are all authors that he lent to his lover, Marie, in the 1870s. See 10 April 1875: *OC*, viii, 92.

longer threatening because it was already in decay.[17] The first of these personal crises was the discovery in 1874 that Arnaudin, now aged thirty, had been having an affair with the eighteen-year-old family servant, Marie Darlanne.[18] Arnaudin's mother was horrified, and arrangements were made for Marie to be sent away, and married to another local man. But the young servant, nourished with ideas from the novels Arnaudin lent her, refused the marriage, and tried to poison herself.[19] Over the next few years, Arnaudin continued to visit Marie in secret, until she was allowed to return to the family home in 1877. For some reason which is not clear in Arnaudin's papers, she left again, but returned permanently in 1880, and remained with him until she died in 1911.[20] They never married nor had any children.

While his diary is remarkable for the absence of emotional and personal details, focusing instead on the hunting outings of which he was so fond, the affair with Marie prompted Arnaudin to reflect grimly on his life:

I am past thirty. I am without a station in life, without money, and without the strength to earn it. I have no more friends: the few who looked kindly on my first steps when my talents seemed to offer hope have distanced themselves one by one, to make place for general indifference. The vacuum that has opened around me cruelly reinforces my sense of social inferiority. I am no longer even treated with basic courtesy. Who cares about me? ... Memories of the past choke me, crush me, and break me.[21]

As if the crisis of his relationship with Marie was not enough, one necessary condition of her return to the Arnaudin household was Arnaudin's mother's sudden death in 1876, itself a source of great pain. Just three years later this was compounded by the death of his brother, Ariste, who left a wife and young son. Mortality is a recurring theme in Arnaudin's diary. With no sense of irony, his diary lamented the passing of family members and acquaintances, but also hunting dogs, and even the family cow.[22] He spent his time alone weeping.

Arnaudin saw the same melancholy in the folk songs he collected, writing that the melodies of 'local poetry' 'seize the heart, and provoke tears, stirring up the

---

[17] Michel de Certeau, Dominique Julia, and Jacques Revel, 'The Beauty of the Dead: Nisard', in *Heterologies: Discourse on the Other*, trans. Brian Massumi (Minneapolis, 1986), 119–36.

[18] The story is told succinctly in Latry, 'Introduction', *OC*, viii, 5–6.

[19] NFA, 2 MI 29/18, ff.25–6; See entries on 29 September, 1 October, and 4 October 1874: *OC*, viii, 66–9.

[20] Latry, 'Introduction', in *OC*, viii, 6. As Eloise Moss pointed out to me, she was probably sent away because she had become pregnant. Arnaudin's diary certainly contains anguished notes about pregnancy scares during their affair.

[21] 23 September 1874: *OC*, viii, 64.

[22] He wrote of the cow: 'So, one by one, everything from my past abandons me.' 25 August 1875: *OC*, viii, 98.

memories that slumbered at the depth of our hearts, replaying the best of the past'.[23] In this way, his own personal disappointments became entwined with romantic ideas about a fading past, motivating him to collect and preserve local traditions. After the crisis with Marie, he fantasized about living a joint life of simple labour, with her collecting folklore for him.[24] From this point on, Arnaudin felt like an outcast within his own class. His parents' attempts to marry him to the daughter of a local bourgeois were unsuccessful, and a tentative foray into business with his friend and folklore informant Henri Vidal (1850–1919) came to little.[25] When he was not working on his folklore collection, much of Arnaudin's energy was eaten up by a series of conflicts over family inheritances, which drove a wedge between him and his widowed sister-in-law, and later his cousin, Michaël Arnaudin. Michaël was everything that Arnaudin was not: financially successful, he had a family and made a career in local politics, eventually becoming mayor of Mont-de-Marsan.[26] Arnaudin felt profoundly disconnected from the local bourgeoisie, of whom Michaël was typical and who prospered in the second half of the nineteenth century. Arnaudin charged them with lacking respect for the past and privileging profits over decency in their haste to complete the forestation of the moorlands.[27]

Forestation and Folklore

The environmental changes in the moorlands during the second half of the nineteenth century might appear fundamental to historians in the twenty-first century, but it is not clear that they were as important to the development of Arnaudin's ideas as he later claimed. There is little evidence from any of his personal writings or recollections that Arnaudin, aged just thirteen in 1857, cared very much about the national law encouraging the forestation of the moors. Guy Latry has pointed out that as late as the 1860s, Arnaudin had no interest in local social conflicts, and thought little of destroying old, ruined buildings for fun, something that would surely have shocked him later in life, when he struggled to document the architectural heritage of the moorlands.[28] It was only at this later stage, and for reasons that were connected to his personal unhappiness, that Arnaudin developed his lament for the vanished open horizons of the old moorlands:

> Now, the moorlands are gone. In the place of the magnificent desert that enchanted our forebears, unfolding under the sky, empty as the earliest ages,

---

[23] NFA, 2 MI 29/12, f.156.   [24] 9 October 1874: *OC*, viii, 69.
[25] On the marriage plans, see 16 November 1875: *OC*, viii, 106; on his business plans, see Latry, 'Introduction: Arnaudin à la lettre', xi.
[26] *OC*, viii, xi–xii; see Arnaudin's letters to Jean-Baptiste Lescarret from 9 April and May 1889: *OC*, v, 116, 143.
[27] Latry, 'Introduction', in *OC*, viii, 4, 10.   [28] *OC*, viii, 4.

the vast plain, without limits where the eye was perpetually dazzled by emptiness... [in place of these] now there is the forest—the industrial forest!... whose suffocating curtain forcibly limits the view, dulls the mind, and prevents it from soaring [away].[29]

Forestation, in Arnaudin's understanding, was a key factor in the social changes that led to the decline of rural traditions, and even language:

Here, as elsewhere, the rupture with the past is now complete...

Nothing remains of our old way of life, which suffused such originality, such primitive simplicity into our old hearths: ideas, traditions [moeurs] and customs, even language itself, with the first shove from outside, all disappeared, all lost their shape or faded in front of our eyes with stupefying speed.[30]

In his autobiographical contribution to Henri Carnoy's dictionary of folklorists, Arnaudin explicitly linked the project of saving what remained of local oral tradition to the threat of a changing landscape:

His obsession was the moorland, with its strange poetry of vast open spaces; from early in his life, until the moors disappeared, invaded by the forest, they were his alone. They belonged to the hare chaser, the duck hunter, waiting on the shores of the lagoons, dizzy from the solitude and empty space. Yet he also sought out the company of the old shepherds, curious about their traditions, their semi-nomadic way of life: he collected their tales, their legends, anything they traditionally talked about around their sheepfolds. Soon his attention turned to songs, and found an abundant harvest at weddings, at the winter spinning bees, and at singing meetings he organized.[31]

The links Arnaudin drew between social change, his own emotional state, primitive nature, and being a pariah are quite similar to the lives of other folklorists across Europe, such as the passionate hunter and Norwegian folklorist Peter Christen Asbjørnsen.[32] Peter Burke and Giuseppe Cocchiara trace this elite interest in popular customs back to the early-modern period, when Europeans became interested in both the 'savages' of the New World and the culture of antiquity.[33] These interests in customs and traditions were maintained in the early nineteenth century by learned societies, such as the Académie Celtique, who were

---

[29] Reproduced in: *OC*, iii, xx–xli, xxxiv.   [30] *OC*, iii, xxi.
[31] Reproduced in: *OC*, v, 169.
[32] Marte H. Hult, *Framing a National Narrative: The Legend Collections of Peter Christen Asbjørnsen* (Detroit, 2003), 14.
[33] Burke, *Popular Culture in Early Modern Europe*; Giuseppe Cocchiara, *The History of Folklore in Europe* (Philadelphia, 1981).

equally interested in archaeology, local history, and folklore.[34] Yet for much of the nineteenth century, France lacked the organized and systematic attempts to collect folklore that were launched in other European countries.[35] Unlike the splintered German lands that sought a unifying cultural identity in tales and legends, or the Nordic countries in search of a vernacular that could justify resistance to occupation by Swedes or Russians, nations like France and England had less political imperative to record folklore.[36] The regionalist agenda of many folklorists came too easily into conflict with the integration necessary for the Grande Nation.[37] The idea of a national folklore had none of the power it had in countries that were subjugated by neighbouring powers, such as Ireland.[38]

But Arnaudin came of age in time to profit from what Nicole Belmont has called a 'renaissance' in folklore studies in France. In 1877, Henri Gaidoz and Eugène Rolland founded the journal *Mélusine*, and in 1886, the year before Arnaudin published his first short collection of tales, Paul Sébillot established a rival journal, the *Revue des Traditions populaires*.[39] Charles Rearick has written that this was the time when the 'folklorists of France...were establishing new standards of scholarship, were increasingly concerned with questions of methodology, and were forming a distinct identity, a discipline of their own'.[40] Arnaudin was closely connected to this new group of folklorists. He corresponded with Paul Sébillot and Henri Gaidoz, the editors of the two most important journals, as well as other researchers such as Henri Carnoy, Achille Millien, Léon Marillier, Paul de Beaurepaire-Froment, and Julien Vinson. At one point, he even engaged in a confusing bilingual correspondence with the English folklorist Edwin Sidney Hartland. Arnaudin's qualifications and methods had much to recommend him to this new generation of more scrupulous folklorists. He was proud that his research presented 'the moorlands through the eyes of a true native', rather than the views of an outsider:

> who knows nothing about our moorlands, who turns up out of the blue, in the time between catching two trains, enlists the help of the first small-town hack

---

[34] Nicole Belmont, *Paroles païennes, mythe et folklore: Des frères Grimm à P. Saintyves* (Paris, 1986), 63–91.

[35] Charles Rearick writes that France 'lagged behind' the rest of Europe. See Charles Rearick, *Beyond the Enlightenment: Historians and Folklore in Nineteenth Century France* (Bloomington, 1974), 18.

[36] Jonathan Roper, 'England: The Land without Folklore?', in *Folklore and Nationalism in Europe during the Long Nineteenth Century*, eds. Timothy Baycroft and David M. Hopkin (Leiden, 2012), 227–54.

[37] See, for instance: Shanny Peer, *France on Display: Peasants, Provincials, and Folklore in the 1937 Paris World's Fair* (Albany, 1998), 138.

[38] Rearick, *Beyond the Enlightenment*, 167; Diarmuid Ó Giolláin, *Locating Irish Folklore: Tradition, Modernity, Identity* (Sterling, VA, 2000).

[39] Belmont, *Paroles Païennes, Mythe Et Folklore*, 90–1.

[40] Rearick, *Beyond the Enlightenment*, 164; For a similar argument, focusing on Brittany, see: Fanch Postic, 'Le Beau ou le vrai ou la difficile naissance en Bretagne et en France d'une science nouvelle: la littérature orale (1866–1868)', *Estudos de Literatura Oral*, iii (1997), 97–123.

they meet, and scoops up a few anecdotes, seasons them with some flourishes, and serves them to the public, who gawp appropriately.[41]

In his dedication to documenting all of the traditional life of the moorlands, Arnaudin was receptive to the ideas of this new group of folklorists. In 1882, he called himself 'an amateur scholar', but by 1900 Paul Beaurepaire-Froment was doing his best to persuade Arnaudin to join the board of *La Tradition* by pointing out that he was hardly unknown in the field of folklore.[42] Arnaudin refused, characteristically preferring to work independently. He was willing to correspond with other authors, and read widely, but he seems to have been terrified to actually work with them. He so feared and resented other researchers, especially those who threatened to trespass on his home region, that one writer has called him 'jealous of the moorlands'.[43] He wrote to the novelist Jean-Baptiste Lescarret that he had to work in secret, 'because I want to be the first to cover this territory, and to present unpublished material'.[44] He especially deplored the rivalry of priests, the 'butchers of the patois', who seemed unable to resist amateurish forays into folklore.[45] He was equally scathing about teachers. He met one who told him that he had helped another folklorist collect proverbs in the moorlands. When Arnaudin asked this teacher what his sources for the proverbs were, he replied that he had read them in a dictionary.[46] Arnaudin constantly worried about rival folklorists such as the abbé Vincent Foix or Eugène Dufourcet, who both had projects to publish the songs of the moorlands.[47]

Yet his desire to be 'first' was in conflict with competing feelings of powerlessness and obscurity. He tended both to play down the importance of his work—talking of 'my poor old shepherd's stories, taken from the most remote parts of the simple and ignorant moorlands'—and yet to also stress how painful and time consuming collecting oral traditions had been.[48] Much of his surviving correspondence is made up of apologies for not responding sooner, and for not being able to help other researchers who had contacted him. This may have been a way of avoiding collaborating on projects he did not value, but it also reflects his own conviction that he could not keep up with his project. He wrote to J.V. Lalanne of his 'natural indolence', and struggled throughout his life with overwhelming

---

[41] Letters from Rolland de Denus, 21 January 1889, and to Paul Sébillot, 13 January 1902: *OC*, v, 92, 174.
[42] See the letter to du Boucher, 3 May 1882 and the letter from Beaurepaire-Froment, 12 June 1900: *OC*, v, 74, 162.
[43] Jacques Sargos, 'Félix', in *Félix Arnaudin: imagier de la Grande Lande*, ed. Jacques Sargos (Bordeaux, 1993), 26.
[44] Letter of 25 March 1885: *OC*, v, 55.
[45] Arnaudin used the word 'déformateurs': NFA, 2 MI 29/3, f.456, 2 MI 29/8, f.34, 2 MI 29/25, ff.160–2.
[46] NFA, 2 MI 29/34, f.365.
[47] Guy Latry discusses this paranoia. See: Latry, 'Introduction', *OC*, v, xiv.
[48] Letter to Raoul Ponchon, May 1902: *OC*, v, 150.

episodes of melancholy.[49] In 1915, he wrote to Victor Dourthe: 'I am going through a crisis of unbearable sadness, which leaves me without power, without energy for even the simplest efforts. I am disgusted by everything, disgusted by life, and by this nightmare of a war, which nothing suggests will come to an end soon.'[50] His resistance to other folklorists was also partly a resistance theory. Arnaudin's published works were resolutely empirical, aiming to showcase the culture and landscape of the moorlands. In his correspondence, he was wary of speculations about the deep temporal roots of folklore, or the relationship between traditions, race, and Darwinism. Where other folklorists published collections as evidence for grand theories about the Indian origins of oral tales, Arnaudin avoided discussions of racial migrations or variations in local physiognomy.[51] Instead, he wrote that 'I have published what I heard around me, without investigating the question of the origins of these traditions. That is all a simple collector can hope for, and—alas!—that is all that I am.'[52]

He was as resistant to the nascent regionalist movement as he was to the grand theories of contemporary folklorists. He did correspond with many other local specialists in the south-west, including the folklorist Camille de Mensignac, and men such as Jean-Baptiste Lescarret, Léonce Couture, Henry du Boucher, Paul Labrouche, and Serge Barranx, who wrote novels about local life, were involved in local academies in Bordeaux, and published regional journals such as the *Bulletin de la Société de Borda*, the *Rebiste gascoune*, and the *Revue de Gascogne*. But Arnaudin kept all of these men and the organizations they represented at a distance.[53] When a group of local writers established a Gascon branch of Frédéric Mistral's Félibrige, the organization for the promotion of Occitan language and culture, Arnaudin maintained fairly cool relations.

Neither was conventional politics an explicit motivation for his folklore collecting. Although his nostalgic view of pre-industrial social relations suggests Arnaudin was strongly influenced by right-wing thinkers such as Maurice Barrès, he is hard to categorize as either a straightforward social conservative or left-wing populist. Despite the folklore movement's subsequent association with right-wing politics, particularly in France after Vichy, the folklorists of the nineteenth century held a range of political opinions from across the spectrum.[54] Many of the best

---

[49] Letter of 3 October 1902: *OC*, v, 323; Latry, 'Introduction', *OC*, v, IX.
[50] Letter of June 1915: *OC*, v, 403–4.
[51] The chief proponent of the Indo-European model in France was Emmanuel Cosquin. See: Emmanuel Cosquin, *Contes populaires de Lorraine comparés avec les contes des autres provinces de France et des pays étrangers* (Paris, 1886); for letters where Arnaudin resisted racial and other theoretical speculations, see his correspondence with J.-B. Lescarret in 1889, and with M. Dallas also in 1889: *OC*, v, 96–100, 111.
[52] Letter of 6 July 1889 to the comte de Chasteigner: *OC*, v, 196.
[53] See: Latry, 'Introduction', in *OC*, v, vii–xxxvi.
[54] The folklorists themselves were conscious of this issue. See the letter from Lafore, 11 May 1896, which stressed that a range of political positions were represented in the new Escòla Gaston Fèbus: *OC*, v, 299.

known, men such as Paul Sébillot, Emile Souvestre, and François-Marie Luzel, were left wing.[55] Arnaudin himself never made any open political commitments, and was horrified to discover at one point that his name had been circulating on a list of possible local political candidates.[56] The moment in his life when a public career was possible had long passed. Like other folklorists, Arnaudin's politics fit poorly to ideas of left and right: although he was often deeply critical of rural elites and the exploitation of agricultural workers, his views were imbued with a fixed conservatism, a distrust of manual labourers, and a belief that things had been better in the past.[57] Arnaudin's only political choice was a negative one: to abstain from local and national politics.

His intellectual interests nonetheless suggest a strong vein of anti-modernist conservatism, which drew on wider currents at the end of the nineteenth century. Arnaudin read the works of Maurice Barrès, who championed 'the earth and the dead', particularly closely, and seems to have been strongly influenced by his ideas about belonging, nationhood, and death.[58] He also read books by Cesare Lombroso, the influential Italian criminologist, who suggested that criminals were individuals who belonged to an earlier stage of human development. Arnaudin was immersed in a fin-de-siècle culture that worried about 'degeneration' and the ways that 'civilization' was a force that corrupted the very bodies of modern citizens.[59] Arnaudin's relationship to this vein of thought exposes a key tension in the nineteenth-century folklore movement in general. Interested in a social process of decline, he constantly individualized these general processes, melding them with his own personal set of disappointments. And yet this highly self-absorbed romanticism became the motivation for producing an archive that reflects the voices of the entire region.

This was always an impossibly vast project. Folklorists today would probably question whether the 'complete harvest' Arnaudin dreamed of was even possible.[60] Especially towards the end of his life Arnaudin talked of the 'very heavy task' that he 'somewhat blindly undertook'.[61] In 1900, he told Paul de Beaurepaire-Froment: 'I live only to finish my work'.[62] In his final years, Arnaudin suffered

[55] Hopkin, *Voices of the People*, 36–7; Shanny Peer, *France on Display*, 2–3.

[56] NFA, 2 MI 29/24, f.566.

[57] See, for example, the folklorist-photographer P.H. Emerson's strongly worded attacks on the inhumanity of local landlords, despite his reactionary politics. Clive Wilkins-Jones, 'One of the Hard Old Breed: A Life of Peter Henry Emerson', in *Life and Landscape: P.H. Emerson: Art and Photography in East Anglia, 1885–1900*, eds. Neil McWilliam and Veronica Sekules (Norwich, 1986), 3.

[58] On Barrès, see: Ruth Harris, *The Man on Devil's Island: Alfred Dreyfus and the Affair That Divided France* (London, 2011), 201–13.

[59] See, for example: Christopher E. Forth, 'La Civilisation and Its Discontents: Modernity, Manhood and the Body in Early Third Republic', in *French Masculinities: History, Culture, and Politics*, eds. Christopher E. Forth and Bertrand Taithe (Basingstoke, 2007), 85–102.

[60] He used the phrase in a letter to Jean Barthélémy, 3 February 1895: *OC*, v, 332.

[61] See the letters to Paul Sébillot and Antoine Degert, 14 and 17 January 1888: *OC*, v, 64, 65.

[62] Letter of 6 July 1900: *OC*, v, 161.

from nose bleeds and vertigo, and his notes suggest he had a stroke. Worried about being paralysed, he armed himself with poison.[63] On 6 December 1921, his fear was realized. Arnaudin died a few hours after the paralysis set in.[64]

The papers he left behind were scattered between different drawers in his house, leading one of the men charged by him with posthumously publishing his writings to talk of 'absolute chaos'.[65] Three posthumous works appeared in the 1920s—two volumes of ethnographic and historical notes entitled *Remnants of the Old Moorlands*, and a photographic album entitled *In the Days of the Stilts*—but most of Arnaudin's papers remained unedited. It took until the 1960s for any systematic attempt to publish the unedited proverbs, narratives, and songs, but even these works were based on a limited selection of the papers.[66] Finally, in 1979 the Arnaudin family donated the majority of the surviving manuscripts to the Parc Naturel Régional des Landes de Gascogne, who in turn entrusted the materials to the Archives Départementales des Landes in 1991. In 1992, Jacques Boisgontier added more documents to the collection, and in 1994 the first volume of a nine-volume complete works appeared. After the final volume of Arnaudin's materials—his diary and natural history writings—appeared in 2003, a further index was produced in 2007. Eighty-six years after his death, the edition finally does justice to his life's work.

Arnaudin's research was as divisive after his death as it was during his lifetime. He himself was jealous, secretive, bitter, and obsessed, and even his mentor Jean-Baptiste Lescarret had some words of criticism for the way Arnaudin fiercely protected his project.[67] After his death, other researchers inherited his painful compulsion, and the complete works were the subject of fierce academic disagreements.[68] The reason why is not hard to see in retrospect. As with the work of other folklorists, Arnaudin's legacy is contested because it amounts to the heritage of an entire region.[69]

Crafting a Terrain

But Arnaudin's manuscripts do not speak with one voice. They are the scene of struggles and arguments. Singers and storytellers would sometimes refuse to provide what he wanted and were often determined to give him things he was

---

[63] NFA, 2 MI 29/24, f.383.   [64] Daugé, 'Félix Arnaudin', 5.

[65] Latry, 'Introduction', *OC*, v, vii; See André Poudenx's comments in: NFA, 2 MI 29/34, f.409.

[66] See: Florence Galli-Dupis, 'Les Fonds Félix Arnaudin (1844–1921), collecteur et photographe des 'Choses de l'ancienne Grande Lande', www.garae.fr/spip.php?article206.

[67] See Lescarret's review of the *Contes*, reproduced in *OC*, v, 105.

[68] These are evident in the uncatalogued papers held by the Parc Naturel Régional des Landes de Gascogne in Belin-Beliet.

[69] See especially the divisive legacy of Luzel in Brittany. Françoise Morvan, *François-Marie Luzel: Enquête sur une expérience de collecte folklorique en Bretagne* (Dinan, 1999).

not seeking. His manuscripts almost betray a fascination with materials Arnaudin himself considered inappropriate, as he compulsively recorded texts which he thought were useless, because they were too obscene, too French, or incomplete. In his manuscripts, attempts at censorship are self-defeating, as he records his own frustrations at finding materials that he did not want.[70] In this way, the manuscripts tell modern readers both how Arnaudin wanted the moorlands to be seen, and the limits of his ability to control the culture he sought to record.

The researcher most familiar with Arnaudin's life and manuscripts, Guy Latry, has called his project nothing less than 'the invention of a region'.[71] The area around the villages of Sabres and Labouheyre known as the 'Grande-Lande' was the part of the moorlands with the sparsest population, the fewest pine trees, and the most open moorland.[72] Before Arnaudin's fieldwork, it was seen as a desert: both physically and culturally empty. He gave the region a cultural identity, asserting its difference from other parts of the department, such as the fertile agricultural lands of the Chalosse in the south, the coastal region of the Marensin, and the area further east around Roquefort, known as the Petites-Landes.[73] He wrote in his notes:

> The Béarnais have a very pretty proverb:
>
> 'Jan Petit made buttons
>
> He didn't make very big ones, but he made very good ones.'
>
> My only ambition is to be as much like Jan Petit as possible. What I mean is that I have deliberately restricted myself... to a relatively small geographical area in order to produce better work.[74]

In his thinking, the limits of this area were linguistic and geographical.[75] Nearby communities that spoke a slightly different patois might as well be in another country. Arnaudin's only interest in the folklore of neighbouring regions such as the Petites-Landes or the Bazadais was to prove that the culture of the 'Grande-Lande'—the true moorlands—was different.[76] This heartland of pastoralism, the region of open skies and wild moors, was where Arnaudin collected folklore.

---

[70] Judith Butler, *Excitable Speech: A Politics of the Performative* (New York, 1997); Pooley, 'Can the "Peasant" Speak?'.

[71] Latry uses the word 'pays'. See: Guy Latry, 'Introduction,' in *Contes des Landes*, ed. Françoise Morvan (Bordeaux, 2011), 20.

[72] See: Guérin, 'Paysan-Résinier de Lévignacq (Landes)'. The map Thore produced at the start of the nineteenth century shows that there were almost no pine plantations in the Grande Lande. See: Jean Thore, *Promenade sur les côtes du Golfe de Gascogne*, 6–7, 177–8.

[73] Arnaudin explained the differences between these regions in his notes. See, for instance: NFA, 2 MI 29/8, f.166.

[74] NFA, 2 MI 29/34, f.363.   [75] NFA, 2 MI 29/21, f.255.

[76] Guy Latry, 'Une Enquête de Félix Arnaudin dans le Bazadais', *Cahiers du Bazadais* (1987), 29–41.

His notes also give some idea of when he did most of his fieldwork. Although there are hints in his diary that Arnaudin was interested in folk songs as early as 1862, when he was just eighteen years old, the earliest notes in his folklore manuscripts are from 1873, when he collected songs from the shepherd Jean Saubesty, known as 'the Boss' (1818–94), and his wife Elisabeth Plantié, known as Babé (1826–1912).[77] Arnaudin made a point of saying in 1912 that some of his fieldwork dated back thirty-five years before.[78] Although this may be true, it certainly does not reflect when he did the majority of his song collecting, if the surviving manuscript notes are to be believed. He was most active between 1885 and 1910, and the last records come from around the outbreak of the First World War. Arnaudin intended to continue after the fighting stopped, and told correspondents that he had suspended his project for the war.[79] By 1918, his health had declined, and there is little evidence he resumed his work.[80]

Over this forty-year period, his interests and methodologies noticeably shifted. His first published piece was an article of 1873 in the *Revue de Gascogne* on 'A Branch of the Pic de la Mirandole Family in the Landes'. The article was an attempt to use a legend that he recorded about a 'wicked lord' in the eighteenth century to supplement the historical record concerning this aristocratic family. As with several other projects, Arnaudin later abandoned this early agenda of supplementing written historical records with the evidence of popular tradition. In 1899, he admitted to the folklorist Paul Sébillot that he had perhaps neglected local legends, since his interest had been drawn to other materials.[81] Magical tales, songs, and photography seem to have vied for Arnaudin's attention in this second stage, but he was much quicker to publish a selection of the tales, which appeared in 1887.[82] The songs and photographs were left aside, and would not in fact appear in print until 1912.

A major factor in this delay was his disappointment with the reception of his short collection of tales. He felt unjustly criticized by writers such as Henri Gaidoz and the abbé Vincent Foix.[83] Partly, the criticisms were based on the nature of the materials. Few of the stories Arnaudin published were completely unknown from other parts of Europe, and he was disappointed to find that the moorlands did not have stories that were completely unique.[84] But several writers also criticized his linguistic notes and his decisions on how to represent the Gascon patois. And even more disappointing for Arnaudin was the silence his collection elicited. Friends

---

[77]   26 January 1862: Arnaudin hid by the roadside in order to listen to a man singing on his way home: *OC*, viii, 36. Jean Saubesty was called 'lou Patroun' in Gascon.

[78]   *OC*, iii, XX.   [79]   *OC*, v, 439–40.

[80]   Although this is what the abbé Daugé claimed in his obituary: Daugé, 'Félix Arnaudin', 4.

[81]   Letter of 12 April 1899: *OC*, v, 145.

[82]   Félix Arnaudin, *Contes populaires recueillis dans la Grande-Lande, le Born, les Petites-Landes et le Marensin* (Paris, 1887).

[83]   NFA, 2 MI 29/20, f.518.

[84]   See his letters to Gaidoz and Barthélémy, 23 November 1888 and 3 February 1895: *OC*, v, 67, 332–3.

tried to reassure him that the public for folklore writings was necessarily small in any case, and Arnaudin also later discovered that his publishers had failed to send review copies to many of the journals that were meant to receive them, but the damage to his pride was done.[85]

The reception of the tales was just the first in a series of disappointments that convinced him that his work was not appreciated in academic circles.[86] In 1918 Arnaudin wrote to Arthur Rossat that he 'did not have many connections with the folklorists any more, because of the cold reception my little book of songs received'.[87] His disappointment must have been even more acute than his feelings over the indifference to his book of tales: since then, songs had been his overriding passion. He wrote to one correspondent that the songs 'are especially close to my heart', and the years after 1887 were devoured by exhaustive song-collecting campaigns, which resulted in 3,620 song texts, collected from at least 517 singers.[88] The difference between this song fieldwork and many of the other projects he embarked on was that he came closest to finishing it. In 1912, the first volume appeared, and Arnaudin also gathered and organized the materials for two more volumes which must have been close to completion in the year before he died.[89]

Throughout this period, other ethnographic projects competed with the songs for Arnaudin's time. He took almost 4,000 photographs, of which just a few are personal. The majority are landscapes, group portraits, and architectural photographs, designed to capture 'the physiognomy of our old country'.[90] At the same time, he was meticulously collecting proverbs, riddles, and charms, and taking notes for a dialect dictionary. While he is known to many people today for his photographs of the old moorlands, specialists do not necessarily see this as his most important work. Jacques Boisgontier and Guy Latry, for instance, have tended to see dialectology as the centre of his project. This has some grounding in his writings, as Arnaudin sometimes emphasized language as the real object of his publications.[91] Nor did he ever completely abandon the interest in local history that he had developed when he was researching the local legend of the wicked lord. He continued to ask his singers and storytellers what they knew about historical events on the edge of living memory, such as the French Revolution and Napoleonic Wars, and even extended his interests to local archaeological finds, such as a haul of coins uncovered in Labouheyre.[92] Like other folklorists, his interests stretched beyond what specialists today might recognize as the strictly ethnological. He kept notes for a book about local hunting—a particular regional

---

[85] See the letter from Landrin, 4 May 1889, and a series of letters concerning the missing review copies: *OC*, v, 136–42.

[86] See for example: NFA, 2 MI 29/12, f.67.   [87] Letter of 5 January 1918: *OC*, v, 454.

[88] Letter to Lafore, 27 April 1896: *OC*, v, 297.

[89] Félix Arnaudin, *Chants populaires de la Grande-Lande et des régions voisines* (Paris, 1912).

[90] Letter to Landrin, 8 April 1888. *OC*, v, 78.   [91] Letter of 12 March 1889. *OC*, v, 109.

[92] Arnaudin became involved in a lengthy correspondence about the coins. *OC*, v, 206–13.

and personal passion—and even had aspirations to write the natural history of the moorlands, sending other specialists plants and insects by letter.[93] Yet popular traditions always came first. Most of his historical and botanical research was left unfinished, and his own notes make it clear that this was because he consciously prioritized his writings on folklore.[94]

Fieldwork Methods

How did Arnaudin go about contacting these singers and storytellers, and what did he do in order to record their songs? To some degree, his notes represent his own choices about what was important about local folklore, and prioritized his own aesthetic and social concerns. In the song manuscripts, he sometimes crossed texts out, writing 'rubbish' across the top of the page. This might be because they were not sung in the local patois or because he thought they were too rude.[95] But, for the most part, these choices were aesthetic. He rejected songs that were 'deformed', 'uninteresting', 'insignificant', or 'very banal, but very well-known', preferring those with tunes that were, as he put it, 'delicious'.[96] As with other folklorists of the period, these aesthetic considerations sometimes sat awkwardly with his desire to be faithful to exactly what his informants said.[97] Like landscape painters, folklorists wanted both beauty and fidelity.[98] Arnaudin himself wrote that he wanted his ethnographic photographs to be 'both as *precise* but also as *artistic* as possible'.[99] In terms of oral traditions, this double imperative was a license to edit and rework the original transcriptions for publication: the rushed and elliptical style of an oral tale or the ruder elements of a folk song would have to be 'polished, and tidied up'.[100]

But before the materials could even be reworked, they first had to be collected. The initial challenge was to find good informants, and there is plenty of evidence that this was far from straightforward for the folklorists. When Arnaudin's mentor the novelist Jean-Baptiste Lescarret tried to collect songs from women working in Bordeaux, they assumed he was teasing them, and refused to help.[101] The English folklorist Alfred Williams was mistaken for a tramp on one occasion and suspected of being a German spy on another.[102] Arnaudin's notes are filled with

---

[93] See his letters of 7 January and 7 February 1887. *OC*, v, 221.
[94] See, for instance: NFA, 2 MI 29/24, f.359.
[95] See, for example: NFA, 2 MI 29/4, ff.9 and 226–8.
[96] See, for instance: NFA, 2 MI 29/1, ff.427, 487, 2 MI 29/2, ff.26, 387, 2 MI 29/3, ff.100, 277, 2 MI 29/4, f.297.
[97] Postic, 'Le Beau ou le vrai'.   [98] Hopkin, *Voices of the People*, 39–41.
[99] The emphasis is in the original. Letter to Alphonse Davanne, 19 April 1887. *OC*, v, 16.
[100] See the letter to Labrouche, 15 September 1888. *OC*, v, 88.
[101] Letter of 27 January 1889. *OC*, v, 97.
[102] Alfred Williams, *Folk-Songs of the Upper Thames: With an Essay on Folk-Song Activity in the Upper Thames Neighbourhood* (new edn, Detroit, 1968 [1923]), 27–8.

anecdotes about informants who he did not dare approach, or who turned out to be useless. His method depended on getting recommendations of singers and storytellers who were known to be talented within their communities. But when he came to record their materials, they might turn out to be dead, or unsuitable. One singer named Cataline had suffered some kind of 'mental disturbance. She thinks one thing, but says something different.'[103] The widow Cigrand, a singer in Mimizan, turned out to be deaf.[104]

Arnaudin's personal acquaintances, on the other hand, offered guaranteed sources of folklore, but needed to be managed even more carefully. Babé Plantié was such a close employee of the Arnaudin family that it fell to her to announce the deaths of relatives to Arnaudin's father, Barthélémy.[105] She was also by far Arnaudin's most prolific informant, providing some 187 song texts and sixteen stories. Yet he wanted to play down her importance in his published writings. Having initially listed her fifteenth in his list of informants, he wrote a note to himself: 'put her further down... delete that... don't give her more fame than necessary. She is not worth it.'[106] With Babé, the motivation for this demotion is not clear. With other informants who also worked for him, the tensions were more obvious. He suspected both Jean Monicien (1866+) and Jean Cazade (1850+) of charging him too much money for the work they did for him, or stealing materials like wood and manure.[107] During the First World War, he was very bitter about the fact that some of his tenants had stopped paying him rent.[108]

Arnaudin did not limit himself to mining the men and women who worked for him for folklore. He also collected from personal friends, his parents, brother, and nephew, and even from lovers. And these relationships could sometimes sour. He fell out with the storyteller Henri Vidal after Henri made some ill-considered statements about a business venture Arnaudin had once undertaken with him.[109] While she never appeared in any of his published writings, it is clear from the manuscripts that his servant and lover Marie Darlanne provided songs, stories, and proverbs. Arnaudin also collected materials from at least one other lover, someone he referred to in the manuscripts as 'Uv'. Perhaps most damning of all is a short note he wrote about a 'pretty woman' named Anna Raymond, which suggests that his folklore fieldwork might have overlapped directly with his sex life. Arnaudin noted she had been 'married for eleven years' before slipping into the Latin that he used for risqué topics to note that she was 'without children (one had died)'.[110] It is not much of a stretch to imagine that Arnaudin was considering a sexual relationship of some kind with Anna.

[103] NFA, 2 MI 29/24, f.56.   [104] NFA, 2 MI 29/20, f.311.
[105] See 9 March 1876: OC, viii, 121.   [106] NFA, 2 MI 29/1, f.14.
[107] See, for example: NFA, 2 MI 29/17, f.38, 2 MI 29/18, f.64.
[108] NFA, 2 MI 29/24, f.395; OC, v, 434.   [109] OC, v, 243–4; OC, viii, 107.
[110] NFA, 2 MI 29/24, f.56.

These personal connections depended on communication technologies that Arnaudin wrote out of his published accounts. Like other folklorists, his project depended on a paradoxical attitude to modern technologies.[111] He talked of the destruction of the old culture by the forces of modernity, railing against trains, teachers, and the newspapers, but his fieldwork was achieved with photographic equipment, a bicycle, the train, and even by car. His photographs were taken at a time when the open moorlands had almost completely disappeared, but he positioned the new technology to capture the vestiges of the landscape of his youth.[112] The train that brought new trade and new ideas to the villages of the former moorlands, consolidating the changes of the 1857 law, was the same train Arnaudin rode to find the oldest storytellers and singers. In some ways, this anti-modernism led Arnaudin to create a static and rigid picture of how life used to be. Like his photographs, his folklore fieldwork was often staged, rather than improvised.[113]

He also depended heavily on letter writing. Sometimes it was singers or storytellers themselves who wrote to him, although it was much more common for a literate son or daughter to record their parents.[114] It can be hard to tell who the 'singer' or 'storyteller' is, and whether the version Arnaudin received was a new performance by someone who was a performer in their own right, or whether men like Joseph Sart, known as Jules (1853–1921) and Henri Vidal simply saw themselves as scribes. These intermediaries tended to come from similar backgrounds to the folklorist himself. Many were men, and most were fairly well off, although his maid and lover Marie Darlanne recorded at least one story for him.[115] Some of the notes in Arnaudin's manuscripts even came from correspondences with other local folklorists, such as the abbé Vincent Foix.

When it came to face-to-face meetings, Guy Latry has gone so far as to call Arnaudin's fieldwork techniques similar to laboratory control, as the folklorist attempted to detail every aspect of how he collected songs and stories. Latry studied the example of the fieldwork Arnaudin did in Souis in 1908, discovering how the folklorist wrote to a local baker, named Bernard Lassévils, with very specific instructions: the singers should be old, female, illiterate, and discreet. They were not required to sing, but merely to recite the songs. In this case, Arnaudin travelled to them, and he often organized similar singing groups in order to collect songs. On other occasions, he would visit individual singers, or persuade them to come to him. In Souis, Arnaudin offered to pay the singers, as long as they could

---

[111] Sargos, 'Félix', 25. For other folklorists with a paradoxical relation to modernity, see for example Victor Smith's use of the trains in the Velay to reach his informants, discussed in: Hopkin, *Voices of the People*, 210–52.

[112] Guy Latry, 'Miroirs voilés: la photographie dans l'oeuvre d'Arnaudin', in *Félix Arnaudin: imagier de la Grande Lande*, ed. Jacques Sargos (Bordeaux, 1993), 146.

[113] Pierre Bardou, 'Lou limajayre', in *Félix Arnaudin: imagier de la Grande Lande*, ed. Jacques Sargos (Bordeaux, 1993), 142.

[114] For instance: NFA, 2 MI 29/5, f.10, 2 MI 29/19, f.485.   [115] NFA, 2 MI 29/11, f.58.

meet his conditions for doing fieldwork, most obviously by keeping it a secret.[116] On other occasions, he took similar care to remain secret, even drawing careful maps that would allow him to discreetly approach informants' houses, as he was fearful of being spotted by suspicious neighbours.[117]

Once Arnaudin had found an informant, he still had to persuade them to perform for him. As his correspondence makes clear, he paid some in cash. Others agreed to sing in exchange for having their portraits done. The singer Catherine Brouqueyre, known as Liya de Bidau, had her daughter-in-law write to the folklorist confirming she had more songs for him. After the signature, she wrote, in a mixture of polite forms with absolutely no punctuation: 'I note with pleasure that if needs be you will bring your camera if you don't mind do as you like'.[118] For at least a few of his literate singers, there was the appeal of seeing their name in print, or receiving a copy of the Folksongs of the Grande-Lande in 1912.[119]

The notes he took once he had set up a meeting can be hard to decipher, but they reveal an obsession with fidelity. The strictness of his techniques is evident in the standards to which he held the men who collected folklore for him. He gave detailed instructions to Jean Barthélémy (1840–1922) for collecting songs from Marie Lorty, known as Maria, femme Dubos (1859+):

Please be kind enough to have her sing, and to copy down *every single word, exactly as she says it*. I don't know if what I sent in my note is an accurate version of the song, so please don't read it to her beforehand. That way you will avoid influencing her memory. The smallest difference in one word could be very important to me. And even if she can only remember a few scraps, and odds and ends, please carefully record them. They may be very useful.[120]

Arnaudin, like other folklorists of the period, was a victim of what David Hopkin has called 'the obsessive nature of collecting [folklore] the constant hope for a new song, a unique variant'.[121] To satisfy this obsession, he used checklists and questionnaires, which he would either go over with his informants, or send to them by post.[122] He also used his most reliable and most helpful informants to go over texts, frequently noting minor variations in the versions of songs or stories

[116] Letter of 26 March 1908: *OC*, v, 339; Latry, 'Une enquête de Félix Arnaudin dans le Bazadais'; Latry, 'Introduction', *OC*, v, XXV.
[117] NFA, 2 MI 29/1, f.148. [118] NFA, 2 MI 29/19, f.485.
[119] For singers who sang in exchange for portraits, see for example the letter of 25 August 1908: *OC*, v, 339. For singers to whom Arnaudin gave copies of the book, see for instance 2 MI 29/279. The English folklorist Cecil Sharp also gave his informants copies of his published versions of their songs and offered portraits in exchange for music. See: Chris J. Bearman, 'Who Were the Folk? The Demography of Cecil Sharp's Somerset Folksingers', *Historical Journal*, xliii (2000), 756–7.
[120] Letter of 23 December 1895: *OC*, v, 332–3. [121] Hopkin, *Voices of the People*, 213.
[122] There are a great many of these questionnaires in the manuscripts. See for example a checklist he sent to two singers in Captieux. They were meant to write whether or not they knew the song next to each title: NFA, 2 MI 29/19, f.474.

they performed.[123] Although he was never as thorough with the tales as with the songs, Arnaudin collected several stories more than once from the same narrator.[124]

He was not above using subterfuge to persuade reluctant informants, and the abbé Césaire Daugé painted a picture of him slyly noting songs and stories: 'Often the storyteller or singer, disconcerted and baffled by the sight of the folklorist's pencil, refused to go on. So he would put his hands behind his back, and write on a piece of paper stuck to his left hand.'[125] This might go some way to explaining Arnaudin's handwriting. When the interaction worked well, he could spend entire days listening to a talented storyteller or singer.[126] Towards the end of his life, however, Arnaudin reflected bitterly about the waste of time, effort, and money much of his collecting had been. He would spend up to a week at a time travelling to see informants, and estimated he had spent forty years of his life and 25,000 francs on his fieldwork.[127]

In pursuit of the traditions of the moorlands, Arnaudin would go almost anywhere within the small region. He collected a great deal of material from men and women outside, in fields, or standing watching sheep by their sheepfolds: 'Between two sheepfolds I found [Jean Bernède, known as] 'the Singer', who sat on the heather with me to sing me some songs'.[128] While the image he liked to project in his published writings of fortuitous encounters is not the whole story, neither are the planned sessions with singers reciting the words to songs. Arnaudin really did collect folklore in everyday situations, like the time a man with a rake wandering through a pine plantation gave him a couplet for a song.[129] This was carried to its extreme in the fieldwork he did for the proverbs and dictionary. In his notes for an introduction to his dialect dictionary, Arnaudin wrote:

> You may note that my examples are often extensive, and *the word* [in question] is swamped by many other words. I did this on purpose [crossed out]. My phrases, which have been taken from the lips of the people, and reproduced absolutely as they were spoken, with absolute precision, will help not only to understand the different uses and specific meanings of the words themselves, but also reflect the cultural reality [of the moorlands].[130]

---

[123] For instance, 'Text carefully checked with Babé'. NFA, 2 MI 29/3, f.81; he also mentioned 'reverifying' songs in two letters to Alexis de Chasteigner, 14 February and 25 July 1889: *OC*, v, 102, 199. Latry highlights Babé's role in checking texts. Guy Latry, 'Représenter dans l'ecriture: Collecte et transcription chez les folkloristes à travers un exemple gascon', *Cahiers de Littérature Orale*, lii (2002), 116–32. Latry also talks of Arnaudin using informants to fill in missing texts. See: 'Une enquête de Félix Arnaudin dans le Bazadais', 37.

[124] NFA, 2 MI 29/11, ff.380, 631.   [125] Daugé, 'Félix Arnaudin', 3.

[126] He spent the whole day with Jean Destruhaut, known as lou Mén, on 24 June 1879, for instance: *OC*, viii, 152.

[127] See his letter to Charles Schweitzer, in October 1889: *OC*, v, 125; NFA, 2 MI 29/12, f.209, 2 MI 29/21, f.168.

[128] 22 or 25 September, 1879: *OC*, viii, 153.   [129] NFA, 2 MI 29/19, f.470.

[130] NFA, 2 MI 29/8, f.15.

He collected proverbs from people passing on the road, or from mule drivers waiting for the train at a level-crossing, from men and women as they worked, and even from people on the train.[131] The annual fairs in villages such as Labouheyre were such fertile grounds for this kind of fieldwork that Arnaudin had a whole series of notebooks on the 'Fairs'.[132] The one place he generally resisted was local inns. Although there are some records of materials he collected there, he was reluctant to go into drinking establishments for his fieldwork. He was disappointed to realize that Marguerite Dubos, known as Maguide (1839+) was an innkeeper: 'She runs a bar, there are always drinkers there, which puts me off, I wouldn't and I couldn't. In fact, I went in on 28 April, the other week, and seeing the drinkers sitting at their tables made me regret the decision immediately.'[133] Nor was this the only source of tension with potential informants. When Arnaudin was collecting material, much was beyond his control, as he often bitterly complained. He was at the mercy of weather, train timetables, and bicycles. But more than anything else, he was at the mercy of the suspicious locals and difficult go-betweens who were the folk. He had problems with singers like Marinette Glize (1849–1916), who refused to come the first time he asked, and did not turn up the second. Marinette herself was not at fault: she had been called away to help at a threshing, but it turned out she had forgotten the songs he wanted anyway.[134] Faced with the challenges of walking long distances or taking inconvenient trains, Arnaudin encouraged his informants to write down their stories and songs, and even those of other people they knew. But this just raised a whole new set of problems. Some persisted in sending him songs in French, rather than the patois he wanted. On one occasion, a local road worker named Jean Pabon told him that the singer Anne Joie (1843+) had lost the list of songs that Arnaudin had asked for. Instead, she had sung some others, as had Pabon's own brother. Pabon added: 'they are charming'.[135] Far from being the sole author of his collection, Arnaudin was entangled in exchanges of money, objects, work, affection, and distrust. His manuscripts tell a story of multiple agencies, as men like Pabon chose what was 'charming' just as much as Arnaudin himself did.

Conclusion

As a folklorist, Arnaudin was relatively typical.[136] Many other middle-class men across Europe in this period found themselves drawn to folk traditions for their connection to a supposedly disappearing past. Their motives and their political inspirations were varied, but many, like Arnaudin, embraced new methodological

---

[131] NFA, 2 MI 29/10, ff.6, 21, 22, 51, 66.   [132] NFA, 2 MI 29/24, 2 MI 29/10, ff.13, 93.
[133] NFA, 2 MI 29/20, f.219.   [134] NFA, 2 MI 29/1, f.42.   [135] OC, v, 334.
[136] Dorothy Noyes, 'Humble Theory', *Journal of Folklore Research*, 45, no. 1 (2008), 37–43.

criteria in order to produce works that would accurately reflect the folk and their lore. Their inspirations and justifications for what they did were not necessarily consistent. Like Arnaudin, other folklorists projected theories of social decline onto their own experiences and confused their own biographies with the progress and pitfalls of civilization. But the importance of this confusion lies in what it bequeaths for historians: the folklorists should not just be the subject of intellectual histories of ideas about popular culture. In their unpublished papers, historians can read both along and against the grain, to construct a conversation between folklorists and folk. Arnaudin's papers reveal a meticulous, detailed, systematic, and careful ethnographer at work, as well as an opinionated, romantic, and nostalgic aspiring author. While Arnaudin's published work was self-consciously shaped to reflect his own interpretation of the changes he saw around him, his notes suggest curiosity, and a willingness to be surprised by local culture and local people. Motivated by a mixture of personal nostalgia, bitterness, regret, and self-aggrandizing heroism, Arnaudin's collection is nonetheless the expression of the culture of a wide range of different men and women, artisans and shepherds, farmers and road builders, servants and soldiers.

Arnaudin held different forms of power over many of these informants, but he was far from omnipotent. The care he took in his fieldwork methods uncovered a range of materials that he actively tried to suppress in his published work. In the manuscripts, historians can find both Arnaudin's ambitions and the reality of his interactions with informants who he sometimes found stubborn and non-compliant, and at other times considered too willing, eager to take on the mantle of folklorist for themselves, and to act as collector in their own right. Having seen these men and women through Arnaudin's eyes, Chapter 3 steps outside of his manuscripts to ask what can be learned about these singers and storytellers that Arnaudin did not know—or was not willing to say.

3

Singers and Storytellers

In his published works, Arnaudin wrote lyrically of the elderly shepherds whose traditional lives preserved the culture of the moorlands even after the triumph of the pines. This chapter asks how accurate this depiction of their lives was. What can we learn from his notes and from other archival sources about things he left out of the books? At the most basic level, who were his singers and storytellers? A broad understanding of their work, their family lives, their education, and social class is a necessary starting point for understanding the songs and stories in Arnaudin's manuscripts.

Other archives tell other stories about these women and men that Arnaudin named, did not name, or could not name.[1] The lives of these singers and storytellers can be pieced together from birth, marriage, and death certificates, military, conscription, and employment records, and notarial acts such as marriage contracts, loans, and sales of land. I have identified 759 different informants mentioned in the manuscripts, although this number is imprecise, as it includes individuals from whom no materials survive in the manuscripts, as well as individuals who are hard to identify in any other sources. Arnaudin often provided full names, ages, and locations for informants, but he was not always so scrupulous, and it was easy for him to record inaccurate information. Sometimes he simply used nicknames or abbreviations, and sometimes the information is simply missing, perhaps lost in the confusion that followed his death in 1921. Of the 759 mentioned in the manuscripts, I have firmly identified 333 in other sources. For the other 426, all I know relies on whatever Arnaudin himself recorded. Sometimes this was as little as 'a young man in the hamlet of Brin'. Often it includes information on occupation and some hints as to who the individual might have been, such as the 'chamber-maid of Joseph Dulau', who was almost certainly the same person as either Marinéte Dupin of Loc-Bielh (b. 1863) or Dorine Bertrande (1868+).[2] Both worked for Joseph Dulau, and Arnaudin recorded the details of both in other notes, so it is impossible to say which he was referring to in his manuscripts.

---

[1] For a similar analysis, see: Bearman, 'Who Were the Folk?'; C.J. Bearman, 'Cecil Sharp in Somerset'.

[2] The young man at Brin was mentioned in NFA, 2 MI 29/1, f.175. Joseph Dulau's chambermaid was mentioned in NFA, 2 MI 29/5, f.327.

Body and Tradition in Nineteenth-Century France: Félix Arnaudin and the Moorlands of Gascony, 1870–1914.
William G. Pooley, Oxford University Press (2019). © William G. Pooley.
DOI: 10.1093/oso/9780198847502.001.0001

The general picture that emerges from this research in other documents presents the singers and storytellers in a very different light to how Arnaudin himself liked to describe them. Folklorists have emphasized that traditions make sense in the contexts where they are handed on. The contexts Arnaudin's informants performed in were not the static pastoralism of the pre-forest moorlands which he tried to reconstruct: his informants were younger, more literate, more familiar with the French language, and more mobile than Arnaudin pretended, the first sections of the chapter will argue. Although his notes do not provide extensive evidence about how traditions were passed on within and beyond local communities, the final section of the chapter suggests some outlines of the conduits along which songs and stories flowed. This research into Arnaudin's informants and the ways traditions were transmitted suggests that, far from belonging to a disappearing and unchanging world, these songs and stories were shaped in the context of new concerns about work and family.

'My Rustic Collaborators'

Many of the tensions described in Chapter 2 stemmed from Arnaudin's resentment of the forcefulness and individuality of his informants. His feelings towards Babé Plantié come across most clearly, as he brooded in his notes on demoting her in his published version of the songs. More broadly, it is telling that, although he very proudly credited his informants at the start of his book of folk songs, the songs themselves were not attributed to specific singers. In fact, Arnaudin showed some frustration with singers, such as Jeanne Garbay, known as Néte de Penalh (1859+), who took liberties with songs, improvising or introducing new verses.[3] Since his death Arnaudin has been seen as a model for ethnographic honesty, thanks to these lists of informants.[4] Arnaudin himself was given to self-congratulation about this, even as he sniped about the unworthiness and ignorance of the informants: 'It is proof of my conscientiousness to have collected songs from over 500 people, and proof of my gratitude/kindness to give their names. Of the 230 I chose to list, probably just five even know they have earned this honour.'[5] Yet, as his note about only publishing 230 of the 500 names makes clear, Arnaudin's book of folk songs did not tell the whole truth about the women and men that he called his 'rustic collaborators', and nor did his book of stories.[6] He systematically edited the details he published about these people to emphasize patois-speaking, elderly men and women, who worked in traditional occupations, such as farming and

---

[3] NFA, 2 MI 29/1, f.44.
[4] Arnold van Gennep used Arnaudin's 1912 book of songs as the example of best practice in terms of naming informants in his influential book on French folklore. See: Gennep, *Le Folklore français*, i, 74.
[5] NFA, 2 MI 29/12, f.58.   [6] Letter of 25 March 1885: *OC*, v, 55.

shepherding, to fit with his vision of the moorlands, and his sense of their inevitable decline. Denis Labeau (1853+), one of Arnaudin's most reliable singers, provides a good example. How the two men met is not clear. They lived near each other in neighbouring villages for many years, but Arnaudin does not seem to have mentioned him in his diary, and never wrote to him. This is probably because he had no need: Denis would have seen Arnaudin regularly on his rounds as a local postman. His job as an employee of the modern state and a distributor of written culture and the fact that he was not even a local explain why it was that Arnaudin never mentioned him in any of his publications, and included scant details about him in his own manuscripts.[7] The postman was typical of the individuals Arnaudin tried to erase from his published works.

Arnaudin pruned his singers and storytellers based on some clear criteria, which can be discerned in his notes. A surname could be enough to exclude an informant. Duviella, Philibert, and Couyon were apparently too 'exotic'.[8] They were not typical enough of local, Gascon-sounding names. Another important reason to exclude informants was the question of which languages they sang or narrated in. French was unacceptable, despite the large volumes of material many of his most trusted informants contributed in the national language rather than the local dialect.[9] Arnaudin also excluded informants for other reasons connected to how he wanted the collections to appear. He worried that both Jean Hazera and Étienne Dupouy might at different points have got in trouble for stealing.[10] He gave up on a man called Labadie because he was 'moronic'.[11]

But Arnaudin's informants were not powerless in this exchange. It is clear that he felt pressure to include certain names, and some informants badgered him. He wrote a short note about the singer Jean Laguë: 'a former resin-worker (now a road mender), born in Geloux, in Petit-Louricat, living in Sabres, 32 years old (12 March 1914). Is determined.' Arnaudin then recorded that Jean Laguë had complained 'But I'm not in there!' Arnaudin noted 'promised' next to the road mender's complaint, suggesting it was his protests that persuaded Arnaudin to include his name in the book.[12] On the other hand, sometimes he rode rough-shod over his informants. He wrote that Marie Labadie, known as Justine, femme Lahari (1882+), was useless since she 'gave me none of the songs I asked for'.[13] Neither did all of his informants want to figure in his published list. Arnaudin

---

[7] Denis is the only person with the correct surname to have lived in the region during the period when Arnaudin was collecting songs. On top of this, there is other evidence that corroborates this identification. Denis the postman was from the right part of the south-west to fit with what Arnaudin said about his accent, and when he got into trouble with the law in 1891, the local notables rallied around Denis, suggesting Arnaudin and his family must have known him. See ADL PS 16 (unsorted documents).

[8] Arnaudin used the word to refer to Marie Pomade, known as Trézine's married name, 'Duviella'. NFA, 2 MI 29/1, f.16.

[9] NFA, 2 MI 29/20, f.294.   [10] NFA, 2 MI 29/20, f.112, 2 MI 29/1, f.16.

[11] NFA, 2 MI 29/19, f.192.   [12] NFA, 2 MI 29/31, f.489.

[13] NFA, 2 MI 29/31, f.490.

wrote that he would include Marie Dulucq, femme Denis (1869+), if she sent the songs promised by her mother, but Marie herself had different ideas, writing to him 'I won't give you my [maiden] name I don't want to'.[14]

Issues around naming mean that many of Arnaudin's informants remain stubbornly hard to identify, especially since many local men and women were known not by their baptismal names, but by nicknames or *chaffres*.[15] Jeanne Barrière (1875+), for instance, was known as 'Cérise' because her mother had craved cherries when pregnant with her.[16] Other people inherited a nickname from their family, so both Pierre Fronsac (1823+) and his wife Claire Baladès (1827–1913) were known as 'Biroun(e)', even though the *chaffre* was based on a story from Pierre's mother's childhood.[17] At least one of the most important informants, 'Cabardès', who provided some ninety-four songs for Arnaudin's collection, is impossible to identify simply from this nickname.[18] Even people who did not have a proper *chaffre*, whether based on an incident from their own life or inherited from their family, were unlikely to use their baptismal names.[19] In the place of the French Christian names such as 'Jean', 'Jeanne', and 'Marie' that they were obliged to write on their birth certificates, many preferred to use names with a more Gascon feel: 'Jouan', 'Maguidote', 'Marinette', or just 'Nette' or 'Néte'. This variety of names means that it is possible that some of the different informants mentioned in the manuscripts are duplicates. Arnaudin sometimes used the maiden names, sometimes the married names, and sometimes the nicknames of his informants. On other occasions, he simply referred to groups of singers from specific villages, groups that must have included the named individuals he collected from there.

I have followed the hierarchical naming practices Arnaudin himself used: while his informants called him by his surname, he called many of them by their first names or nicknames. I have chosen to reproduce this inequality rather than erase it, because it draws attention to the fundamental dynamic of the ethnographic encounter. It also has the advantage of giving the historian insight into the most symbolically important identity of these people, the names that their communities bestowed on them.[20]

There are also ninety-six 'informants' mentioned in the manuscripts from whom no song or story texts survive. In many cases, Arnaudin recorded that these individuals knew songs and stories, but either he never got around to

---

[14] NFA, 2 MI 29/4, f.240.   [15] Lescarret, *La Vie dans la Grande-Lande*, 59–60.
[16] NFA, 2 MI 29/1, f.48.   [17] NFA, 2 MI 29/8, f.507.
[18] It could be his or her patronym, but it seems unlikely given that no one with this name was married in the Landes during this period. It could also be a nickname based on the hamlet where this mysterious singer lived. Tantalizingly, there is a hamlet in Labouheyre called 'Cabardos'. The patronym is Galician.
[19] On the significance of these naming practices, see: Françoise Zonabend, 'Pourquoi nommer?', in *L'Identité: Seminaire interdisciplinaire*, ed. Claude Lévi-Strauss (Paris, 1977), 257–79.
[20] Zonabend, 'Pourquoi Nommer?', 268, 271.

collecting them, or the notes have been lost. In some cases, the information they provided was actively negative, such as when informants told the folklorist that all of the local songs had disappeared. The vast majority of these informants only provided a few songs or stories for his collection. Over half provided just one or two songs, and very few provided large numbers of songs.[21] Arnaudin did not collect enough stories to come to many firm conclusions about repertoire sizes, but it is telling that over half of his storytellers told him just one.[22] Traditional culture was spread very thinly between a great many people.

And these people did not fit the stereotypes that Arnaudin himself suggested. Like other folklorists, Arnaudin sought out the oldest informants, and tended to emphasize elderly singers and storytellers in his published writings. But, as Guy Latry has pointed out, the informants Arnaudin actually found did not always conform to his vision of the 'old shepherds' who supposedly made the best storytellers. On one occasion, he asked a local innkeeper in Cazalis to provide elderly singers, but when he turned up, he found two young girls, Augustine Latrille (1893+) and Marie-Jeanne Rouchaleou (1895+), known as Marguerite.[23] The majority of Arnaudin's informants were actually younger than the folklorist himself.[24] This is not to say that none of his informants were very old. The oldest, Marie Duvic, was born in 1799. But he also collected from very young informants. The youngest, one of his youthful singers from the trip to Cazalis, Marguerite Rouchaleou, was born almost a century after Marie Duvic, in 1895. Another of the youngest informants, Rose Dubos, was born in 1889. She died on 22 January 1983. The singing tradition had not disappeared before Arnaudin made his collection, nor did it vanish with the last of his singers. Other folklorists collected songs in the moorlands throughout the twentieth century.[25] Despite deliberately seeking out older informants, and despite repeatedly claiming oral culture was doomed in his lifetime, Arnaudin collected folklore from individuals who lived into the second half of the twentieth century.

Perhaps the most striking thing about the list of informants Arnaudin produced for his 1912 edition of songs is the gender imbalance. He was especially attached to an image he constructed of collecting songs from women as they spun, going so far as to stage photographs of all-female spinning bees to illustrate his books. In the introduction to the 1912 edition he claimed songs were traditionally led by

---

[21] This fits with what other researchers have found in comparable collections. See, for instance: Timothy R. Tangherlini, *Interpreting Legend: Danish Storytellers and Their Repertoires* (New York, 1994), 59–60.

[22] Again, this is in line with what other writers have suggested, particularly about tales. Very few narrators know many tales. Most tell just a few, and are capable of remembering some that they would not often perform themselves. Dégh, *Folktales and Society*, 50, 168.

[23] Latry, 'Une Enquête de Félix Arnaudin dans le Bazadais'.

[24] See the charts in: Pooley, 'The Singing Postman'.

[25] See, for instance: Sylvain Trébucq, *La Chanson populaire et la vie rurale des pyrénées à la Vendée* (Bordeaux, 1912); Patrick Lavaud, *Lo Medòc de boca a aurelha* (Bordeaux, 2011).

women in the moorlands, and his list of singers reflects this idea that singing was a gendered tradition.[26] Less than a quarter of the 227 singers in his published list were men, whereas 265 of the 702 informants I have identified, or well over a third, were men. This could be partly explained by the fact, noted by other folklorists, that women are more likely to sing and men are more likely to narrate, especially the complicated magical tales.[27] But even when it came to the singing, Arnaudin slightly exaggerated the role of women, and played down the importance of male singers.[28] This bias towards excluding men fits into his concerns about social changes: men tended to be better educated, and had more opportunities to engage with print media, politics, and new forms of employment. They were also more likely to be his friends and social equals. They were, therefore, in his view, less representative of the true local tradition.

The information available about the working lives of his informants present a similar contrast to what the folklorist himself said. Arnaudin liked to depict himself 'wandering from moor to moor in search of the old shepherds' and of the six storytellers he mentioned in his 1887 book of tales, three were pastoralists.[29] They were also a favourite subject of his photographs, which posthumously became his best-known work, appearing in history books and even on the local road signs in the area. The shepherds represented the old way of life destroyed during Arnaudin's lifetime by the victory of the pines, so he dressed his subjects like the shepherds of his youth, in sheepskin jackets, and had them perch on traditional stilts. But 'shepherd' may not have been the descriptor that made most sense to working people when official documents asked for an occupation. Pastoralism was not a separate lifestyle and the men who guarded sheep were not, as Bernard Traimond assumes, all bachelors.[30] They were not even all men: Arnaudin photographed women guarding sheep, and it seems probable that children were responsible for looking after some animals in the moorlands, as they were elsewhere in France. Neither was pastoralism a fixed and permanent identity. Individuals might pass through a stage working as a shepherd and then find other work. It is easy to be seduced by the fictions of census recording. A man who worked for a wage as a shepherd would be called a shepherd on official documents, but a man who was a head of household but who spent much of his time minding sheep might not be.[31] As Francis Dupuy has pointed out, the number of men in Callen in 1856 who were called shepherds in the census would only be enough to look after about 1,100 sheep, but there were five times as many in the commune.[32] One of Arnaudin's storytellers, Jeanne Dupart, known

---

[26] OC, iii, XXVI.
[27] Tangherlini, Interpreting Legend, 59, 68; Dégh, Folktales and Society, 91–2.
[28] Of the 478 identifiable singers, 147 were men.   [29] Arnaudin, Contes populaires, 5.
[30] Traimond, 'Le feu est dans la lande'.   [31] Lescarret, La vie dans la Grande-Lande, 135.
[32] Francis Dupuy, Le Pin de la discorde: Les rapports de métayage dans la Grande Lande (Paris, 1996), 142.

Fig. 3.1 Shepherds on stilts watching their flocks, courtesy of the Musée d'Aquitaine

as Marianne Hailloune (1824–86), was married to a man who official documents insistently referred to as a 'ploughman', yet Marianne Hailloune told Arnaudin a story about her dead husband and his sheepdog.[33] Is it fair to call him a shepherd? All families depended on sheep to fertilize their crops, and pastoralism was part of a shared world of work.[34] Shepherds, quite simply, were not a class apart.[35] This helps to explain why the vast bulk of Arnaudin's informants were simply called farmers (*cultivateurs*) by official documents. In this sense, the demography of his singers and storytellers simply reflects local life: most of the population did list their primary occupation as farming.[36]

Along with the farmers who provided the majority of the songs and stories he collected, artisans, employees, and tradesmen were quite important to his fieldwork. Like the chart of the age of his informants, this makes it clear that Arnaudin tried to play down the role of certain types of people in his fieldwork. An obvious category is tradesmen and innkeepers, who are completely absent from his published works, but turn out to represent twenty-one of the 759 informants in the manuscripts. Many individuals were both. Romain Magnes, known as Martin

---

[33] *OC*, viii, 558.

[34] See Sargos for the family division of labour: *Histoire de la fore^t landaise*, 216, 328.

[35] And I have found no evidence that the shepherds, alone of all the local population, abstained from fighting the fires, as Traimond claims. Traimond, 'Le Feu est dans la lande', 337–8.

[36] For more detail, see the charts in: Pooley, 'The Singing Postman'.

(1861+), for instance, was a some-time baker and some-time travelling fishmonger according to the folklorist's own notes, and the 1921 census called him a hotelier.[37] Arnaudin's 1912 list, on the other hand, simply called him a landowner. Bartenders made obvious informants. They knew lots of local people, and would have had plenty of occasions to learn songs and stories, but Arnaudin, as previously mentioned, was nervous about collecting songs from innkeepers. Yet, in reality, these travellers, merchants, and innkeepers were more numerically important to his fieldwork than the shepherds. Artisans also provided a significant amount of material to Arnaudin.[38] Neither did his professed horror of the effect of priests and schoolteachers on local traditions prevent him using at least two priests and a teacher as correspondents. Despite the complete absence of soldiers from his published writings, it is clear from conscription records that at least fifteen of his informants had served in the army. There are also many more servants in the manuscripts than in his published writings.

The clearest way in which he remodelled the occupational diversity of his informants, however, was by playing down the importance of industrial workers and employees of the railways and the state. If many of the villages he collected folklore in were straightforwardly rural, the important exception is Labouheyre, where the folklorist himself lived, and where he collected many of his materials. Labouheyre swelled from a village with a population of just 460 people two years after his birth to 2,265 individuals by his death in 1921, officially becoming a town. The reason for this dramatic growth was the creation of the Bordeaux–Bayonne railway line. As early as 1881, the railway fostered a much more diverse range of industries and occupations in the town than in the surrounding villages that did not have railway stations. The 1881 census for Labouheyre reveals a whole range of occupations that are completely unrepresented in other villages. Arnaudin collected folklore from industrial workers, such as three men who worked in the local forges, and another man who he called simply a 'worker'. There were even more employees, though he tried to exclude their influence from his publications. Next to Marie Lalanne (1852+), Arnaudin wrote in his notes 'Delete: the wife of a shepherd, but mother of an officer, a postman and a mid-wife!'[39]

Despite his misgivings, he could not resist recording materials from two midwives, one rural policeman, a health officer, and two clerks. Another ten of his informants were road menders or employees of the French department of transport, not to mention several more who were married to road menders. Such individuals worked for a salary, to fixed hours, for the state. If they died, their widows had the right to expect a pension. These might sound like small numbers when compared to the mass of his informants who were simply farmers, but many

---

[37] NFA, 2 MI 29/1, f.18; ADL 6 M 152.
[38] Craftsmen have often been singled out for their narrative skill. Dégh, *Folktales and Society*, 68–9.
[39] NFA, 2 MI 29/1, f.40.

more of these farmers had brothers and sisters, children and grandchildren who also took jobs as employees. These jobs as local functionaries often required reading skills, and different attitudes to work and leisure, and essentially made these rural men 'Frenchmen', even as they continued to transmit traditional culture.[40] Men like Arnaudin's some-time employee Jean Cazade (1850+) moved between the worlds of rural labour, military service, and state employment. Many of the Breton folklorist Paul Sébillot's informants similarly went on to take administrative jobs or work for the railways.[41] Whatever Arnaudin himself said about his folklore informants, this makes it clear that many of them were actively involved in the changes to the region. Marie Baladès, known as Marichoun (1821–95), for instance, took a cottage in the experimental colony built at Solférino by Napoleon III. Arnaudin relied on the singing postman, Denis Labeau, to check versions of several songs.

One of the most striking examples concerns the man who had become mayor of Labouheyre by 1853. Although he started life as a cobbler, he soon progressed to owning a local inn, before taking work as an agent for the forge in Pontenx at the railway station in Labouheyre. This important informant who provided Arnaudin with information about language, songs, hunting, and the landscape and environment of the old Landes was his own father, Barthélémy (1816–93). Like many of his informants, and despite his protests against the changes to the region, Arnaudin was imbricated in a web of connections with other men and women who embraced new occupations. Many of his best informants occupied similarly middling positions. Jules Sart (1853+), for instance, was the illegitimate son of a local labouring woman, but went on to become a clerk working for the local quarries, as well as Arnaudin's friend, confidant, and an informant for his collections. The folklorist also collected from local merchant families, such as the Lacave and Dulas families, and other individuals who were at least as well off as he was, such as Mariane de Mariolan and Martin Magnes. He even went into business with one of his best informants, Jean Vidal, known as Henri (1850–1919). Arnaudin was not simply an outsider peering in to the oral cultures of the Landes, he was a participant, even noting his own versions of songs, and questioning other informants based on his own recollections of stories. Like the railway workers, road menders, employees, and bartenders he collected folklore from, Arnaudin does not fit the neat image of the disappearing rural folk presented in his own writings.

It is harder to know what role social class played in Arnaudin's romance of the moorlands. A comment in the introduction to the 1912 edition of folk songs hints that, for Arnaudin, folklore was partly a window into a past before social divisions, or at least divisions between bourgeois and workers. Presenting an example of a conversation with a shepherd-storyteller he digresses to comment on how close

[40] Weber, *Peasants into Frenchmen*.   [41] Hopkin, *Voices of the People*, 107.

masters and servants used to be.[42] When he wrote these words in 1912, he may have been thinking of the strained relationships he himself had with his employees, sharecroppers, and tenants.[43] But he might also have been thinking of the wave of syndicalist protest that rocked the region from the 1880s onwards. The triumph of the pine was a victory for the local landowning class, and especially the bourgeoisie, many of whom made their fortunes at the expense of the sharecroppers, who became a wage-paid 'proletariat of the forests'.[44] Rather than a survival of feudalism, sharecropping in the region became a tool of proletarianization. Arnaudin clearly preferred to present a picture of informants that were labourers and sharecroppers, rather than landowners or professionals. Few official documents specify the landowning status of individuals, but the information available suggests that he collected from slightly more smallholders and property owners than his 1912 list admits. Nonetheless, the majority of his informants were sharecroppers. Many of them were called resin collectors by Arnaudin or on official documents. It seems likely that some of these men and women were involved in these first stirrings of class conflict in the region.

Few of Arnaudin's informants could be considered truly marginal.[45] Other French folklorists found semi-professional and professional beggars to be particularly rich sources.[46] There is ample evidence from Arnaudin's ethnographic writings that begging was not uncommon in the Moorlands, yet there is only one example of a song he collected from a beggar.[47] As with so many aspects of local traditional culture, it is likely that the reason Arnaudin chose not to rely on these marginal figures came from a belief that their peripatetic lifestyles would not have represented an authentic expression of the 'old moorlands'.

Networks

Just as he romanticized the occupations of his informants, Arnaudin produced a selective vision of the conduits along which traditions travelled, playing down the influence of print culture and geographical mobility, and emphasizing oral communication in stable face-to-face communities. There is little evidence in Arnaudin's notes that any of his informants adapted traditions from visual

---

[42] *OC*, iii, XXIII.   [43] NFA, 2 MI 29/24, f.395.

[44] Sargos, *Histoire de la forêt landaise*, 205; Dupuy, *Le Pin de la discorde*, 212–14.

[45] Bottigheimer, 'Fairy Tales, Folk Narrative Research and History', 147–9; Dégh, *Folktales and Society*, 72.

[46] For instance, Victor Smith's singer and storyteller, Nannette Lévesque. See Marie-Louise Tenèze and Georges Delarue eds, *Nannette Lévesque, conteuse et chanteuse du pays des sources de la Loire* (Paris, 2000); William G. Pooley, 'Independent Women and Independent Body Parts: What the Tales and Legends of Nannette Lévesque Can Contribute to French Rural Family History', *Folklore*, cxxi (2010), 190–212.

[47] On begging, see the material from the dictionary discussed in Chapter 4, which presents the point of view of the labouring poor: *OC*, vii, 160, 165, 310, 356; NFA, 2 MI 29/3, f.277.

sources, but the influence of words from printed sources is easier to detect. Influence, however, is not the same thing as dominance.[48] Marie-Louise Tenèze has shown that oral animal tales are related to medieval works such as the *Roman de Renart*, yet have a flavour all of their own.[49] Similarly, Paul Delarue found that the French oral versions of ATU 333 'Little Red Riding Hood' shared common elements that did not appear in Perrault's literary version, suggesting the oral tradition had some degree of independence from the cheap print versions that spread across eighteenth-century France.[50] Martyn Lyons suggests there is little evidence that rural people ever read the stories from the cheap, popular pamphlets known as the *Bibliothèque bleue* aloud at the evening gatherings known as *veillées*.[51] Yet there had clearly been a two-way process of borrowing and appropriation between writing and oral tradition in Europe since at least the early-modern period.[52] In Edmond About's novel *Maître Pierre*, set in the Landes, the mayor of Bulos, a grasping social climber, learns his proverbs from almanacks, and Arnaudin suspected some of the songs he collected of deriving from the same source.[53] He disliked other songs because they 'stink of Navarrot and Despourrins', Béarnais literary figures from the eighteenth and nineteenth centuries. Some of the tunes his singers sang derived from printed music.[54]

The general picture from Arnaudin's manuscripts suggests that many people had at least a passing familiarity with writing, but that the majority of songs and stories were transmitted through informal oral networks, not unlike those through which the Great Fear of 1789 spread, where authority, as Georges Lefebvre put it, was not dependent on 'official status of any kind'.[55] In the introduction to his collections, Arnaudin emphasized the oral transmission of folklore, and it is unsurprising to find that most of his informants, and especially his older informants, were unable to sign their wedding certificates.[56] Nonetheless, many of Arnaudin's younger informants could write.[57] Whether or not songs and stories

---

[48] See Oscar Cox-Jensen's comments about news from the Napoleonic Wars competing with tales of fairies in conversation. Oskar Cox Jensen, 'The Travels of John Magee: Tracing the Geographies of Britain's Itinerant Print-Sellers, 1789–1815', *Cultural and Social History*, xi (2014), 209–10.

[49] Marie-Louise Tenèze, 'Aperçu sur les contes d'animaux les plus fréquemment attestés dans le répertoire français', in *Lectures and Reports: Fourth International Congress for Folk-Narrative Research in Athens*, ed. Geōrgios A. Megas (Athens, 1965), 569–75.

[50] Paul Delarue, 'Les Contes merveilleux de Perrault et la tradition populaire', *Bulletin Folklorique d'Île de France*, xiii (1951), 195–201, 221–8, 251–60, 283–91, 348–57, 511–17.

[51] Martyn Lyons, *Readers and Society in Nineteenth-Century France: Workers, Women, Peasants* (Basingstoke, 2001), 136.

[52] Adam Fox provides an overview: *Oral and Literate Culture in England, 1500–1700* (Oxford, 2000), 413.

[53] About, *Maître Pierre*, 161; NFA, 2 MI 29/3, f.351.   [54] *OC*, iv, 151, 636.

[55] Georges Lefebvre, *The Great Fear of 1789: Rural Panic in Revolutionary France*, trans. Joan White (New York, 1973), 148.

[56] Of 362 individuals who I have found putting their names to documents, just 146 could sign.

[57] This is entirely consistent with the picture presented by Furet and Ozouf of regions of poor literacy catching up with better-educated regions in the nineteenth century. François Furet and Jacques Ozouf, *Reading and Writing: Literacy in France from Calvin to Jules Ferry* (Cambridge, 1982).

were orally transmitted, many of the singers and storytellers had some familiarity with writing.[58] But it was not reading where they learned folklore.

When performers were able to tell Arnaudin where they had learned songs and stories, the sources were normally close to home: the most commonly mentioned in Arnaudin's notes were parents. On three occasions, informants mentioned learning songs from their mothers, and on two more they mentioned learning stories from them.[59] 'Fillon Dumartin' told Arnaudin she learned a story about the French Revolution from her mother-in-law.[60] Sometimes it was parents more generally who were named as sources for traditions. Mariane de Mariolan (1822–1916) told the folklorist: 'All the tales I have told you, I learned them at home, from my father, from my mother...at the evening gatherings to shuck corn'.[61] 'Jeanne Durrous' also mentioned her father as a source for a song, and Marie Baladès, known as Marichoun (1821–95), once mentioned that her father had known a song which she could not remember.[62] There is less evidence for the cultural influence of grandparents in rural society suggested by Marc Bloch.[63] Just one storyteller passed on a story from her grandmother.[64] Sometimes, the direction of cultural flow was reversed across the generations. 'The Boss', Jean Saubesty learned a story about a stolen pig from his son, who in turn had learned it from another boy.[65]

For the most part, however, informants told the folklorist they had learned traditions when they were children, or long ago.[66] Marie Ducout, femme Duluc, known as Caroline (1839+) remarked to Arnaudin of one song: 'I knew it long before I was married'.[67] These childhood recollections and family transmissions took place at the evening work and social gatherings known in France as *veillées*. The *veillées* were above all the place for the long tales which required concentration on behalf of both narrator and audience.[68] At the same time, men and women would shuck corn, spin, or mend tools.

These gatherings of neighbours and family spawned miniature networks of close acquaintants that can be traced in Arnaudin's fieldwork. One cluster of singers and storytellers were related to Arnaudin's neighbour, the carpenter Michel Colin (1836–1906). Michel's marriage to Marie Raynaud in 1858 made him the son-in-law of the singer Pétronille Marsan, known as Filhoun, veuve

---

[58] Other folklorists have recently stressed that literacy and literary culture is not necessarily the enemy of oral culture. See, for instance: Beiner, *Remembering the Year of the French*, 23, 76, 95, 255–6, 258, 291, 303.

[59] NFA, 2 MI 29/2, f.328, 2 MI 29/3, f.27, 2 MI 29/4, f.252, 2 MI 29/17, f.87, 2 MI 29/11, f.368.

[60] *OC*, viii, 557.   [61] NFA, 2 MI 29/11, f.368.

[62] NFA, 2 MI 29/3, f.293, 2 MI 29/1, f.240.

[63] Marc Bloch, *The Historian's Craft*, trans. Peter Putnam (New York, 1964), 40.

[64] NFA, 2 MI 29/3, f.411.   [65] NFA, 2 MI 29/11, f.607.

[66] See, for example: NFA, 2 MI 29/2, f.328, 2 MI 29/3, f.27, 2 MI 29/4, f.134, 2 MI 29/4, f.175.

[67] NFA, 2 MI 29/1, f.439.

[68] For examples of informants who mentioned performing at the *veillée*, see: NFA, 2 MI 29/11, f.368, 2 MI 29/24, 46, 2 MI 29/20, f.195.

Raynaud (1816–98) and brother-in-law of the singer and narrator Catherine Raynaud, femme Barbé (1844+). Catherine Raynaud's son and daughter-in-law also became informants for Arnaudin's folklore collecting. Michel Colin himself was one of his most varied informants, telling him a range of jokes and legends, as well as singing songs. As a carpenter, Michel was uniquely positioned to explain technical terms relating to woodwork and vernacular architecture to Arnaudin, and as his neighbour, he was readily available. This proximity and expertise is reflected in his importance in the dictionary notes. Arnaudin also collected from dynasties of singers and storytellers, such as Elisabeth Broustra (1829–1910), her daughter Marie Lestruhaut (1851+), and granddaughters Anna Loubeyre (1887–1907) and Marie Loubeyre (1872+). These miniature networks were safely local. Bounded within the family, they represented the kind of purity of local tradition that Arnaudin sought.

Yet his desire to preserve what he saw as a disappearing world led him to overemphasize ideas of static communities. Other researchers have found that typical folklore informants are not well rooted, and that the most mobile individuals in traditional societies are also the ones best known for singing and storytelling.[69] Craftsmen, soldiers, and beggars learned stories and songs on their travels, so it is not necessarily surprising to see that the 'traditional' culture of the moorlands that Arnaudin sought was transmitted by women and men who travelled around and beyond the moors. Despite his own claims about focusing all of his attention on a limited geographical area, the official record reveals that many of Arnaudin's singers and storytellers were born outside the moorlands, including Denis Labeau, the singing postman. Many of them moved around both within and even sometimes beyond France. At least nine of the 759 lived part of their lives in Bordeaux, and there are also more extreme examples. One of Arnaudin's closest friends and singers, Pierre Larrouy (1816–83), was known as l'Afrique because he had served as a medical orderly in the French army in Algeria. Another singer, Jean Gellibert, known as Jouanès, Antoine, or Pouton (1853+), also served in Africa, and the husband of yet another, 'Jeanne Latappy', worked for the administration in the Congo.[70] Even those who never left the country were fairly mobile across the moorlands, due to the system of sharecropping which dominated local agriculture. Since sharecroppers owned neither their land nor even their tools or animals, it was quite common to change location regularly, in search of better landlords, or larger farms. 'The Boss' Jean Saubesty and his wife Babé Plantié, two of Arnaudin's most important informants, could be considered typical. Between their marriage in 1844 and moving to work for the Arnaudin family in 1875, Babé and Jean successively farmed six different

---

[69] Dégh, *Folktales and Society*, 68–9, 79.
[70] On 'l'Afrique', see: NFA, 2 MI 29/2, f.451. I found Jean Gellibert's military record in ADL R P/307. On Jeanne Latappy's husband, see: NFA, 2 MI 29/14, f.11

shareholdings around the moorlands.[71] This mobility fostered rather than hindered the transmission and perpetuation of traditional culture.

The singers and storytellers Arnaudin spoke to mentioned many different occupations as sources for songs and stories, from workers, to tailors, to carpenters, labourers, road menders, shepherds, and even a monk, although most traditions were probably learned from farmers, whose occupation simply went unremarked.[72] Among occupations that were commonly named as sources were servants, with two singers and one storyteller claiming they learned from domestic help.[73] Servants were a privileged point of access for middle-class folklorists into working-class culture, as David Hopkin has explored.[74] But their positions as intermediaries, who moved between households, villages, and age groups, also made them particularly important conduits for traditional cultures, in a similar way to the postman, Denis Labeau. The beggars, innkeepers, grocers, and fishmongers also played similar roles as go-betweens, even more mobile than the labouring population. 'Romain' or 'Martin' Magnes, for instance, was especially useful to Arnaudin. Not only did he sing, but he had a cart, and later a car, which he used to deliver fish around the moorlands.[75] This may have been how he developed such a rich song repertoire, and it was also useful to Arnaudin when he wanted to do fieldwork.

As with other aspects of Arnaudin's attitudes to folklore, there were paradoxes to his hunt for the perfect informants. Mobility made for extensive repertoires, but threatened Arnaudin's sense of authenticity. In a similar way, loquaciousness might seem like a virtue when collecting oral traditions, but Arnaudin was suspicious of verbose informants. He distrusted the grocer Anne Joie (1843+), for instance, because he worried she would tell everyone about his song collecting.[76] In a similar way, the ability to read and write that made the postman Denis Labeau, as well as the road workers, soldiers, and midwives such good intermediaries also threatened the purity of the materials Arnaudin sought. Even as his fieldwork took advantage of the growth of letter writing spurred by migration and military conscription, he tried to play down the importance of literate intermediaries, attempting, for instance, to exclude the road mender Jean Laguë (1881–1971).[77] Jean Laguë is doubly interesting because he was also married to a seamstress. Cloth workers, like road menders and soldiers, were especially useful to Arnaudin because they were often literate, but there were also longstanding

---

[71] NFA, 2 MI 29/24, f.417.

[72] NFA, 2 MI 29/1, f.81, 162, 474, 2 MI 29/3, ff.281, 287, 2 MI 29/11, ff.398, 481, 625.

[73] NFA, 2 MI 29/4, f.68, 2 MI 29/5, f.285, 2 MI 29/11, f.660.

[74] Hopkin, Voices of the People, 20; David M. Hopkin, 'Intimacies and Intimations: Storytelling between Servants and Masters in Nineteenth-Century France', Journal of Social History, 51, no. 3 (February 2018).

[75] Arnaudin photographed this car.   [76] NFA, 2 MI 29/20, ff.147, 151.

[77] NFA, 2 MI 29/31, f.489; Lyons, Readers and Society in Nineteenth-Century France, 151.

cultural associations between seamstresses, tailors, and raunchy singing.[78] Oral traditions were caught up in circulations of cloth, money, letters, and people, in networks that were both traditional and innovative, relying on established connections, yet also exploiting new modes of transport.

Conclusion

Whatever Arnaudin himself liked to say about a traditional culture that was static, homogenous, and harmonious, his notes reveal mobility, malleability, and tensions. These tensions that existed between the folklorist and his 'rustic' and often reluctant collaborators dealt in the issues of 'modernity' and 'tradition' of the kind that have been at the heart of historical debates about the nineteenth-century countryside since the appearance of Eugen Weber's *Peasants into Frenchmen*. But the value of Arnaudin's notes is not that they tell historians anything new about the fluidity between 'modern' activities and 'traditional' lifestyles in the nineteenth century. As a range of historians have argued, the countryside was never sealed off from outside influences, and mobility had long been a part of rural life.[79] The point is that this was even true for traditional singers and storytellers. Far from being left behind by the changes of the nineteenth century, many of the most knowledgeable or skilled traditional performers were younger, more literate, and more engaged with the wider contexts of French and global history than Arnaudin himself wanted to admit. If folklore always makes sense in context, then the context in which these traditions were performed, adapted, and passed on was not the static and unchanging past that Arnaudin lamented. Instead, this folk culture made sense in an evolving present, where ideas and experiences of the body itself were changing. It is this shared culture of the body that Chapter 4 explores.

[78] Paul Sébillot, 'Les Couturières', in *Légendes et curiosités des métiers* (new edn, Paris, 2000); Verdier, *Façons de dire, façons de faire*, 246–51.
[79] For one of the clearest statements of this view, see Charles Tilly, 'Did the Cake of Custom Break?', in *Consciousness and Class Experience in Nineteenth-Century Europe*, ed. John Merriman (New York, 1979), 17–44. See also Agulhon, *The Republic in the Village*, and James Lehning, *The Peasants of Marlhes: Economic Development and Family Organization in Nineteenth-Century France* (Chapel Hill, 1980).

4

Body Talk

When people in the nineteenth-century moorlands talked about their bodies, which body parts did they mention and what metaphors governed their understandings of their own flesh?[1] Any answer to this question provides confusing evidence for the big narratives of the historiography of the body. The notes Arnaudin assembled for an unfinished dictionary of the local patois reveal no triumph of biomedical understandings, no sexualization of diverse bodily practices, no transgressive folk body 'civilized' by elites. Instead, labourers, shepherds, and housewives talked humorously and ironically about a body threatened by violence and ground down by physical toil. If this was a step on the road towards the 'modern' body discussed in the Introduction, it was only in the sense that rural people dreamed of growing larger and standing taller.

These changes in bodily experiences and aspirations stand in an ambiguous relationship to linguistic changes. In his unpublished notes Arnaudin wrote passionately but fatalistically about the decline of the Gascon language, demanding 'we should let the patois die their glorious deaths, without taking the idiotic pleasure of disfiguring them in their final hours'.[2] Historical linguists understand the passion of statements like this: language plays a key role in senses of identity, and especially regional identities threatened by national languages, as Gascon was by French.[3] But what historians know less about is how this sense of identity was not only conceived, but lived and performed through the body. In everyday experience there was a bond between dialect and flesh, speaking and experiencing. The men and women Arnaudin lived among transmitted their own understandings and uses of their bodies through the dialect that they spoke, a dialect that grew out of their experiences, unlike a standardized national language, such as French. This dialect was highly localized, creating meanings that reflected the landscape, local agricultural practices, and social structures. The notes Arnaudin assembled to write a dictionary are like a template of everyday bodily meaning, both the shadow cast by countless personal experiences, and a repertoire of strategies for dealing with new situations. These notes are something between a phenomenology, an aesthetics, and a morality of local bodies.

---

[1] For similar questions, see: Roy Porter, 'History of the Body Reconsidered', in *New Perspectives on Historical Writing*, ed. Peter Burke (2nd edn, London, 2001), 242.

[2] NFA, 2 MI 29/8, f.53.

[3] Mari C. Jones and Ishtla Singh, *Exploring Language Change* (London, 2005), 85.

Body and Tradition in Nineteenth-Century France: Félix Arnaudin and the Moorlands of Gascony, 1870–1914. William G. Pooley, Oxford University Press (2019). © William G. Pooley. DOI: 10.1093/oso/9780198847502.001.0001

Arnaudin himself had a keen sense of the rootedness of Gascon, believing that it expressed local meanings that French could not. French, in his words, was 'monotone...a heavy paraphrase' of the 'concise and vivid patois'.[4] Linguistic anthropologists have agreed that these locally elaborated meanings of folk speech were untranslatable because they expressed a whole relationship to the world.[5] As a native speaker of this dialect who also spoke French, Arnaudin is a special kind of guide into the elaboration of rich and complex local meanings. Considering how bodily experiences, and especially internal processes, tend to recede from conscious perception, his dialect notes reveal a surprisingly subtle vocabulary of body parts, not just limited to hands, heads, and hearts, but focusing attention on lips, ankles, necks, genitals, and the anus.[6] The notes are filled with the bodies of the women and men whose speech Arnaudin recorded, and reflections on the bodies of the people they knew. Many local terms refer to bodily skills, labour, postures, and gestures, and the notes are often closer to a choreography than a lexicon. These words do not simply reflect the biological reality of the body: they actively construct bodies, shaping what people perceive and the range of actions available to them.

There is a surprising coherence to this body talk. As a list of words largely divorced from everyday uses, notes for a dictionary might not seem like an obvious place to find unity in bodily experience. But the way a dictionary works by translating meanings, cross-referencing other words, and drawing on example sentences draws connections between different body parts and activities. And when it comes to folk traditions of the body, this is not simply a fiction of how dictionaries are compiled. Body parts were understood in relation to one another, not simply as higher or lower, more internal or external, but even as analogous. For instance, in Gascon the 'eye tooth' is the canine, and the 'eye without the pupil' is a euphemism for the anus.[7] Arnaudin's notes give insights into the metaphors that organized different bodily experiences into coherent frames of reference through metaphor.[8] Rather than a fragmentation of body parts into independent concerns, and rather than separate histories of, for instance, sexuality, working practices, ageing, nutrition, and violence, how these different domains interfere with one another draws attention to the underlying object that is concerned by all of them: the body.

Some aspects of this body might appear familiar. Men and women spoke of bodies that 'wore out' like cloth.[9] Much of their attention was focused on the head, eyes, and mouth, while the interiors of their bodies receded from consciousness.[10] And yet this sense of familiarity is deceptive. As many historians have

---

[4] *OC*, viii, 551.
[5] Benjamin Lee Whorf, *Language, Thought, and Reality: Selected Writings of Benjamin Lee Whorf* (Boston, MA, 1956), 134–59.
[6] Leder, *The Absent Body.*   [7] *OC*, vi, 287; *OC*, vii, 134.
[8] George Lakoff and Mark Johnson, *Metaphors We Live By* (Chicago, 1980).   [9] *OC*, vi, 26.
[10] This is very similar to the account of bodily experience in: Leder, *The Absent Body.*

emphasized, we need to pay attention to how alien even our recent ancestors' lives were.[11] Speech focused on body parts that might surprise us, and there were notable absences in this discourse as well, things historians might expect them to talk about which they do not. If many societies today are cultures of the hand, this was a culture of the legs and back, a world that put more emphasis on gravity, dragging the body down towards an unforgiving earth. Much of this might confirm what historians expect about the bodily culture of the rural labouring classes. There is a great concern with hunger, fatigue, labour, and clothing, which fits neatly with what previous historians have had to say about how folk cultures reflect the fairly miserable existence of nineteenth-century 'peasants'.[12] But there is also a creativity to this concrete language, with its physical metaphors of skin, tools, clothing, pine trees, and the landscape. This everyday speech is both poetic and polemical.

'From the Mouth of the People'

At first glance, the dictionary notes are an unpromising source. The fragments Arnaudin recorded do not add up to a finished dictionary, and the modern edition is the result of the editorial work of a team of local specialists.[13] A dictionary could appear to be a relatively static, anonymous, and monolithic source, which gives too little insight into how different people spoke and in what contexts, as well as how their speaking was changing over time. Yet the notes are not as motionless as they might seem. Dictionaries perform a work of translation, creating correspondences and internal references between different words, even within the same language. Arnaudin's lexicographical notes are no exception. They are the scene of struggles between different languages, struggles between men and women, and subtle statements about class and occupational identity.

As a native speaker of the local patois Arnaudin had strict ideas about its purity. For his dialect research he confined his attention to the immediate space around the town of Labouheyre where he lived his whole life. For him, villages much further away than Sabres, Commensacq, or Pissos were different linguistic regions. In particular, he felt there was a dialect specific to what he called the 'Grande-Lande', the area that was largely unforested at the start of the nineteenth century, and dominated by agro-pastoralism. This extremely local focus has the

---

[11] Robert Darnton, *The Great Cat Massacre*, 4; Hopkin, *Voices of the People*, 2; Goldstein, *Hysteria Complicated by Ecstasy*, 5; Hull, 'Review', 75; Barbara Duden, *The Woman beneath the Skin: A Doctor's Patients in Eighteenth-Century Germany*, trans. Thomas Dunlap (Cambridge, MA, 1991).
[12] Darnton, The Great Cat Massacre, 9–73; Judith Devlin, *The Superstitious Mind: French Peasants and the Supernatural in the Nineteenth Century* (New Haven, 1987); Eugen Weber, 'Fairies and Hard Facts: The Reality of Folktales', *Journal of the History of Ideas*, xlii (1981), 93–113.
[13] See: Juan Miró, 'Introduction: le legs lexicographique et grammatical de Félix Arnaudin', in *OC*, vi, xxii.

advantage of concentrating attention on a key moment: the transition from the agro-pastoralism of the old moorlands to the mixed economy of sylvo-agro-pastoralism, combining sheep and farming with resin farming in the industrial pine forest. Nor are Arnaudin's dictionary notes as divorced from contexts and real speakers as historians might assume. Rather than just lists of Gascon words with their French translations, his dictionary notes consisted of example phrases and ethnographic explanations, designed to make it easier to understand terms and ideas which lacked French equivalents. He wrote that 'my phrases, taken from the mouth of the people, and reproduced faithfully, with absolute exactitude, not only serve to better illustrate the many ways a word can be used and its exact meaning, but reflect aspects of cultural mores'.[14] Although he did write question-naires for some informants, the evidence from his dialect notes shows that most of them were taken on the fly, from what he referred to as 'chance meetings'.[15]

Gascon was the language of everyday life, not just for the poorest labourers, but for middle-class families, such as the Arnaudins themselves. The local clergy even delivered sermons in Gascon.[16] If the patois was spoken across the social scale, it is nonetheless noticeable that most of the identifiable informants for Arnaudin's dialect notes were sharecroppers, labourers, artisans, and farmwives. The names that recur most often in the notes are the names of his own sharecroppers, such as Babé Plantié, Jean Cazade, and Jean Monicien. The dictionary is strongly marked by the voice of these poor labourers, for whom the most important everyday experience was physical work. Many of the phrases Arnaudin included to illustrate word meanings refer to the misery of agricultural toil: 'Poor people like us, we work hard and hope things turn out all right, we have no other concern.[17] [We are] several heads [people] lumped together, we live as we can, work more than we can, both mornings and nights, we aren't happy, us poor earth-scratchers.'[18] It was probably from these workers and shepherds that he collected a range of derogatory terms for the local grandees, known in Gascon as the *moussuralhe*, or gentlemen.[19]

His linguistic informants were not limited to male farm labourers. Michel Colin (1836–1906), a carpenter who lived next door to Arnaudin in Labouheyre, provided a lot of information concerning woodwork and building terms. Arnaudin also included notes from his own father, Barthélémy, and other local bourgeois. He showed some ethnographic interest in women's work, and recorded many notes from his maid and lover, Marie Darlanne, as well as Babé Plantié, Talinote Laporte (1814–1904) and Maria Daugé (b. 1874).[20] These female

---

[14] This unfinished note trails off: NFA, 2 MI 29/8, f.15.   [15] *OC*, v, 102.
[16] Lescarret, *La Vie dans la Grande-Lande*, 221.   [17] *OC*, vii, 176–7.
[18] *OC*, vii, 78.   [19] *OC*, vii, 109.
[20] For example, see a whole range of notes Arnaudin recorded from Marie Darlanne about spinning: NFA, 2 MI 29/24, f.81. 'Talinote Laporte' was called 'Catherine' on her birth certificate, and when Arnaudin knew her, was the widow Lacave. 'Maria Daugé' was named 'Jeanne' on her birth certificate, and was married to Jean Monicien.

informants imparted a sense of a life spent constantly patching things up, performing the 'little jobs' that had to be done around the household.[21] Arnaudin also reproduced a lot of 'children's talk', including terms for animals, family members, and body parts, although he did not mention any child informants in his dialect notes.

Instead, as with his folklore collecting in general, he preferred the oldest speakers he could find, men and women like Babé Plantié, Talinote Laporte, Antoine Dupuch (b. 1808), and Elisabeth Poudens, known as Beroun (femme) Dulas (1813–1904), born in the first quarter of the nineteenth century. This search for the oldest words extended into research in local historical documents, but Arnaudin was not interested in vocabulary that was no longer used. He worried that people might think his dialect notes were a pastiche of a dead language, but he tried to emphasize that all of the words he included were ones that had been used up until recently.[22] His was an ethnographic and not an historical project. For instance, he came across the unfamiliar word *perpau* used in several contracts from the eighteenth century from the nearby village of Pontenx. By chance, the next day Jean Monicien used the very same word in conversation, and explained it meant a fence post.[23] Only then was the word worth including in the dictionary, since Arnaudin's chief interest was language in its living context.

The dictionary notes convey a sense of this place, through references to local vernacular architectural forms, such as different types of sheepfold and housing, and agricultural practices concerning sheep farming and arable farming. The notes also include references to the forest fires which devastated the region in the second half of the nineteenth century, and a refined vocabulary of sticky, wet mud, lagoons, and flooding, reflecting the poorly drained landscape of the moorlands.[24] The notes are also marked by the agricultural and traditional calendar of plantings, ploughings, and harvests. As throughout Europe, saints' days are used as reference points for changing annual contracts, finding new work, and performing specific agricultural tasks. The notes also reveal the omnipresence of conflicts, not just between classes, but also within families. There is a recurring concern with the breakdown of authority in the household, with fathers who 'wear the yoke'.[25] A series of euphemisms refer to conflicts within local communities. People are said to 'hardly stop' if they meet in the street, or to say a 'loud Mass'. Their 'dogs don't hunt together'.[26] Rather than being a static picture of the

---

[21] On Marie's comments about patching, see 'pourpougna': *OC*, vii, 211. On the 'little jobs,' see 'tchictchac': *OC*, vii, 316.

[22] NFA, 2 MI 29/8, f.159.   [23] *OC*, vii, 176.

[24] For references to forest fires, see: *OC*, vi, 37, 235; for references to mud, see for example 'bardis', 'baréyre', baudane', 'desenhagna', 'enhagna', 'enleda', 'hagne': *OC*, vi, 97, 97, 106, 294, 330, 331, 462–3; and: 'tchaflic', 'tchampoulh-tchampoulh', and 'tcharné', as well as example phrases which mention mud in passing: *OC*, vii, 308, 309, 312, and 37, 77.

[25] *OC*, vi, 77, 185, 186–7, 219, 300, 301, 442; *OC*, vii, 86, 89, 137.

[26] *OC*, vi, 50, 151, 166, 185, 500; *OC*, vii, 79, 88, 195, 252, 335.

language of the old timers, the dictionary depicts a world of bitter struggles between rival factions, different families, and angry individuals.

Arnaudin worried about the death of the patois. Although some people still speak Gascon today, at the end of the nineteenth century its future looked bleak. Arnaudin believed it was in the process of becoming extinct, as his comments about the 'glorious death' of the patois made clear.[27] Like other minority languages, such as Breton, Gascon was marginalized and made to seem 'a language of the past, fit only for backward peasants'.[28] Arnaudin's response to this was not that of the revivalists of the *Felibrige* literary movement, who championed Occitan languages. He deliberately rebuffed the advances of Béarnais writers such as Miquèu Camelat who wanted to give a new life to local languages in literary works.[29] Arnaudin, in typical melancholy fashion, had no interest in revitalizing the language. Instead, he sought to preserve its purity, battling the influence of both French and other patois, and complaining bitterly about examples where old words were replaced by new ones. For example, when a sweet seller moved from the largely French-speaking town of Bordeaux to Mios, in the Gascon-speaking moorlands, the population of the village copied her pronunciation of the word sweet, saying 'bonbon' instead of 'boumboum'. Disgusted, Arnaudin wrote: 'And there goes yet another word, buried to make way for a completely illogical and stupid variation.'[30]

In many ways, this anecdote sums up the linguistic changes that were happening in the region. As the old agricultural economy was supplanted by the trade in pine resin, the local population were confronted with new consumer possibilities. The strong links of family and village became interlaced with many weaker links which permitted dialects and languages to cross-fertilize even more easily than they no doubt always had.[31] Arnaudin may have resented this, but there was little he could do about it. In a paradox typical of the Janus-faced project of the folklorists, his obsession with the purity of his local dialect led him to pay more, rather than less, attention to loans from other languages and the changing pronunciation and lexicon. This concern with change inflects the dictionary notes with a surprisingly mobile picture of local speaking. Historians writing today cannot simply believe, as Arnaudin did, that the patois embodied an 'older' or more 'traditional' attitude to the world. While patois songs and proverbs were often lexicographically conservative, tending to preserve words that had fallen out of everyday use, the notes Arnaudin collected also suggest the patois

---

[27] NFA, 2 MI 29/8, f.53.

[28] Lois Kuter, 'Breton vs. French: Language and the Opposition of Political, Economic, Social, and Cultural Values', in *Investigating Obsolescence: Studies in Language Contraction and Death*, ed. Nancy C. Dorian (Cambridge, 1989), 76.

[29] *OC*, v, 295–327.   [30] NFA, 2 MI 29/8, f.153.

[31] On weak ties as the vehicle of language change, see: James Milroy and Lesley Milroy, 'Linguistic Change, Social Network and Speaker Innovation', *Journal of Linguistics*, xxi (1985), 339–84.

was evolving to meet new demands. The dialect notes reflect the culture and experiences of a cross-section of the population of the moorlands in a period of change.

Body Parts and Fluids

The dialect notes fit with the picture that medical historians have drawn of men and women in the eighteenth and nineteenth centuries paying an increasing attention to the head and face, at the expense of their bowels.[32] Yet a picture of bodily experiences based only on understandings of illness and health cannot do justice to the details and ephemera of quotidian body parts. Arnaudin's notes make it clear that the head had not won the absolute victory over the bowels that medical historians might suspect.

The meanings of the body parts on the head itself had little to do with the triumph of reason. The eyes make an interesting example, standing out both for the frequency with which they were mentioned and their symbolic polyvalence. It made sense to think of the holes and marks in everyday objects such as fountains, bread, cheese, and pine trees as having 'eyes'.[33] Since the bubbles of fat in soup were known as eyes, a 'blind soup' was one without enough fat in it.[34] The fact that eyes were everywhere was not necessarily a good thing. They might carry some positive connotations, for instance being associated with talent in financial affairs: to remove the rheum from your eyes meant to become rich.[35] But, in general, these omnipresent eyes were dangerous, even violent. Arnaudin did not collect much material on the evil eye, but he did record vocabulary referring to looking at someone maliciously.[36] 'To make someone see' meant to make them suffer.[37]

The other parts of the head got comparatively short shrift in everyday discussions of the body. The only example Arnaudin recorded concerning ears compared them to the wattle of a cockerel.[38] Noses were more popular, being associated with both pride and curiosity. A 'nosing' means a peek, or a short visit, while a 'stench' is a word for someone proud, or an *arriviste*.[39] Hints from supernatural narratives suggest that, as during the medieval period, the nose was the site of identity, a target for violence, perhaps even a metaphor for the genitals, and a sign of honour.[40] Due to their association with the horns that identified

---

[32] Porter, *Flesh in the Age of Reason*, 60; Roy Porter and Georges Vigarello, 'Corps, santé et maladies', in *Histoire du Corps*, eds. Alain Corbin, Jean-Jacques Courtine, and Georges Vigarello (3 vols, Paris, 2005–6), i, 340.
[33] *OC*, vii, 134.   [34] *OC*, vi, 12.   [35] *OC*, vii, 31.   [36] *OC*, vi, 46.
[37] *OC*, vi, 5–6.   [38] And a ploughshare. See above. *OC*, vi, 81.   [39] *OC*, vii, 118, 224.
[40] Valentin Groebner, *Defaced: The Visual Culture of Violence in the Late Middle Ages* (London, 2004), 72–8.

cuckolds, foreheads are even more closely associated with such ideas of sexual honour.[41] Cheeks typically played the role of indicators of health or drunkenness.[42] Beards, jaws, chins, and throats are all mentioned, but did not hold the interest of body parts such as the neck or the eyes. Hair, on the other hand, had many more figurative meanings. To have a tuft on the top of your head is to be proud, while hair that is too long on the nape of the neck is known as the 'chick'.[43] To 'make hair' is to fight, while 'having good [body] hair' means having a resilient constitution.[44]

The mouth was undoubtedly the most discussed part of the head, whose symbolisms derive from violent connotations as much as the obvious importance of talking and eating. Everyday speech tended to conflate these nutritional and linguistic meanings, so a 'good mouth' meant a good appetite, and making a 'fat mouth' at someone meant approving of them.[45] A bell with a clapper made an obvious comparison to the tongue within the mouth, but local speech was most interested in lips and teeth, body parts that stood in for a number of aspects of interpersonal relations.[46] Like the head, there was more than one term used in Gascon to refer to the lips.[47] Lips carried a variety of meanings. They might stand for the whole face, as in the story of a man who earned himself and his house a nickname: 'He gave [his wife] two slaps on the lips. "Here! Riu!" he said with the first. "Rau!" he said with the second. People found out about it and called him *lou Riu Rau*. And the name stayed with the house.'[48] To 'put something on someone's lips' meant to blame or reproach them, in the same way one could talk in English of throwing something in someone's face.[49] Lips were also associated with kissing, pouting, and laughing, and someone with thin lips was considered severe.[50] These multifunctional, sensitive, and emotional lips are a far cry from the brutal stereotype of 'peasant' bodily survival found in the work of a previous generation of historians. Teeth, on the other hand, were more straightforward in their meaning. Again and again, references to teeth refer to biting, and by extension, harsh words, viciousness, anger, and audacity.[51] Here, as in other parts of Europe, teeth seem to have meant hardness.[52] The variety of other words used to refer to teeth—combs, shovels, nails or keys, rakes—implies euphemism was necessary to avoid the aggression evoked by mentioning teeth.[53]

These violent teeth have little to do with the rise of the head. As in earlier periods, the head held little interest for the patois. It is true that there were two different words for 'head', and several humorous analogies for the skull, such as the pumpkin, or the spinning top, but there were actually very few symbolic

---

[41] *OC*, vii, 325.   [42] *OC*, vi, 8; *OC*, vii, 203.   [43] *OC*, vii, 224, 193.
[44] *OC*, vii, 226; *OC*, vi, 149.   [45] *OC*, vi, 147.   [46] *OC*, vi, 105.
[47] *OC*, vii, 205, 311.   [48] *OC*, vii, 251.   [49] *OC*, vii, 205.
[50] *OC*, vi, 64; *OC*, vii, 205, 206.   [51] *OC*, vi, 56, 177, 340, 342, 358, 440.
[52] Stark, *The Magical Self*, 306.   [53] *OC*, vi, 229, 366; *OC*, vii, 145, 186.

associations with heads.[54] Arnaudin recorded no patois word for the brain.[55] Rather than talking of thoughts in the brain, local people talked of ideas weighing on the stomach.[56] Rather than thinking in terms of a dualism between mind and body, local speech used the same word to mean healthy and well thought out.[57] As in the early-modern period, somatic feelings and specific bodily organs were strongly associated with emotions.[58] Jealousy was thought to keep the body warm.[59] The heart was especially rich for thinking about these feelings. A heart that had been moved signalled surprise or worry, and reassurance meant returning the heart to its place, perhaps in reference to the widespread belief that folk healers could guide wandering organs back into order.[60] A heart that was 'locked up' caused distress or sadness.[61] The liver was thought to be the seat of anger. Someone with their liver 'turned around' was furious.[62] In fact, anger was the most commonly mentioned emotion, although there is no sign that in the moorlands it was positively valued, as it was, for instance, in other parts of rural Europe.[63] Anger was referred to as being like vinegar, venom, or having the devil between your eyes or in your boots.[64] It is harder to know what to make of the attitudes to envy and jealousy which underpin so many local stories about stealing pumpkins and pigs, and cuckolding husbands. Bizarrely, to be jealous was likened to being ticklish.[65] What is clear is that the emotional palette of the local dialect was relatively unvaried, with a much greater focus on the negative emotions of anger and jealousy than on positive feelings.

Everyday speech about the stomach was richer even than talk about the heart or liver. Exhaustion was felt in the stomach, and the very idea of not feeling well was expressed as a stomach 'out of place'.[66] The most recurrent model for internal digestion was the mill, as if human bodies ground their food internally.[67] When it malfunctioned, the stomach might need to be washed out.[68] The multitude of phrases referring to different types of stomach contrasts with the paucity of language to describe the trunk or torso as a whole.[69] Arnaudin noted only one word, the 'belt'.[70] While it is true that attitudes to the internal organs and emotions owed something to old models of bodily experience, these feelings did not dominate everyday talk of the body.[71] Although organs such as the heart and stomach were thought to be able to move, there was little interest in the fluids Barbara Duden discovered in eighteenth-century women's medical complaints.

---

[54] OC, vii, 108; OC, vi, 222, 272.   [55] OC, vi, 266.   [56] OC, vi, 387.   [57] OC, vii, 280.
[58] Duden, The Woman beneath the Skin, 89, 91; Goldstein, Hysteria Complicated by Ecstasy, 13; Ulinka Rublack, 'Fluxes: the Early Modern Body and the Emotions', History Workshop Journal, liii (2002), 1–16.
[59] OC, vii, 174.   [60] OC, vi, 235, 233.   [61] OC, vi, 229.   [62] OC, vi, 486.
[63] Stark, The Magical Self, 57, 220.   [64] OC, vii, 179; OC, vi, 302, 321.
[65] OC, vii, 263.   [66] OC, vi, 342, 264; OC, vii, 48.   [67] OC, vii, 100, 102–3.
[68] OC, vi, 360.   [69] OC, vi, 112.   [70] OC, vi, 223–4.
[71] See: Duden, The Woman beneath the Skin, 107–9; Porter, Flesh in the Age of Reason, 235; Jan Goldstein has argued that this early-modern body survived into the nineteenth century. Goldstein, Hysteria Complicated by Ecstasy, 14, 48.

Neither was the flexible and enduring language of humouralism predominant, as it was in eighteenth-century medicine. Dryness and wetness were only occasionally mentioned. Shepherds worried about their sheep drying out, and dryness was associated with emaciation, and harsh feelings.[72] Yet they do not seem to have been everyday concerns. There is just one reference to bile in the dictionary.[73] Blood was hardly discussed in terms of illness at all, with the exception of the vulnerability of menstruating women.[74] Instead, blood was about heredity. 'His parents keep a close eye on him, but he has mischief in his blood.'[75] In terms of the other bodily fluids, there was surprisingly little interest in sweat, although it was referred to as 'garlic sauce'.[76] It was not recommended to take off your clothes after sweating.[77] Snot, on the other hand, was known by a variety of terms, including, bafflingly 'woodcock'.[78] Spitting was not often mentioned, but vomiting was the source of one of the most striking word plays of everyday speech: 'to make the arse a cuckold'.[79] The lack of figurative language concerning tears is also surprising, especially since it is clear from Arnaudin's own diary as well as the dictionary notes that tears were shed abundantly, especially when people died.[80] When Marie was sent away in 1880, not only she and Arnaudin, but also his father and their sharecropper all cried as she was leaving.[81]

If the head had not won the battle for supremacy, neither did the internal organs and fluids dominate everyday body talk in the way they did in early-modern experiences and descriptions of illness. Speakers were notably imprecise about specific organs, mentioning only hearts, livers, and stomachs. The lungs were not even allowed their own terminology, being instead called the 'white liver'.[82] The recesses of the body were simply not as important as the face and head, nor the skin. Perhaps it is unsurprising that illness is nowhere near as important in the dictionary notes as it is in the historiography of medicine and the body. Studying the eighteenth-century notes of the physician Johann Storch, Barbara Duden found that Storch's patients did not discuss the daily grind of labour very much, but instead saw disease and poor health in terms of sudden shocks and calamities. This is the opposite of Arnaudin's informants who worried about everyday work and barely discussed sudden illnesses, just as they barely discussed the internal workings of their own bodies which were so important to Storch's patients.[83] His informants did talk of bumps and shooting pains, referred to as 'onions' and 'showers', and sometimes mentioned accidents, like a knee broken while threshing.[84] The commonest complaints were coughing, rashes, and boils, but there was also mention of a range of illnesses which have now practically disappeared from western Europe.[85] Pellagra, a fatal skin disease caused by

---

[72] OC, vi, 332, 351; OC, vii, 12.   [73] OC, vi, 480.   [74] OC, vii, 265.
[75] OC, vii, 265, 325.   [76] OC, vi, 25.   [77] OC, vi, 280.   [78] OC, vii, 102–7.
[79] OC, vi, 353, 250.   [80] OC, vii, 599.   [81] OC, viii, 163–5.   [82] OC, vi, 486.
[83] Duden, The Woman beneath the Skin.   [84] OC, vi, 78, 28; OC, vii, 406.
[85] OC, vii, 344, 293.

malnutrition, was known as the 'illness of Bascons', since the fountain in the village there was said to heal it.[86] The dictionary also mentions folk remedies for conditions such as whitlows.[87]

But, in general, sickness and injury seem to have been forbidden topics. The editors of Arnaudin's dictionary note that the very language of illness was in a sense taboo, so that it was dangerous to use the real names of specific conditions.[88] And sickness was felt to be the lot of the poor. The word for ticks—*pistole*—came from the name of a small coin: ticks, therefore, were the salary of the goatherd.[89] There was even a specific term for someone who complained too much about their health.[90] There is little sense from everyday speech of a 'modern' attitude where suffering was becoming unacceptable and avoidable.[91] Little faith was put in medicine:

> 'You should go to the doctor. Even if he doesn't heal you, he will relieve you somewhat.'
>
> 'Well, he will certainly relieve my wallet.'[92]

The figurative language of health and sickness can be hard to understand today. The idea that an old man could want a 'healthy' or 'clean' interior might be comprehensible, but what does it mean to be 'as healthy as a nail'?[93] The use of animal illnesses such as the *amourrau* to discuss human sickness might make sense, but why would being 'unbound' mean being ill?[94] There is an irreducible otherness to figures of speech concerning bodies that hold no meaning for modern readers, and whose associations are forever lost. 'Making almanacs' means to faint, 'making foxes' to throw up, and 'returning to your old lips' means returning to where you used to live.[95] These opaque languages of the body are clearly divorced from what medical historians have been able to say about a body undergoing fundamental conceptual reorganization through medical discourses.

The Unbridled Body

If the rise of the head so apparent from medical history is a poor guide to the symbolic complexities of everyday rural speech about bodies, what is the overall picture? Concerns about the unbridled body are central, as is an obsession with the vertical plane.

---

[86] *OC*, vi, 428.   [87] *OC*, vii, 352.   [88] *OC*, vii, 79.
[89] *OC*, vii, 196.   [90] *OC*, vii, 186, see also 198.
[91] See, for instance: Alain Corbin, 'Douleurs, souffrances et misères du corps', in *Histoire du Corps*, eds. Jean-Jacques Courtine, Georges Vigarello, and Alain Corbin (3 vols, Paris, 2005–6), ii, 273.
[92] *OC*, vii, 84.   [93] *OC*, vii, 22, 280.
[94] *OC*, vi, 30, see also 68, 283.   [95] *OC*, vi, 45; *OC*, vii, 205, 245.

Bodies are unbridled in the sense of inflicting and undergoing violence, and there is also some evidence of the transgressive, yet fecund and joyful bodies that Mikhail Bakhtin found in the work of Rabelais.[96] Like Rabelais' characters, this nineteenth-century everyday speech sometimes suggests that people inhabited a violent, drunk, and sexually explicit body that exceeded its own limits. Everyday speech talked of the ways laughter opened the body to the world around, and the obsession with the skin discussed in Chapter 5 also suggests that the interiorization considered typical of the 'modern' body was not yet complete.[97] Like early-modern patients and magical practitioners, the men and women of the moorlands lived their skins as vulnerability and experienced their bodies as open to a dangerous environment.[98] This is best summed up by a phrase people would use to avoid giving offence: 'Don't think I mean to hurt you by touching you'.[99] 'To have someone's skin' is to get revenge, and an 'ironing of the skin' is a beating.[100] People also talked of 'skinning' words or mispronouncing them, or used the word 'pelt' as an insult for women.[101] Skin was useful for thinking about poverty, so to be skinned meant to be left penniless.[102] 'Misery,' people said, 'has brought him out in boils.'[103]

The general violence of the phrases in the dictionary is striking. There are at least forty-three different paraphrases for 'to beat'. Carding the wool, feeding the cattle, removing fleas, shaking the husk, harvesting rye, moving the wisp of straw, putting on the shirt, receiving logs, peeling, or taking to someone's hair could all mean administering a beating.[104] What stands out from these phrases is the importance of the skin as a site of violence, and the importance of agricultural metaphors for beating. Perhaps most shocking to modern readers is the casual attitude to this violence. One woman told Arnaudin: 'My husband—God rest his soul—did everything to me. He hit me, he bruised me, he slapped me!'[105] Another woman who lived near the folklorist commented approvingly about a man who beat his wife: 'It's no bad thing to give a piece of meat a good beating. Then it won't be so puffed up.'[106] Interpersonal violence, and especially within marriage, seems to have been somewhat expected, even banal.[107] Yet the inventiveness of language for violence suggests it was nonetheless problematic. A rich vocabulary of alternative ways to talk about assaults on skin was one way to avoid the provocative implications of directly evoking violence.

---

[96] Bakhtin, *Rabelais and His World*.

[97] The clearest statement of the 'interiorization' hypothesis is: Le Breton, *Anthropologie du corps et modernité*. On laughter as 'opening up', see: *OC*, vi, 345.

[98] Duden, *The Woman beneath the Skin*, 120–3; Stark, *The Magical Self*, 67, 154–7.

[99] *OC*, vii, 337.   [100] *OC*, vi, 243; *OC*, vii, 47.   [101] *OC*, vi, 346; *OC*, vii, 179.

[102] *OC*, vi, 297.   [103] *OC*, vi, 266.

[104] *OC*, vi, 5, 19, 27, 140, 143, 146, 158, 166, 185, 198, 199–200, 219, 236–7, 369, 382, 410; *OC*, vii, 47, 67, 111, 117, 143, 157, 158, 159, 161, 166, 169, 170, 186, 204, 219, 224, 226.

[105] *OC*, vii, 584.   [106] *OC*, vi, 471.

[107] Although perhaps not as commonplace as in the example of the Gévaudan, which is the central theme of Claverie and Lamaison, *L'Impossible mariage*.

Alcohol, on the other hand, was a constant reference point. Arnaudin, other local elites, and travel writers tended to see the question in stark terms. Either the local population were remarkably sober, as Arnaudin and the novelist Edmond About claimed, or they were unrestrainable alcoholics, as the early nineteenth-century travellers such as M.J. Thore and Jacques Grasset Saint-Sauveur maintained.[108] The evidence from the dictionary notes suggests that Arnaudin's rosy view was either dishonest or self-deluding. His notes mention at least fifty-six different phrases referring to being drunk. To talk in mixes, to raise your sail, to have a servant, to climb the vines, to load up the cart, to be fixed, or to suffer from *perpite*, a disease that normally affects chickens, can all mean being drunk.[109] When Arnaudin and his friend Duport saw a man asleep under a tree on Ash Wednesday, Duport suggested to the folklorist that Mardigras—the personification of Carnival—had hit him on the head.[110] There was even a specific word for a drunk person's vomit.[111] Drunkenness appears in unexpected examples, so the phrase Arnaudin used to illustrate 'care' was: 'Drunk as I was, I took care to look where I was putting my feet.'[112] Figuratively, drunkenness was associated with being 'bewitched', 'ripe', and 'full'.[113] Drinkers have 'wine noses' and rosy cheeks.[114] They even 'sweat wine from [their] eyes'.[115]

There is more than a hint of Rabelais to this, especially considering how raunchy or even smutty the songs that will be discussed in Chapter 7 were. As in Rabelais' writings, there is a free play of rude and fertile images to this sexuality, but perhaps even more interesting is how different it is to a post-Freudian, genital sexuality.[116] The rudeness of the body may have been distributed differently in this culture, considering that one of the longest entries in the dictionary, rivalled only by 'eye' and 'resin collecting', is the word *cu*, a word endowed with the same flexibilities of meaning as its English equivalent, 'arse'.[117] The 'farter' was used for a number of offensive phrases, such as telling people to defecate elsewhere, or to go and 'tan your arse'.[118] The standard response to an uninvited question was 'blow in the arse', and idiots were referred to by the same phrase.[119] But arses were also used to refer to miserliness, and sickness. To be ill was to be 'arse in the air', and to be miserly was 'to shit with half the arse'.[120] And rather than being a rude

[108]   About, *Maître Pierre*, 54; NFA, 2 MI 29/17, f.181 and 2 MI 29/21, f.151; *OC*, vii, 399, 401, 405, 407, 608, 612; Thore, *Promenade sur les côtes du Golfe de Gascogne*, 189; Jacques Grasset Saint-Sauveur, 'Les Landes de Bordeaux: Moeurs et usages de leurs habitants', in *Les Landes de Bordeaux: moeurs et usages de leurs habitants, suivi de Voyage dans le Département des Landes*, ed. Guy Latry (Pau, 2004), 57–8.
[109]   *OC*, vi, 6, 8, 99, 100, 109, 110, 114, 119, 123, 124, 147, 168, 212, 220, 273, 294, 317, 319, 320, 324, 334, 336, 388, 428, 439; *OC*, vii, 11, 31, 60, 108, 117, 130, 157, 164, 176, 183, 191, 192, 193, 196, 202, 275, 277, 287, 291, 316, 317, 327, 343, 354.
[110]   *OC*, vi, 277.   [111]   *OC*, vi, 178.   [112]   *OC*, vii, 291.
[113]   *OC*, vi, 320; *OC*, vii, 60, 202.   [114]   *OC*, vi, 8; *OC*, vii, 117.   [115]   *OC*, vii, 317.
[116]   This argument is a focus of: Goldstein, *Hysteria Complicated by Ecstasy*, 5.
[117]   *OC*, vii, 133–4.   [118]   *OC*, vii, 180; *OC*, vi, 177–8, 52.
[119]   *OC*, vi, 142.   [120]   *OC*, vi, 178–9, 267.

term in itself, *cu* seems to have been adaptable. In some contexts it was closer in meaning to 'back': 'He has turned his arse to his neighbours'.[121] A 'low-arse' was someone with short legs.[122] This proliferation of anal simile suggests that arses were a common part of speech. Mouths, on the other hand, could be more obscene. Arnaudin's notes certainly include a rude word for the mouth, and the historian Anne-Marie Sohn has suggested that kissing was considered more erotic than touching someone's genitals in this period.[123]

Rather than evidence of popular ignorance concerning sexual anatomy, as Anne-Marie Sohn would have it, this points to a different sexual toponymy of the body.[124] Arnaudin seems to have had no trouble discovering words for vaginas and penises, which were respectively referred to as 'flies', and 'packets' or 'little chaps'.[125] Just because this language of sexuality was often shrouded in euphemism and innuendo does not mean that people lacked knowledge about sex and sexual organs. The judicial sources Sohn relies on may produce a view of popular sexuality skewed towards people who were abnormally ignorant about bodily functions, since such individuals may have been more likely to be victims of sexual attacks. Whatever the case, because of the culture surrounding sexual assaults in the court system, it would have been in the interests of victims to downplay their sexual knowledge in order to emphasize their innocence. The problem with Sohn's account is that it essentially agrees with Michel Foucault when he argues that the nineteenth century saw the triumph of a new way of understanding human bodies: sex. Where they part ways is in how they understand this shift. For Foucault, sex became a trap, an eternal lure at the heart of human interactions.[126] For Sohn, this new sexual knowledge was profoundly liberating, giving people a language to understand and enjoy their bodies. But Arnaudin's dialect notes, relatively isolated as they are from the clinics, sexologists, and psychologists Foucault was interested in, already have their own polymorphous and omnipresent symbolism of sexuality. It was just a different one to our own. Sexual anatomy was neither the benevolent gift to the popular classes Sohn claims, nor the poisoned chalice Foucault and his followers have tended to believe.

Instead, sexual meaning was spread unevenly through the whole body. To say a woman fell on her back implied that she was promiscuous.[127] The mouth was not only considered erotic in its own right, but likened to the vagina, which was called a 'blower'.[128] But it was above all else the legs and feet that carried sexual meanings. Being married was referred to as 'having a thorn in your foot'.[129] Women were prized for their thighs, calves, and strong buttocks: 'She is a beautiful woman, and hard-working. What thighs she has!'[130] The dictionary mentions few

[121] *OC*, vi, 266, 125.   [122] *OC*, vi, 267.   [123] Sohn, *Du Premier baiser à l'alcôve*, 94–5.
[124] Ibid., 11–37.   [125] *OC*, vii, 110, 151, 195.   [126] Foucault, *The History of Sexuality*, i, i.
[127] *OC*, vi, 378.   [128] *OC*, vi, 141.   [129] *OC*, vi, 67.
[130] *OC*, vii, 64, 64, 65, 73, 74.

other body parts admired for their beauty. There is no material on beautiful hair, and the sexualization of the breasts does not seem to have fully overcome their association with nursing.[131] The verb meaning to breastfeed figuratively meant 'to put up with something'.[132] On the other hand, at least one song talked of the beauty of a woman with a thin waist and a raised breast.[133] A throwaway comment from a man named 'Ducom' suggests that men may have discussed the beauty of the furrows in women's necks, and there are also mentions of the beautiful gait of a woman walking.[134] But there is no material about what women looked for in men in the dictionary notes, and the only hints from the songs are verses that talk of the 'darling stick' of a young soldier.[135]

One thing that is clear is the close association between clothing and sexuality, an association perhaps not surprising in a culture where absolute nudity was probably very rare, and certainly not considered necessary for sex.[136] As one informant remarked to Arnaudin, 'Clothes cover so many sins'.[137] In an image combining the importance of both feet and clothing to sexuality, women who had had sex before marriage were said to be 'down at heel'.[138] A thorn in the foot was also a euphemism for pregnancy.[139] Pregnant women were said to be 'on a trip', 'grafted', 'fat', or 'thick'.[140] What these evocative analogies and descriptions reveal is not the misunderstandings of a pre-medical knowledge of the body, as Sohn suggested, but a playful language of the body that depends on euphemisms and misdirection. Even as body parts were enumerated individually in songs involving counting, they were linked together into a coherent bodily system.[141] And at the centre of that coherence stood certain enduring concerns with skin, the lower body, and uprightness.

'The Earth Calls to Them'

High to low has long been an organizing principle for human embodiment, but it is a principle that takes on special meaning in agricultural societies that depend on back-breaking labour.[142] Nicole Pellegrin has talked of a 'dream of uprightness' that dominated the bodily experiences of eighteenth-century labourers.[143] Early-modern elites cultivated an upright posture which distinguished them from

---

[131] On sexualized breasts, see: Corbin, 'La Rencontre des corps', 192.   [132] OC, vii, 215.
[133] OC, iv, 439. Typically, the singer sang not 'breast' but 'stomach'.
[134] OC, vii, 543; OC, vi, 32.   [135] OC, iv, 63–5.
[136] See, for instance: Sohn, Du Premier baiser à l'alcôve, 84–5. The close link between clothes and the body itself is a commonplace of the literature on the early-modern period. See, for instance: Duden, The Woman beneath the Skin, 47.
[137] OC, vii, 270.   [138] OC, vi, 292.   [139] OC, vi, 119.
[140] OC, vi, 121, 332.   [141] See, for instance: OC, iii, 124.
[142] Lakoff and Johnson, Metaphors We Live By, 14–21; For a historical example, see: Goff and Truong, Une Histoire du corps au moyen âge, 88–9.
[143] Pellegrin, 'Corps du commun, usages communs du corps', 127.

manual labourers, but these same labourers were still living out this bodily difference in the nineteenth century.[144] For these workers the body was a burden, pulling them down ineluctably toward the ground. This helps to explain why, despite being commonly mentioned body parts, arms and hands were remarkably limited in their symbolism, almost uniquely referring to labour. As in English and French a 'hand' can mean a worker or some help, and words involving 'hand' have to do with the use of tools, hand-les, and hand-ling.[145] Whenever arms appeared in the dictionary, it was in reference to manual work. An armful also means the working capacity of a family, while 'arm oil' means labour.[146] Arnaudin illustrated one word with the telling phrase: 'My arms are killing', meaning the speaker was too tired to work.[147] Labourers took a necessary pride in the power of their own hands, criticizing soft hands as being 'hands of butter'.[148]

The most common metaphors for understanding body parts were neither drawn from religion nor the animal kingdom, but tools. Most were agricultural. Teeth, for instance, were referred to as shovels or nails. Ears, noses, and bones were all likened to ploughs.[149] Other analogies were drawn with domestic implements. The frying pan of the knee referred to the kneecap, and the head was called a pot or a soup tureen.[150] Some body parts were compared to agricultural work. The mouth is like the hole a bean is planted in.[151] 'To clean out the stables' figuratively means to blow your nose.[152] Unkempt stubble is called *arpaliu*, after a tough weed that must be removed from meadows before mowing in order to prevent it spreading its seeds.[153] The dialect notes are filled with specific terms referring to agricultural gestures which have no modern English or French equivalent: to spread manure, or to perform the cuts in the bark of the pine tree necessary to collect resin.[154]

And it was an agricultural tool that provided a key metaphor for the labourers' battle with gravity: people were ironically said to be 'as straight as a sickle'.[155] Locals talked of themselves as literally 'bent', their noses to the ground. But bending was also figurative. A 'bend' meant a habit, something the very body had become accustomed to.[156] As they so often do, a proverb plays on the figurative implications of the literal: 'Whoever stoops too much becomes bent'.[157] This bent body pays attention to parts that have no equivalent in modern speech. The *hope*, for example, is the part of the back between the shoulder blades,

---

[144] Georges Vigarello, 'The Upward Training of the Body from the Age of Chivalry to Courtly Civility', in *Fragments for a History of the Human Body*, eds. Michel Tazi Feher, Ramona Naddaff, and Nadia Tazi (3 vols, New York, 1989), ii, 148–97; Herman Roodenburg, *The Eloquence of the Body: Perspectives on Gesture in the Dutch Republic* (Zwolle, 2004).

[145] *OC*, vii, 66, 67–9. An interesting exception is 'the Spanish handkerchief', a figure of speech meaning hand. See: *OC*, vii, 106.

[146] *OC*, vii, 157, 130.   [147] *OC*, vii, 156.   [148] *OC*, vii, 66.

[149] *OC*, vi, 81, 134, 229; *OC*, vii, 131, 145.   [150] *OC*, vii, 143, 340; *OC*, vi, 139.

[151] *OC*, vi, 183.   [152] *OC*, vi, 356.   [153] *OC*, vi, 46.   [154] *OC*, vi, 356, 433–4.

[155] *OC*, vi, 311.   [156] *OC*, vii, 201.   [157] *OC*, vi, 4.

a part especially important for lifting and carrying burdens.[158] Lifting and carrying were undoubtedly important ways of thinking about the body in this rural society. In a similar way, the neck was very important in everyday speech. This importance derives from the neck's ambiguity as a body part that aspires to strength, power, and rigidity, yet reveals weakness. To be 'neck-hanging' meant to lack energy.[159] Swearing by the neck, which was also common, suggests the other aspect of this weakness, the vulnerability of the neck to injury and assault.[160]

Uprightness was the focus of particular attention in this historical period. With advances in agricultural technology, the bent backs of rural labourers were destined to disappear.[161] For the people Arnaudin talked to in the second half of the nineteenth century, however, these bent bodies were a reality, the price the elderly paid for a lifetime of labour:

'Poor Talinote, she'll soon be very old. She walks leaning on a stick, her nose to the ground.'
'The earth is calling to her.'[162]

As proverbs put it, old age is like a forty-pound weight on each leg.[163] These physical postures carried moral and aesthetic meanings. As in many European languages, to be proud was to keep the head held high.[164] Attractiveness was associated with an upright posture, so people could talk of 'A handsome man, and very upright'.[165] This association of beauty and the upright posture may help to explain the great importance attached to legs in everyday speech. There are a multitude of terms and phrases which focus on thighs, feet, ankles, knees, and legs in general. In the vertical plane of the body, legs necessarily play a special role. Perhaps unsurprisingly, the word for foot is also used to refer to stability, solidity. To be on your feet is to be in control.[166] This biomechanical experience was extended to social experiences, so 'foot' was also used to mean an individual's position in society.[167]

The importance of legs is evident from the role they play in giving nicknames to the inhabitants of different villages. Despite the fact that many of the labourers in the moorlands were mobile, moving from village to village year by year in search of different shareholdings, they themselves believed that the region was made of micro-regions that differed in their very bodies. People from Gastes, Pissos, Commensacq, and Trensacq were thought to have black feet, while people from

---

[158] *OC*, vi, 487.   [159] *OC*, vi, 238.
[160] See for instance, the example from 'M[arie]': NFA, 2 MI 29/10, f.6.
[161] Pellegrin, 'Corps du commun, usages communs du corps', 136.
[162] *OC*, vii, 600; this is not the only example of a similar phrase. See, for instance, the reference to years wearing the elderly 'Nirot' down: *OC*, vi, 488.
[163] See proverbs nos 2042 and 2043. *OC*, ii.   [164] *OC*, vi, 4.
[165] *OC*, vi, 25.   [166] *OC*, vii, 164.   [167] *OC*, vii, 165.

Arjuzanx, Arengosse, Ygosse, and Villenave had red ones.[168] The seasonal workers who travelled from the Limousin could be recognized by their feet.[169] Even within a large village, such as Sabres, one hamlet might be known for having big buttocks, fat stomachs, and short legs.[170] Legs, more than any other part of the body, were central to rural concerns about sex, identity, and labour, and the importance of standing and bending they indicate was not limited to cultural representations. The 'dream of uprightness' governing bodily understandings also directly affected their postures and gaits. In the photographs Arnaudin took, local bourgeois appear seated in rigid positions. Many of the labourers, on the other hand, stood around, sometimes in staged portraits, and sometimes as they went about their work. They leant on tools, or other people, or stood with their hands on their hips, supporting their weight. Men put their hands in their pockets, while women tended to fold theirs when their portraits were taken.

These are the postures of working men and women. When the protagonist of Edmond About's novel *Maître Pierre* was asked if his work keeps him entertained, he replied that it both does and does not.[171] His attitude seems to reflect the ambivalence most men and women in the moorlands felt towards their labour. It is difficult to imagine that many people would have agreed wholeheartedly with the phrase Arnaudin used to illustrate the word *desaneya*, to chase away boredom: 'Work chases away boredom'.[172] In fact, working people worried that they might forget that they laboured under this burden. Like donkeys, they might grow accustomed to it.[173] Far from being ignorant of the toll this took on their bodies, the phrases from the dictionary show that people worried about their physical resilience: 'She died, young as well: she was worn out by work, bad weather, rain, dew, and hard life'.[174] Men and women wanted to be hard like iron, or at least 'well-woven'.[175] 'I won't live long, I'm too soft,' someone told the folklorist in conversation.[176] And yet many of the men and women who contributed materials to his fieldwork lived long, and extremely hard-working, lives. The storyteller Jean Pédéluc (1842–1919) retired in 1902, having done thirty-seven years of road mending. He wrote to his employers that 'he felt very tired now, and quite unable to do his work well'.[177] Women rarely had the luxury of the pension men like Jean could expect. Marie Couloudou (b. 1854) was still working as a day labourer at the age of sixty-seven in 1921.[178]

For these workers, this resilience was not just personal, but social. Bodies were at the service of a family exploitation and subject to the demands of the greater good of the household. Bodily resources were understood in terms of a 'limited

---

[168] *OC*, vii, 172, 176.   [169] *OC*, vii, 47.   [170] *OC*, vi, 267.
[171] About, *Maître Pierre*, 218.   [172] *OC*, vi, 289.   [173] *OC*, vi, 19.
[174] *OC*, vii, 132; The idea that people were not aware of the toll labour took on their bodies can be found in: Duden, *The Woman beneath the Skin*, 141.
[175] *OC*, vi, 478, 74.   [176] *OC*, vii, 208.   [177] ADL 1 S 10, 'Ponts et chaussées'.
[178] ADL 6 M 159, 'Recensement de la Population: Labouheyre'.

good', something that was not only expendable, but often won at the expense of others.[179] 'To be able' also meant to surpass, and could be used to refer to someone overcoming someone else, or being taller than them.[180] Fatigue was thought of like a physical object that was picked up and carried.[181] Tiredness was not just a matter of bodily strength, but also emotional feeling. Exhaustion was a synonym for sadness or melancholy.[182] But the sharecroppers Arnaudin talked to often expressed a judgemental bodily morality that focused on vices such as laziness and clumsiness, more than on positive values such as strength and skill. Laziness was the moral language of verticality. It could be read from a slouching posture, and lazy people were said to have their ribs the wrong way round. With vertical ribs, of course, bending over would be impossible.[183] Clumsiness, on the other hand, was associated with injury, paralysis, and stupidity. In a culture where so much relied on physical work and so little on refined intelligence, to be clumsy was to be an idiot. There was little differentiation between physical and mental agility.[184]

The concern with the vertical was also associated with the growing realization in the nineteenth century that overworked and undernourished agricultural labourers were shorter than the rest of the French population. Horrified visitors to the moorlands wrote of the tiny bodies of the local population, who were 'much shorter than middling; they seemed as thin as if their bodies had stagnated'.[185] But these concerns with the admittedly tiny bodies of the population were not just confined to the men who sought to reform the agriculture and health of the moorlands over the nineteenth century. They also had roots in local culture. Local speech was filled with references to body size, people who were 'weary of growing' or 'born the year of the drought'.[186] The muted but firm concern about hunger that is found in the dictionary confirms what anthropometric historians have written about the links between malnourishment and growth. Being hungry was such a constant that it was used figuratively to refer to any kind of desire.[187] Nothing was larger than hunger.[188]

While it is clear that the terms referring to short people are insults, corpulence was not such a straightforward issue. Arnaudin actually presented beautiful and fat as synonyms, and some of the phrases in the dictionary praise women who were 'as fat as pears'.[189] Other phrases are clearly critical of fatness.[190] At least one provides evidence of a new cult of slenderness: 'She is so narcissistic that she is starving herself to remain slender'.[191] Georges Vigarello and Richard Holt have argued that the nineteenth century was the period when the association between

[179] Foster, 'Peasant Society and the Image of Limited Good'.   [180] OC, vii, 207.
[181] OC, vi, 27.   [182] OC, vii, 189.   [183] NFA, 2 MI 29/10, f.6; OC, vi, 236–7.
[184] OC, vi, 380, 418; OC, vii, 160, 165, 183, 197, 307, 320, 332, 334.
[185] Sargos, Histoire de la forêt landaise, 81–2; The quotation is from: Thore, Promenade sur les côtes du Golfe de Gascogne, 183; See also: About, Maître Pierre, 27.
[186] OC, vi, 346, 354, 471; OC, vii, 198, 220, 226, 275, 311, 314, 326, 332, 349, 353, 359.
[187] OC, vi, 465.   [188] OC, vi, 445.   [189] OC, vi, 118; OC, vii, 77, 521.
[190] OC, vii, 49, 61, 99, 120, 150, 161, 321.   [191] OC, vii, 46.

Fig. 4.1 A pine plantation, courtesy of the Musée d'Aquitaine

roundness, authority, and beauty was breaking down, so perhaps the ambivalence in Gascon speech is evidence of a period of changing attitudes to fat.[192] Whatever the case, it is interesting that all of the references to corpulence concern women. Food and body size were issues that were discussed with reference to women more than to men.

The paradox and the potential of the dialect notes lies in the fact that these men and women, despite the difficult conditions of their lives, also turned their bent bodies to more satisfying ends. On the one hand, Arnaudin talked of the 'terrible labour' of threshing, and recorded grim notes from Michel Colin about the exhaustion occasioned by this annual task.[193] But, on the other hand, he also emphasized play at work, recording details of the tricks men and women would play on each other during the threshing. Two men might seize a woman and pretend to thresh her instead of the crop, giving everyone involved opportunities to touch each other in ways not normally permitted in everyday life.[194] Even in a region such as the moorlands, where agricultural labour was especially tough, nutrition standards were especially poor, and the upright body carried extra emotional and social weight, everyday speech could express more hopeful possibilities.

---

[192] Georges Vigarello and Richard Holt, 'Le Corps travaillé: gymnastes et sportifs au XIXe siècle', in *Histoire du Corps*, eds. Alain Corbin, Jean-Jacques Courtine, and Georges Vigarello (3 vols, Paris, 2005–6), ii, 321–2.

[193] *OC*, iii, xxxiii; *OC*, vii, 405.   [194] *OC*, vi, 111–12.

It could also express a pessimistic attitude to contemporary exploitation. The best example of this is the many ways that folk speech compared the human body to a pine tree. Like humans, pine trees have a trunk and a heart.[195] Pine trees even have eyes, legs, and faces, words used to refer respectively to the top of the tree, its lower branches, and the surface where it was cut for resin.[196] When bitten by mosquitoes, human skin becomes knobbly, like the bark of a pine tree.[197] The word used in the patois for tears—*oli*—is the same word used for pine resin.[198] This analogy was important because it governed how both reformers and locals came to think about the possibilities of human bodies in the region.[199] For the reformers, draining and cleaning up the local landscape would save the health of the population, just like draining the waterlogged roots of a tree. For the locals, however, the analogy took on slightly different implications, also linked to bodily health, but more aligned with their own experiences of ageing, exhaustion, and physical and moral uprightness.[200] The phrase *esta abiat a pin pérde* literally refers to the process whereby a pine tree is sapped to death, but figuratively it was used to refer to an individual who abandoned themselves to bad behaviour.[201] An analogy which, in the writings of reformers, provided the justification for the drastic intervention in local agriculture after 1857, provided local people with another justification for experiencing their bodies as a precious and limited resource. This is partly because the pine tree was a profoundly double-edged metaphor for human bodies. The straight, tall trunks of healthy pines were an image of everything that the labourers wanted to be, but the way the pines were sapped to death provided a powerful metaphor for the all-too-human exploitation of the sharecroppers by the landowners in the region.

Language Change

This picture of a malnourished, violent, and rowdy peasantry who dreamt of standing taller was not unchanging. The link that bound local ways of working, moving, and experiencing to the patois also meant that as bodily conditions changed, so did the language. Labourers had new ways of being smutty, which are explored in Chapter 6, new concerns about labour and exploitation, discussed in Chapter 8, and changing concerns about bodily boundaries, analysed in

---

[195] *OC*, vii, 357; *OC*, vi, 248.   [196] *OC*, vii, 134; *OC*, vi, 425, 199.
[197] *OC*, vi, 150.   [198] *OC*, vii, 130.
[199] Examples from novels include: About, *Maître Pierre*, 71; François Mauriac, *Thérése Desqueyroux* (Paris, 1927), 71–2.
[200] The two examples the dictionary gives for the word 'arraca', to not grow well, are a child, and a pine tree. *OC*, vi, 48.
[201] *OC*, vi, 7–8.

Chapter 5. But Arnaudin firmly resisted the evidence before him that traditional cultures and languages too could change, complaining that the new 'bric-a-brac' spoken by local men and women 'suits their lips like a flute suits a goose's beak', but he was powerless to stop the transformation.[202] He filled his notes with references to those feudal terms which, against the odds, survived into contemporary speech, such as the tax known as the *dime* or the *tape*, the grain-rationing system.[203] He was even interested in how locals remembered the emigrations of the revolutionary years, or the drought of 1803–4.[204] They still used the word *camalét* to mean a good-for-nothing, a tribute to the fame of the brigand executed in Bordeaux in 1789.[205] Many people preferred the term *arché* to the modern word *gendarme*.[206] He was less interested in how the patois had adapted and adopted new terms, including a whole range of vocabulary based around technological advances both in resin farming and arable farming. To 'make the resin' figuratively meant to make a fortune, a meaning that must have developed as resin prices soared during the American Civil War.[207]

Much of this adaptation was forced. Gascon, after all, was a threatened language. As is so often the case, most local people learned to speak both the patois and French. As the status of French increased, sociolinguists would suggest that Gascon would undergo processes including simplification, reduction, grammatical interference, phonological interference, and even lexical interference.[208] It is true that Gascon was losing words, with some only conserved in songs. These tended to be words relevant to the old feudal social order, or types of textile and clothing that were no longer in use.[209] It is also true that words were imported from French to fill 'lexical gaps'.[210] New words were needed for recent arrivals in the region, such as asparagus and mules.[211] But many of the changes to the patois involved a Gascon word being replaced by what Arnaudin called 'gallicisms'. Needless to say, this was not a completely new phenomenon, and he himself was aware that many of the linguistic borrowings from French into Gascon dated back to the fifteenth or sixteenth centuries.[212] Nonetheless, it is clear that these changes accelerated in the nineteenth century, leaving no domain of speech untouched. Mari Jones has suggested that topics such as the weather, the house, the family, and animals tend to be the most resistant to lexical imports, while technology is quite often composed only of imports.[213] In the case of the dialect of

[202] NFA, 2 MI 29/8, f.49.   [203] *OC*, vi, 262, 302, 403, 445, 449; *OC*, vii, 303.
[204] *OC*, vi, 287; *OC*, vii, 282.   [205] *OC*, vi, 183.   [206] *OC*, vi, 42.   [207] *OC*, vii, 130.
[208] Jones and Singh, *Exploring Language Change*, 84–91.
[209] *OC*, vii, 66, 145, 211; *OC*, vi, 435, 436–7.
[210] Jones and Singh, *Exploring Language Change*, 31.
[211] *OC*, vi, 370; *OC*, vii, 111.   [212] *OC*, vi, 219, 269, 430.
[213] Mari C. Jones, *Jersey Norman French: A Linguistic Study of an Obsolescent Dialect* (Oxford, 2001), 141–52.

the moorlands, this model does not seem to fit well. Terms for food were changing rapidly, as were terms for products whose production may have been moving outside the local community, such as umbrellas, candles, chairs, and clogs.[214] So were religious terms, and the vocabulary used to describe local artisans and working practices.[215] People no longer referred to sharecroppers as *bourdilés* but used the Gallicism *matayé*.[216] Even the names for family members, and the very word for 'man'—*omi*—had been affected by French.[217] As if to rub it in, the word for 'old'—*ancién*—was a gallicism.[218]

There is some evidence that the patois was conservative when it came to the body. Modern French, English, and Gascon all derive their word for skeleton from the Greek, as if the meaning of bones themselves change little over millennia.[219] Other examples suggest Gascon words were replaced by Gallicisms except when they applied to bodies. The word for strong—*hort*—was losing ground to French in all of its figurative meanings, but remained the preferred word to describe someone who was fat.[220] The Gallicism *curt* may have replaced the Gascon word for heart when it came to card games, but when it came to the human organ, *co* was still used.[221] But the body was far from immune to Gallicisms. *Fésse* was imported from French to mean 'buttock', and blood had changed gender in Gascon under the influence of French.[222] Suffering had become inflected by French, so speakers said *soufért* instead of *soufrit*.[223]

It is not quite fair to call this language death, however. Part of the nature of the patois had always been their diversity. The imports and borrowings from French and other dialects that Arnaudin abhorred had always been part of how Gascon dialects developed. What is more, languages under threat may actually become richer, as speakers respond by coining new words, and displaying lexical virtuosity.[224] In the case of the Gascon of the moorlands, this might involve applying old terms to new situations. The phrase *ha courre le pet*, for instance, referred to the custom of taking the skin of a pest animal a hunter had killed from door to door to collect donations. After the introduction of democratic elections, it came to be used to refer to politicians canvassing voters.[225] Neither was Gascon incapable of coming up with new terms, which referred to new bodily realities. The bumpy and uncomfortable local trains came to be known as the 'arse-bruisers'.[226]

---

[214] *OC*, vi, 27, 114, 204, 219, 442, 470; *OC*, vii, 153, 182.
[215] *OC*, vi, 33, 49, 65, 200; *OC*, vii, 98, 110, 218, 301.
[216] *OC*, vi, 147.   [217] *OC*, vi, 326; *OC*, vii, 130, 303.   [218] *OC*, vi, 32.
[219] *OC*, vi, 377.   [220] *OC*, vi, 488.   [221] *OC*, vi, 270.
[222] *OC*, vi, 402; *OC*, vii, 265.   [223] *OC*, vii, 288.
[224] Susan Gal, 'Lexical Innovation and Loss: The Use and Value of Restricted Hungarian', in *Investigating Obsolescence: Studies in Language Contraction and Death*, ed. Nancy C. Dorian (Cambridge, 1989), 329–30.
[225] *OC*, vii, 179.   [226] *OC*, vii, 77.

Conclusion

The everyday bodies of Arnaudin's dictionary notes fit poorly into the grand narratives of the historiography of the body. Instead of interiorization, medicalization, or sexualization, people discussed bodies made up of a pointillist array of body parts: legs, feet, teeth, lips, eyes, and arses. The topics historians favour, such as sexuality, were spread between these different body parts, found in odd places, and yet the changeable interior and humoural model of the early-modern period does not seem to fit the picture either. This may be a vertical body, but this has less to do with the rivalry between the head and the stomach than with the fundamental importance of the legs, prized for their beauty and praised for their power. This was a body of skin and bones, in its obsession with the threat to integrity, its emphasis on solidity, its fear of and fascination with teeth. Above all else, talk of the body was talk of the incessant demands and exhaustion of labour, resentment of a social and physical world that pulled people down to the ground. But in the metaphor of the pine tree lies a clue that such a body was not simply a survival of a pre-modern subsistence world, but the product of a very specific squeeze: the dramatic social and environmental changes of the moorlands in the second half of the nineteenth century, the arrival of the industrial forest, and the consequences it had for local life.

There are absences of this everyday speech that can be hard to understand. What to make, for instance, of the almost complete absence of both sheep and stilts, symbols of the agro-pastoralist lifestyle, from everyday metaphors and discussions of the body? Why was there so little explicit consideration of corporeal beauty, beyond the importance of legs? Nor are dead bodies the central concern they had apparently been in western Europe over such a long period.[227] Even more puzzling is the relative poverty of references to religion when discussing bodies.

To understand these absences, everyday speech needs to be replaced in its most meaningful contexts. One key area of tension is obvious: gender. All of the references to physical beauty and fatness are to women. Even descriptions of gesture carry sexed meanings: a verb meaning to spread your legs in an indecent way is only applied to women.[228] Everyday speech was misogynist, filled with terms for malicious, unkempt, lazy, gossipy, or otherwise transgressive women.[229] The sexuality and fertility of women's bodies threatened the social order.[230] Yet at the same time, the ways that everyday speech summarized the differences between men and women's bodies was open to question. All of the examples Arnaudin collected about drunkenness for his dictionary referred to men. Yet in the most

---

[227] Pellegrin, 'Corps du commun, usages communs du corps', 117; Caroline Bynum, 'Why All the Fuss about the Body? A Medievalist's Perspective', *Critical Inquiry*, xxii (1995), 27.

[228] *OC*, vi, 357.

[229] *OC*, vii, 105, 271, 294, 304.

[230] This is a running theme in: Verdier, *Façons de dire, façons de faire*.

popular songs Arnaudin collected, women often sang of getting drunk, and of a sexual licence that everyday speech heavily criticized. These kinds of tension can be traced to the identities of specific singers and storytellers, who often lived idiosyncratic experiences of embodiment. Chapter 5 turns to an example of this, a legend teller named Marichoun, who used the widespread sense of sensitivity around skin to talk about her own family experiences as a vulnerable woman in a society of shifting boundaries.

5

Monstrous Bodies

In 1891, Marichoun Lescarret was fifty-eight years old, but she still vividly recalled the time she almost saw a werewolf as a child. She had been sent to bed one night without her dinner for getting lost on her way to the well, and from where she was tucked up in bed, she could hear her father and some men and women who worked for the family shucking maize in the kitchen, an activity traditionally associated with storytelling and other entertainments. But on this particular evening, the story was real. The workers noticed that something was bothering the dogs and, peering out through their windows, they realized it was a werewolf. The best plan the worried men and women could come up with was to shoot at the beast, but it slunk off, apparently unharmed. And this was not the end of the story. It turned out that the same werewolf was harassing some of their relatives, hanging around their house at night, and licking the trough in an outhouse. The father of this related household had a better plan than shooting at the animal. Along with his son, he trapped the beast in an outhouse, beat it up, and burnt its muzzle. The following day, he came to see Marichoun's father to suggest that they go to the tavern in town to confirm his suspicion that the innkeeper was the werewolf. Sure enough, when they got there the suspect was badly injured on his face, and very angry with the man who had beaten up the beast. They parted on bad terms, with Marichoun's father telling the innkeeper he was nothing but a 'rotten werewolf'.[1]

Although Marichoun herself was a child at the time of the events, the story she told was deeply personal, a typical example of what folklorists have sometimes called 'memorates', in order to distinguish them from the friend-of-a-friend attribution of many legends.[2] If legends offer historians a kind of folk historiography, or a view of historical change 'from below', a personal story such as Marichoun's offers something a little different, a more individual and experiential reflection on the changing boundaries of everyday life in the moorlands.[3]

---

[1] NFA, 2 MI 29/11, ff.86–7. The story appears in a heavily edited form in: *OC*, i, 280–3.
[2] Linda Dégh and Andrew Vazsonyi, 'The Memorate and the Proto-Memorate', *Journal of American Folklore*, 87 (1974), 225–39.
[3] Beiner, *Remembering the Year of the French*; David M. Hopkin, 'Legends and the Peasant History of Emancipation in France and Beyond', in *Storied and Supernatural Places: Studies in Spatial and Social Dimensions of Folklore and Sagas*, eds. Ülo Valk and Daniel Sävborg (Tartu, 2018); David M. Hopkin, 'Paul Sébillot et Les Légendes Locales: Des Sources Pour Une Histoire 'Démocratique?', in *Paul Sébillot (1843–1918): Un Républicain promoteur des traditions populaires*, ed. Fanch Postic (Brest, 2011).

Body and Tradition in Nineteenth-Century France: Félix Arnaudin and the Moorlands of Gascony, 1870–1914.
William G. Pooley, Oxford University Press (2019). © William G. Pooley.
DOI: 10.1093/oso/9780198847502.001.0001

What is interesting about her account is not its historical accuracy about the period in the late 1830s or early 1840s when it took place, but how an individual like Mariane used this recollection in the present, in 1891. The legend, as the folklorist Bill Ellis has put it, is '*potential* fact', a story that happens within 'the group's conception of the real world' but somehow challenges 'the boundaries of what the world is or should be'.[4] As Linda Dégh has pointed out, this means that disagreement over the truthfulness and accuracy of the story is not incidental to these stories: 'disputability is not only a feature of the legend, it is its very essence, its raison d'être, its goal'.[5] In the example of the story Marichoun told, this is not just a description of how everyday boundaries were experienced: it is a criticism and a complaint, addressed to a community who were expected to respond in some way to how she felt about domestic spaces, bodies, family, and the household as both a physical reality, and an imagined experience.

Changing Places

The forestation of the moorlands lies in the background of this argument about community. This would not surprise historians who have explored the tight links between the formation of rural political identities, cultural senses of community, and the privatization of the commons.[6] But for an individual like Marichoun, forestation itself is a less important subject of debate than its social consequences. The story, Marichoun told Arnaudin, happened when she was a child, so took place before the 1857 law was even passed, let alone implemented. A brief detail that she mentions confirms that her sense of temporal distance was related to this change at a very straightforward level. 'In those days,' Marichoun explained at the start of the story, 'the houses weren't surrounded by big pine trees like they are now, and they had little windows' which allowed Marichoun's family to spot the werewolf as it prowled around outside.[7] This anchoring of her own memory in a historical chronology divided into before the triumph of the pines and after is a throwaway comment, a clarification of how it was that someone inside a house could have seen across the landscape. If the werewolf itself is the subject of the debate of the legend, the pine trees hardly bear discussing, but could pass between storyteller and listener as a shared reference point.

Arnaudin did not find many traditions that explicitly dealt with the transformation of the local environment through forestation. The one example he did collect

---

[4] Bill Ellis, *Aliens, Ghosts, and Cults: Legends We Live* (Jackson, 2001), 6, 11.
[5] Linda Dégh, *Legend and Belief: Dialectics of a Folklore Genre* (Bloomington, 2001), 3.
[6] Jones, *Politics and Rural Society*; Matteson, *Forests in Revolutionary France*; McPhee, *Revolution and Environment*; Whited, *Forests and Peasant Politics in Modern France*.
[7] NFA, 2 MI 29/11, f.86.

was a story about the 'wicked lord of Luë' told by a woman called Mariane de Mariolan:

> They say that in the olden days there was a wicked Lord in the village of Luë, who was very hard on the poor. This lord owned a large span of lands, woods, and moorland around Luë, but he forbade the shepherds and goatherds to graze their flocks there, or even to allow them to pass through.
>
> One morning, he had gone to see a plot of land that he had planted with pines, not far from the hamlet of Hidéou, and he found a goatherd there with his flock. When the goatherd saw the lord, he tried to turn his goats around, but the lord, mad with rage, fell upon him, and chased the goatherd and his goats, driving his horse on the poor man's heels. The unfortunate goatherd soon asked for mercy:
>
> 'Take pity, my lord. Forgive me, for the love of God...'
>
> But the gentleman took no mind of the goatherd's words: the more he begged, the more the lord bore down on him.
>
> 'Will you do this again, you brigand?' the lord kept saying. 'Will you ravage my pine plantation again?'
>
> He chased the unfortunate goatherd like this for more than a quarter of a league, at the speed of his horse's trot. In the end, the goatherd grew angry: he took his rifle (in those days shepherds and goatherds always had a rifle with them on the moors, as defence against the wolves), and without warning, he fired on the lord, and left him dead on the spot.
>
> Immediately afterwards, seized by fear, the goatherd fled, and was never seen again in the parish. No-one cried for the wicked lord, and since that time the poor folk of Luë were free to graze their flocks where they wished on the moorlands.
>
> Because justice was never done for the lord, the heather never grew back on the spot where he was killed, and the sand there is stained red to this day.[8]

There are several obvious differences between Mariane's legend of the wicked lord and Marichoun's story of the werewolf. Although both are explicitly historical, anchored in a specific time frame that the narrator spells out, Marichoun's story is both more personal, and deals with a more shocking manifestation of the supernatural. Mariane's story, on the other hand is distanced, both socially and temporally from her own experience.

Where Marichoun talks of a personal recollection, even one that was mostly about something that happened to her father, Mariane's story of the wicked lord is

---

[8] This is one of the rare occasions where the original transcription of the story does not survive in Arnaudin's manuscripts. This French version would undoubtedly have been edited by Arnaudin, and may even have been translated from Marianes's Gascon. See: *OC*, i, 295.

told in a depersonalized voice: 'They say that in the olden days there was a wicked Lord in the village of Luë, who was very hard on the poor.' Where the audience is invited to wonder with Marichoun about the shocking and troubling existence of a monster within their own community, the audience to Mariane's story is offered a more complicated identification. 'No one cried for the wicked lord,' and it would be easy to assume, as Jacques Sargos has, that Mariane's story was told for and from the point of view of 'the poor folk' of the moorlands, or even the shepherds: 'This story reveals a war: the eternal conflict between rich and poor, perhaps, but adapted to the moorlands as a war between shepherds and smallholders, on the one hand, and the landowners who owned the forest.'[9] There is a problem with this reading of the legend. Mariane herself is clear that the goatherd has committed a crime. The landscape itself is indelibly marked by the fact that he was never brought to justice. This complexity in the moral significance of the story comes both from the history of the region as a whole and from Mariane's own life. As the Introduction suggested, identifying the winners and losers of forestation is hard. Individuals adapted to the new challenges and opportunities of the pine forest, and did not necessarily act consistently in defence of a customary common good, or as entrepreneurs.[10]

Mariane's own life provides a good example. Born in 1822 into an extended family in the village of Escource, Mariane ended up inheriting the family farm in the hamlet of Jurman where she was born.[11] Aged nineteen, she was married to Jean Bouzats, and the couple went on to have at least six children.[12] She lived in the same house in Jurman until her death in 1916, and during her life, her 'semi-bourgeois' family bought communal moorlands, and planted them with pine trees.[13] This casts an entirely different light on the story of the goatherd driven to murder, and it is worth reflecting on the fact that Mariane was no silent partner in these transactions. Unlike many of Arnaudin's singers and storytellers, she continued to be known by her father's name even after her marriage to Jean Bouzats, strongly suggesting that she was a powerful *daüne*, a Gascon word used for the female head of a household, especially a matriarch. When the family lands were being reorganized in 1861, it was Mariane, and not her husband, who signed the notarial document.[14] In some senses, Mariane's own life was much closer to that of the wicked lord than the desperate goatherd. This helps explain why the

---

[9] Sargos, *Histoire de la forêt landaise*, 424.
[10] See Karl Jacoby's concept of the 'moral ecology': *Crimes against Nature: Squatters, Poachers, Thieves, and the Hidden History of American Conservation* (Berkeley, 2001), 3.
[11] In 1819, a few years before her birth, her grandfather, mother, father, uncle Charles (a black-smith), his wife, and several of her cousins were all living in the family house. See ADL 6 M 93, 'Recensement de la Population: Escource'.
[12] See ADL 1 MIEC 94, 'État civil: Escource', for the births of her children between 1848 and 1866.
[13] The plot was originally sold in 1836. It was Jacques Boisgontier who called Mariane 'half-bourgeois' in *OC*, i, xix.
[14] See ADL 3 E 52/94, 'Étude notariale Dominique Bacon à Labouheyre', 3 March 1861.

story is run through with such ambiguity. It expresses a hatred of those who are 'very hard on the poor', but perhaps it only does so to excuse the actions of those who own moorlands but also sympathize with the shepherds and practise pastoralism themselves, as Mariane's family did.

This also helps to explain the temporal distancing in her legend. Arnaudin was very interested in the fact that a feudal lord really was murdered around the time that Mariane suggested.[15] But there is nothing to suggest from the historical record that the murder was connected to forestation or the kinds of conflict over pastoralism that were so common throughout rural Europe at this time. Mariane used the widespread legend form of a feudal lord punished for his cruelty to explore a problem that was really contemporary: how to reconcile the interests of pastoralists and forestry.[16] The feudal lord is worthy of a legend not so much because of a long-remembered hatred of feudalism, but because he can be used instead of the contemporary figure of the 'half-peasant, half-bourgeois' that Mariane herself represented.[17] The legend debates the appeal of solidarity with the shepherds by someone whose interests would sometimes have conflicted with them. This tension is the one that would have made sense to Mariane's life, caught as it was between the 'poor folk' and the landowners. Marichoun's story of the werewolf, on the other hand, situated the challenges of this transition in a different set of spheres: the household, domestic space, literal physical boundaries, and the metaphorical boundaries of the body itself.

The Werewolf Tradition

What did werewolves mean to other people at the time? Werewolf stories are, on the one hand, banal, even boring, and—at least according to folklorists—widespread, and yet at the same time, dramatic, extraordinary, and shocking. The werewolf of lore and legend is a far cry from the savage beasts or tragic heroes of twenty-first-century fiction. Caroline Walker Bynum has reminded medievalists that marvels and monsters like this were never as common as the abundant secondary literature might suggest.[18] Our fascination with werewolves owes more to Hollywood than it does to what recent Europeans—people like Marichoun—have believed about shapeshifters.[19]

[15] Félix Arnaudin, 'Une Branche des Pic de la Mirandole dans les Landes', *Revue de Gascogne*, 14 (1873), 259–67.
[16] There is no catalogue of legend types, but on these legends, see: Paul Sébillot, 'La Noblesse et le Tiers État', in *Le Folk-Lore de France*, Vol. IV (1904), 281, 291.
[17] See Boisgontier's phrase in: *OC*, i, xix.
[18] The problem is not quite the same for modern historians, who have tended to assume the belief in werewolves had completely disappeared. On the medieval problem, see: Caroline Walker Bynum, *Metamorphosis and Identity* (New York, 2001), 93.
[19] Willem de Blécourt has recently made a very similar point. See: Willem de Blécourt, 'Monstrous Theories: Werewolves and the Abuse of History', *Preternature: Critical and Historical Studies on the Preternatural*, ii (2013), 188–212.

It is hard to know for sure how widespread discussions of the possibility of lycanthropy were. The clerics, administrators, and amateur ethnographers who investigated 'popular superstitions' at the time often claimed werewolves were everywhere. The village priest in Commensacq, near where Marichoun lived, for instance, exclaimed: 'If the inhabitants of the village had as much faith in the tenets of Catholicism as they do in witches and werewolves, they would be the best parish in the diocese!' Another local priest and folklorist of the Landes, Vincent Foix, agreed with him, going so far as to claim that in the small village of Bascons where he lived there were at least twenty-seven suspected werewolves. Folklorists in other parts of France made similar, if less dramatic claims about the widespread belief in shapeshifters. Speaking of the Anjou, one writer claimed that 'There is not a single village where the belief in lycanthropy is not still firmly entrenched, and where stories about werewolves are rare.' Others referred to a 'throng of stories' or 'host of examples' that they could have reproduced, if they had chosen to do so.[20]

Where are all of these stories? It seems that the folklorists published relatively few from among the 'throng' at their fingertips. Including a few that were edited posthumously, such as Marichoun's story, for the whole of France I have found only fifty narratives about werewolves collected from named narrators before 1945, and another eighty-three from unnamed sources in the same period. Compare this to the huge number of 'short local legends' that appeared in the *Revue des Traditions Populaires* after the editor, Paul Sébillot, asked his readers to send in stories they had collected about local landmarks, statues, or saints: within ten years, he published over 10,000.[21] Werewolves were not that popular.

No doubt there are other published narratives about shapeshifters that I have not found, as there is no exhaustive bibliography of French supernatural folk-lore.[22] It also seems likely that the folklorists decided that some of the 'host of examples' they did discover were too trifling to bother publishing. Without the impetus of a Paul Sébillot, these stories went untranscribed, were destroyed as uninteresting, or slumber on in regional archives, unpublished. And there is

[20] For Commensacq, see: Abbé Dumartin, 'Monographie Paroissiale: Commensacq', 1000 J 65, ADL, 36; Vincent Foix, *Sorcières et loups-garous dans les Landes* (new edn, Belin-Beliet, 1988), 49–50. For similar claims from elsewhere, see A.-J. Verrier and R. Onillon, *Glossaire étymologique et historique des patois et des parlers de l'Anjou*, 2 vols (Angers, 1908), ii, 477. For the claim about the Anjou, see: Camille Fraysse, 'Au Pays de Baugé', *Revue des Traditions Populaires*, xx (1905), 12. And for other examples, see: Camille de Mensignac, *Notice sur plusieurs coutumes, usages, préjugés, croyances, superstitions, médailles, prières, remèdes, dictons, proverbes, devinettes et chansons populaires du Département de la Gironde accompagnée d'un questionnaire* (new edn, Marseille, 1999), 175; L. Huibert, reproduced in: Louis Queyrat, *Contribution à l'étude du parler de la Creuse. Le Patois de la région de Chavanat* (Guéret, 1924), 348.

[21] Hopkin, 'Paul Sébillot et les légendes locales'.

[22] The section in van Gennep's bibliography is a start, but it does not even cover all of the werewolf narratives he must have come across in the tale and legend collections he mentions elsewhere in the same book. See: van Gennep, *Le Folklore Français*, iv, 515–18; another point of departure can be found in: Lise Andries, 'Contes du loup', in Jean de Nynauld, *De la Lycanthropie, transformation et extase des sorciers (1615)*, eds. Maxime Préaud and Nicole Jacques-Chaquin (Paris, 1990), 197–217.

always the possibility that folklorists did not ask about werewolves, whether because they thought them silly, a dangerous topic, or boring. What makes this unlikely is the recurring role played by 'witches and werewolves' in the discourses outsiders employed to talk about rural culture. Folklorists undoubtedly went looking for these stories, and yet they found very few legends of lycanthropy. Historians might, therefore, imagine that the folklorists' rural informants were unwilling to talk to them about a topic as fraught as werewolves. Perhaps they feared the ridicule of outsiders, representatives of the town, and the educated middle classes. This was what Jeanne Favret-Saada argued about witchcraft beliefs during the nineteenth and twentieth centuries.[23] But witchcraft makes an interesting comparison to lycanthropy, since, despite what Favret-Saada claimed, many of the folklorists' informants did talk to them about sorcery. Sometimes, storytellers even used the danger inherent in the topic to make threats against the ethnographers.[24] And witchcraft was a recurring problem for the criminal justice system, both in the cities and towns, and in the countryside. During the period when Arnaudin and the French folklore movement in general were at their most active, there were often more than ten cases a year reported in the national newspapers. At least sixty-four different cases were mentioned in the press in the 1880s alone, and another fifty-seven in the 1890s. In many of these trials, witnesses, victims, and defendants were resolutely unrepentant about their belief in sorcery.

Serious accusations of lycanthropy, on the other hand, were rare in court.[25] The 1925 'werewolf of Uttenheim', mentioned by Montague Summers in his sensationalist book *The Werewolf*, was never called by that name by any of the participants in the case, and the idea that the witches involved had transformed themselves into animals was only a small part of a much more complex set of beliefs about night visions and sleep paralysis.[26] In the mid-nineteenth century, from 1830 to 1855, there were eight mentions of werewolves in criminal cases, but in none was the accusation of lycanthropy seriously explored by any of the participants, whether defendants or prosecution. The identification of a werewolf was offered as an excuse for murder in three cases, but a case from Bourg in 1830 was typical in how little weight this carried in court. When a neighbour tried to intervene to stop Jean Goyard savagely beating his wife's brother after a night of drinking, the murderer shouted: 'Let me be: he is a werewolf!' This detail was left unexplored, and he never provided any further explanation for the motivation for

---

[23] Jeanne Favret-Saada, *Deadly Words: Witchcraft in the Bocage*, trans. Catherine Cullen (Cambridge, 1980), 64–5.

[24] Pooley, 'Can The "Peasant" Speak?'.

[25] Letuaire does mention a case of a man in Toulon prosecuted for dressing up as a werewolf in 1830, although I have not been able to find any record of this. See: Pierre Letuaire, *Les Cahiers de P. Letuaire, 1796–1884*, ed. L. Henseling (3 vols, Marseille, 1976), ii, 49–50.

[26] Montague Summers, *The Werewolf* (London, 1933), 238.

his crime. The court decided to take it into account that he had been drinking, and was not of entirely sound mind.[27] In two other cases, the fact that criminals had ranted about werewolves, or even attempted to shoot at them, was provided as evidence that they were mad.[28] No defendant successfully argued that their belief in werewolves excused their actions. This situation is a marked contrast to the little-studied ways that witchcraft was legitimized by the French criminal justice system: witchcraft was so real to so many people that it had to be taken seriously by the courts. Werewolves, on the other hand, were rare and ridiculous, and belief in them was a sign of madness, or backwardness. The 1925 Uttenheim case was considered by contemporaries to be a complete outlier, and there was widespread disbelief that anyone still gave credit to ideas of shapeshifters.

Among the folklorists, there was a strong sense that the belief in lycanthropy was disappearing. The story Robert Hertz collected in the trenches of 1915, for instance, was considered a tall tale by some of the soldiers who heard it. They did not deny the existence of the *guérou*, but doubted that the storyteller's father could have seen one: 'Those things belong to the old times. It's been sixty or seventy years since anyone has seen one.'[29] The folklorists proposed that the spread of the telegraph, railway and rifles killed off the belief, while more recent writers have suggested the advent of the theory of evolution made it untenable.[30] One narrator told Georges-Michel Coissac that 'the world has grown too subtle' for werewolves, while another nineteenth-century folklorist confidently wrote that the werewolf had 'completely disappeared'.[31] Writing in 1912, the folklorist Henri Cormeau claimed that 'werewolves no longer romp through the rural imagination'.

Yet it is worth questioning how absolute this decline really was. In a move characteristic of many other folklorists, Henri Cormeau went on to say that although belief in the werewolf was fading, 'the generation who are on their way out still believed'.[32] Perhaps, as Jeanne Favret-Saada suggested for the belief in witchcraft, belief did not simply disappear, not least since wary informants tend to distance themselves from direct statements that could open them up to mockery from outsiders.[33] After all, in 1947 Claude Seignolle was told that a local werewolf in Guyenne had only died five years before.[34] Charles Joisten continued to collect narratives about werewolves into the second half of the twentieth century.[35] Some

---

[27] *Gazette des Tribunaux*, 27 September 1830, 1091.
[28] *Gazette des Tribunaux*, 14 November 1845, 51, and 26 January 1848, 302.
[29] Robert Hertz, 'Contes et dictons recueillis sur le front parmi les poilus de Mayenne et d'ailleurs, campagne de 1915', *Revue des Traditions Populaires*, xxxii (1917), 89.
[30] Georges-Michel Coissac, *Mon Limousin* (Marseille, 1978), 295–6; Beresford, *The White Devil*, 194–235; Brian Regal, 'Where Have All the Werewolves Gone?', *Fortean Times* (2010).
[31] Coissac, *Mon Limousin*, 293; Letuaire, *Les Cahiers de P. Letuaire*, ii, 49.
[32] Henri Cormeau, *Terroirs mauges: miettes d'une vie provinciale* (Paris, 2000), 358.
[33] Favret-Saada, *Deadly Words*, 64–5.
[34] Claude Seignolle, *Contes populaires de Guyenne* (2nd edn, Paris, 1971), 226.
[35] Charles Joisten, Robert Chanaud, and Alice Joisten, 'Les Loups-garous en Savoie et Dauphiné', *Le Monde Alpin et Rhodanien*, i–iv (1992).

narrators claimed that their stories dated back to the feudal period, but many more storytellers in the nineteenth and twentieth centuries referred to events that had happened to their parents or grandparents, or took place forty or fifty years earlier. Marichoun's story was not the only werewolf legend set in the recent past, but such accounts were rare.

The Poverty of Horror

Werewolves are not what modern readers might expect. One of the first odd things that the most sensitive folklorists remarked about werewolves was how banal they were.[36] Consider how inoffensive Marichoun's werewolf was: he appeared in inappropriate places at inappropriate times, and behaved like an animal. This appears mild compared to the vitriol and physical violence to which he was subjected in retaliation. Both this behaviour and its severe punishment are typical of stories across France. They rarely attack people, and when they do, they fare worse than their victims. Even animals have relatively little to fear from werewolves. Although dogs and cats are at risk of being devoured by them, this seems to have more to do with the werewolf's disgusting habits than his violence. Werewolves have an insatiable appetite for inappropriate food, such as filth, pig slop, or carrion.[37] While seven of the nineteenth-century sources do refer to werewolves ravaging flocks of sheep or herds of cattle, even more suggest that they eat animals that local people never would, such as 'little dogs' and cats. In one short anecdote Arnaudin recorded, Talinote Laporte recalled a local man who had to stop threshing so that he could vomit up seven dogs he had consumed during the night.[38] The werewolf was disgusting rather than terrifying.

In fact, the werewolf had very little to do with real wolves in the nineteenth century, perhaps reflecting the decreasing importance of wolves in the French countryside.[39] This represents a major point of departure from the early-modern demonological accounts of lycanthropy. Early-modern demonologists were aware that not all shapeshifters turned themselves into wolves, recognizing that they could become cats, or even pigs and other domestic animals.[40] Nonetheless, almost all of the literary accounts deal with humans who are turned into wolves,

---

[36] For instance: Dr Drouet, 'Le loup-garou en Limousin', *Revue d'ethnographie et de sociologie* (1911), 147.

[37] Eugène Sol, *Le Vieux Quercy* (Aurillac, 1930), 93–4; Arnaudin collected a story about a werewolf who eats carrion. See: NFA, 2 MI 29/11, f.88.

[38] NFA, 2 MI 29/11, f.90.

[39] The absence of wolves, so the argument goes, is why the British Isles has no werewolf tradition. Matthew Beresford, *The White Devil: The Werewolf in European Culture* (London, 2013), 130.

[40] Jean de Nynauld, *De la Lycanthropie, transformation et extase des sorciers (1615)*, eds. Maxime Préaud and Nicole Jacques-Chaquin (Paris, 1990), 67; Charlotte Otten, ed., *A Lycanthropy Reader: Werewolves in Western Culture* (Syracuse, 1986), 80–1.

and most authors agree that real wolf attacks probably lay behind the werewolf accusations that led to the criminal trials in the early-modern period.[41] In the narratives collected since the nineteenth century, the picture is different. Many narrators were uncertain about what exactly the beast was, talking of 'a shapeless animal' or a 'bizarre mass'.[42] Only seven narrators specified that the shapeshifter turned into a wolf. By contrast, the narratives mention sixteen humans who became dogs, as well as eleven cats, nine sheep, five horses, four goats, three pigs, a bull, a donkey, a rabbit, and a hare, suggesting that Ronald Hutton is right to argue that 'werewolves' are really part of a much wider tradition of human-animal shapeshifters known in many cultures.[43] Marichoun's story is typical in that she explicitly calls the beast a *loup-garou*, but goes on to refer to it throughout as a 'dog'. In another story Arnaudin collected from Marichoun, the point was made even more forcefully. When a local man decided that a dead cow would provide the perfect opportunity to wait for a chance to shoot some wolves, he was disappointed to find that only dogs appeared to eat the carcass. His disappointment turned to surprise when he heard the dogs talking to one another in Gascon, and arranging to meet later the same day for a drink in the local inn. The man took the opportunity to go to the inn himself and identify the werewolves, with whom the family never did business again.[44] By the time Arnaudin was collecting stories like this, the connection between the violence of real wolves and the figure of the werewolf had become so weak that it was almost meaningless. In the twentieth century, Charles Joisten found there was no correlation between areas in the Alps that were still affected by wolves and mentions of wolves in the shapeshifting narratives he collected.[45]

The werewolf was known by many names in the different parts of France, but there are nonetheless underlying similarities between the *garou*, the *varou*, *elbrou*, *lebrou*, *lebrette*, and *birette*. Some folklorists did confuse these beings with other supernatural figures, such as the *meneur de loups*, who had the power to control real wolves, but also witches, fairies and goblins, the Devil, or the Wild Hunt.[46] Nonetheless, the tradition has coherence: the werewolf was a human who by some means or another is turned into a horrifying animal, normally at night, and who

---

[41] Caroline Oates, 'Metamorphosis and Lycanthropy in Franche-Comté, 1521–1643', in *Fragments for a History of the Human Body*, eds. Michel Tazi Feher, Ramona Naddaff, and Nadia Tazi (3 vols, New York, 1989), i, 305–63; Michel Meurger, 'L'homme loup et son témoin. Construction d'une factualité lycanthropique', in Jean de Nynauld, *De la Lycanthropie, transformation et extase des sorciers (1615)*, eds. Maxime Préaud and Nicole Jacques-Chaquin (Paris, 1990), 143–79.

[42] Foix, *Sorcières et loups-garous dans les Landes*, 50; Alfred Micha, *L'Ourthe et l'Amblève* (Liège, 1919), 37.

[43] Ronald Hutton, *The Witch: A History of Fear, from Ancient Times to the Present* (New Haven, 2017), 262–78.

[44] NFA, 2 MI 29/11, f.88.

[45] Joisten et al., 'Les Loups-garous en Savoie et Dauphiné', 50.

[46] This is why Andries includes even phenomena such as the animal-bridegroom of the fairytale tradition in her survey of werewolves. See: Andries, 'Contes du loup'.

provokes disgust among a community. Most were men.[47] The fact that they were not wolves seemed to cause little concern to the narrators, who maintained that this was what the *garou* was. This was clearly quite a different phenomenon to the mysterious and violent 'beasts' that terrorized the Cévennes (1809), or Chaingy (1814), Cézallier (1946–51), and most famously, the Gévaudan (1764–7).[48] It was also markedly different from the violence and drama of early-modern werewolf accounts, which frequently featured 'rape, incest, murder, savage attacks, and cannibalism'.[49] As the medieval author Marie de France put it: 'A werewolf is a savage beast/while his fury is on him/he eats men, does much harm,/goes deep in the forest to live'.[50] This literary werewolf is both more dramatic, and more easily defined than the folk traditions of the nineteenth century.

Beyond the feeling that the werewolf was—to use Marichoun's term—'rotten', legend tellers were generally vague about the most basic details of what a werewolf is, and whether they were to blame for their metamorphosis. As one folklorist pointed out, legend tellers were frustratingly imprecise about what he called 'the actual workings of the metamorphosis of man into werewolf'.[51] Dr Drouet, who wrote one of the most in-depth investigations of the werewolf, expressed a similar dissatisfaction: 'The very nature of the beast, its essence I might say, is only conceived in vague terms. And the peasants do not respond well to questions about this, since they do not see the point.'[52] When storytellers were explicit, the most common way to become a werewolf involved putting on some kind of skin, a method mentioned in fourteen stories and by five of the folklorists. Another two stories mentioned getting undressed. In a story collected by Henri Carnoy in Picardy, a man changed himself into a werewolf by ducking himself in a pond.[53] Other common methods of transformation included ointments, which were mentioned by three of the folklorists and in three stories, and belts, which were used in four of the stories and mentioned by one of the folklorists. All in all, storytellers evoke uncertainty about how werewolves transform, because uncertainty is the meaning of their stories.

This also helps to understand why legend tellers had such a different attitude to the folklorists when it came to blaming or excusing the werewolf. There were some narratives which explicitly blame the werewolf, or link his actions to diabolism.

---

[47] Sixty-six of the examples I have found refer explicitly to male werewolves, while just twenty-four mention women who were turned into animals. What is more, many of these women seem to have been more akin to what we would recognize as witches, individuals who deliberately use their maleficent powers to harm others. Charles Joisten, for instance, was adamant that most werewolves were men. Joisten et al., 'Les Loups-garous en Savoie et Dauphiné', 47.

[48] Andries, 'Contes du loup', 201; Jay M. Smith, *Monsters of the Gévaudan: The Making of a Beast* (Cambridge, MA, 2011).

[49] See the chapbooks about Stubbe Peeter in: Otten, *A Lycanthropy Reader*, 51, 69–76.

[50] Cited in: Bynum, *Metamorphosis and Identity*, 170.

[51] Henri Gelin, *Légendes de sorcellerie* (Liguge, 1898), 5.

[52] Drouet, 'Le loup-garou en Limousin', 146.

[53] Henri Carnoy, *Littérature orale de la Picardie* (Paris, 1883), 106–8.

Thirteen of the stories featured examples of individuals who were condemned to be werewolves for crimes such as stealing sticks, or having sex before marriage, but the storytellers were much less likely to talk of satanic dealings, magic books, and blasphemy than the folklorists were.[54] Eleven folklorists mentioned pacts with the Devil, while only five legend tellers offered this as an explanation for metamorphosis. Folklorists such as Camille de Mensignac declared that in some villages, children who were baptised by the priest before he had said mass risked becoming werewolves. According to this logic, the priest was impure until he performed this rite, 'since he was probably sleeping with his maid'.[55] Yet these religious explanations for the aetiology of shapeshifting were less popular with storytellers. Being the son or grandson of a priest was mentioned by a few of the folklorists but none of the legend tellers. This was part of a wider pattern, whereby storytellers had less interest than the folklorists in how exactly the transformation occurred or why. With the notable exception of the storyteller Nannette Lévesque, who told the folklorist Victor Smith two long, fantastical, and violent stories about werewolves who seem to have represented her own repressed violent urges towards her family, most storytellers did not discuss the subjective guilt or shame of the shapeshifter.[56] Like Mariane, most legend tellers struggled to know who to blame. Their stories were not about the guilt of the werewolf, but what the possibility of transformation challenged: the social order, boundaries, and bodily integrity.

That is not to say that the stories were uninterested in who the werewolf was. The narrative core of most legends was about identifying the transgressor by injuring their skin. In many of the stories this marked the body of the werewolf, who could then be identified the next morning by looking for the person in the community who bore the same injury as the beast.[57] Marichoun's story is a good example of this process, which folklorists have called 'repercussion'.[58] Just as Marichoun's family recognized the werewolf by his burnt face, many other stories talked of injuries to the face, ears, and forehead. It was even more common for stories to tell of how breaking a werewolf's skin ended the metamorphosis.[59] Several specifically mentioned injuring the nose, such as this anonymous account collected in Anjou:

There was a woman from near Beauvau who saw a big black cat come into her house each evening and try to eat the dinner she was making. One day, annoyed

---

[54] The stick thief is found in: Léon Pineau, 'Le Folklore de la Touraine: Le loup-garou', *Revue des Traditions Populaires*, xvii (1902), 579–80; the werewolves whose fault seems to have been in extramarital sex are in: Tenèze and Delarue, *Nannette Lévesque*, 85.

[55] Mensignac, *Notice sur plusieurs coutumes, usages*, 175.

[56] See: Tenèze and Delarue, *Nannette Lévesque*.

[57] Hutton, *The Witch*, 265.

[58] wBynum, *Metamorphosis and Identity*, 74; Joisten et al., 'Les Loups-garous en Savoie et Dauphiné', 119.

[59] On breaking the skin to cure the werewolf, see: Joisten et al., 'Les Loups-garous en Savoie et Dauphiné', 81. Interestingly, the Joisten collection suggests feeding werewolves was a more important method for curing them than wounding them. I have found no trace of this in other sources.

with the persistence of the animal, she hit it on the nose with the handle of her knife, making it bleed. In a flash, it turned into a human, much to the amazement of the woman, who found herself face to face with one of her cousins from the town.[60]

Werewolf stories were about the uncertainties and violence of what the psycho-analyst Didier Anzieu has called the 'skin-ego'. People like Marichoun feared and abhorred the transgressions of skin and identity that the werewolf represented. As one nineteenth-century folklorist wrote: 'in the old days, our hearty farmers had very sensitive skin'.[61]

In some ways, this sensitive skin belongs to the deep history of the human body. Repercussion features in classical, as well as in medieval and early-modern sources.[62] In Petronius' *Satyricon*, which dates from the first century CE, Niceros tells his companion Trimalchio how he saw his master turn into a wolf. While under this form, he was injured by another servant. When Niceros returned home he found his master 'lying a-bed like an Oxe in his Stall, and a Chirurgeon dressing his neck. I understood afterwards he was a Fellow that could change his Skin, but from that day forward, could never eat a bit of Bread with him, not if you'd have kill'd me.'[63] Yet, in spite of what has sometimes been assumed about the time-lessness of shapeshifting, the nineteenth- and twentieth-century werewolves were not exactly the same as their ancient ancestors.[64] The modern storytellers pre-sented narratives that were less extravagant, less religious, and less violent, but more banal, and more intimate than the sources that survive from earlier periods. Rather than a wild beast, the werewolf was a domestic disturbance. His appear-ance signalled concerns about identity and skin that were specific to the changes in rural private spaces, but not obvious to outsiders, whose gaze was drawn to the more dramatic projects to reform the exterior landscape.

Religion, Gender, and Family

The folklorists identified werewolves with certain areas of France, and with a receding past. Very often, they were collected in the parts of France that were thought to be wildest, such as moorlands where Marichoun and Arnaudin lived, Brittany, the Nivernais, and the Massif Central. Yet authors such as Lise Andries

---

[60] Fraysse, 'Au Pays de Baugé', 12.

[61] He was talking about sensitivity to nicknaming. See: Charles Beauquier, *Blason populaire de Franche-Comté: Sobriquets, dictons, contes, etc.* (Paris, 1897), 5.

[62] Bynum, *Metamorphosis and Identity*, 174; Oates, 'Metamorphosis and Lycanthropy in Franche-Comté', 39.

[63] Otten, *A Lycanthropy Reader*, 233.

[64] Andries suggests the tradition is relatively unchanging. See: Andries, 'Contes du loup', 197.

and even Arnold van Gennep were a little too hasty to write off regions they claimed had no werewolf tradition, such as the Dauphiné or Savoie.[65] Moreover, it is clear that werewolf traditions did travel, as when they were recorded by folklorists in the industrial town of Saint-Étienne, or the metropolis of Bordeaux, or in the trenches of the First World War.[66] As traditions moved, so too did their meanings. In the Alps, for instance, Charles Joisten and his collaborators found that the geography of werewolf narratives demonstrated connections between feudal heritages, the hunting of wolves, the ravages of the glass-making industry, and politicization.[67] Other werewolves could take on even more modern guises. In the late nineteenth century, the villages on the outskirts of the industrial town of Saint-Étienne were plagued by a werewolf who apparently scared one woman to death.[68] It is hard not to see this beast through the lens of fears about the immigrant industrial workers, or as a reflection of the resentments these workers themselves felt towards religiously motivated social reformers. When it was finally caught and forced to confess, the werewolf revealed it was under the control of the clergy.

This was a common theme in werewolf stories. Especially for the folklorists in more devout parts of France, the werewolf had particular religious connotations, which meant narratives of lycanthropy could be used to debate the merits of Catholicism, and express anti-clerical sentiments. In Normandy, the first folklorist to mention traditions about a rite known as 'quérimonie' was a former Girondist with a dislike for the Catholic Church, Louis du Bois. According to the account he gave, under the old regime, when a crime was committed it was within the clergy's power to excommunicate any witnesses who did not come forward. These unfortunate souls would become werewolves, or so the 'credulous grandmothers' would tell their 'terrified grandchildren'.[69] In the twentieth century, Jean Cuisenier claimed that locals even told him that the *quérimonie* had occasionally been revived in more recent times.[70] These associations between sin, werewolves, and penance were not as strong in the nineteenth and twentieth centuries as they may have been in the medieval period, but they cropped up in accounts from the Limousin, Mayenne, Auvergne, Guyenne, Creuse, Quercy, and the Beauce.[71] Léon

---

[65]   In fact, Charles Joisten found a rich haul there. See: Joisten et al., 'Les Loups-garous en Savoie et Dauphiné'; Andries, 'Contes du loup', 198; Arnold van Gennep, *Le Folklore du Dauphiné, Isère. Étude descriptive et comparée de psychologie populaire*, 2 vols (Paris, 1932), ii, 552.

[66]   Albert Boissier, *Carnets d'un folkloriste, 1910–1953* (2 vols, Saint-Didier-en-Velay, 1990), i, 130; Hertz, 'Contes et dictons'; Mensignac, *Notice sur plusieurs coutumes, usages*, 175.

[67]   Joisten et al., 'Les Loups-garous en Savoie et Dauphiné'.

[68]   Boissier, *Carnets d'un folkloriste*, i, 130.

[69]   Louis Du Bois, *Recherches archéologiques, historiques, biographiques et littéraires sur la Normandie* (Paris, 1843), 300.

[70]   Jean Cuisenier, *Récits et contes populaires de Normandie* (2 vols, Paris, 1979), i, 54.

[71]   For example: Coissac, *Mon Limousin*, 293; Hertz, 'Contes et dictons', 89; Antoinette Bon, 'Le Seigneur loup-garou. Légende de l'Auvergne', *Revue des Traditions Populaires*, v (1890), 216–18; Seignolle, *Contes populaires de Guyenne*, 225; Louis Guibert, 'Histoires de sorciers', reproduced in: Queyrat, *Contribution à l'étude du parler de la Creuse*, 347–8; Sol, *Le Vieux Quercy*, 92–3; Félix Chapiseau, *Le Folk-lore de la Beauce et du Perche* (Paris, 1902), 219.

Pineau recorded a story about a woman in the Touraine who was changed into a werewolf after witnessing another local cutting off a donkey's ear. Since she failed to come forward after the local priest had pronounced an 'ommonitouère', she became a shapeshifter.[72]

Perhaps the piety of these werewolf beliefs appealed to the many early folklorists who were also clerics.[73] But perhaps it was simply the Voltairean Du Bois' misfortune to collect folklore in a region where the association between Catholicism and werewolf beliefs was mutually reinforcing. In other, more anti-clerical regions, the priesthood played a much darker role in popular narratives about lycanthropy. Around Toulon it was rumoured that the fear of werewolves was a convenient excuse for priests to extort money in exchange for masses.[74] Charles Joisten collected evidence of similar suspicions in the lower valleys of the Alps in the twentieth century.[75] Werewolf stories could deal in the rural repercussions of the kinds of tensions between Catholicism and scepticism that raged in politics and education in nineteenth-century France.[76] Coissac reproduced a particularly pithy example:

Near Ambazac, they say, there was a priest...who was dressed in an animal skin, and ran around the countryside in the evenings to scare people and put the fear of God in them. Piety through terror. F***ing shoot the bastard, people said, and you'll soon see if it's the priest.[77]

As narratives of the out-of-the-ordinary, werewolf stories allowed storytellers to talk about difficult topics, such as religious conflict, with their social superiors.

In Marichoun's case, it was not religion, but gender and the family that lay at the heart of her story. In Marichoun's stories as in her life, the remaking of the physical environment was also associated with the remaking of families. Many of the stories Marichoun told Arnaudin evoke a bygone period of extended families. She told him about a time her brother was bewitched, or about the time she herself was ridden by a hag when visiting family members.

Most importantly, she set her werewolf story in the context of an extended household of family members and sharecroppers, who would have lived in a fairly large house, like the one in Fig. 5.1. This extended co-habiting family was declining in the period when she told these stories. Where agro-pastoralism was highly labour intensive, and relied on all of the different family members to perform complementary tasks for the good of the whole household, the newer

[72] Pineau, 'Le Folklore de la Touraine: Le loup-garou', 579.
[73] David M. Hopkin, 'Les Religieux et la culture vernaculaire en Europe au XIXe siècle: François Cadic dans son contexte', in *François Cadic—un collecteur vannetais, 'recteur' des Bretons de Paris*, ed. Fanch Postic (Morbihan, 2011).
[74] Letuaire, *Les Cahiers de P. Letuaire*, ii, 49.
[75] Joisten et al., 'Les Loups-garous en Savoie et Dauphiné', 126.
[76] The literature is extensive, although perhaps the best introduction is: Harris, *Lourdes*.
[77] Coissac, *Mon Limousin*, 296.

Fig. 5.1 A typical traditional house in the moorlands, courtesy of the Musée d'Aquitaine

forms of employment, such as resin collector, roadmender, or railway worker paid an individual salary, encouraging a shift to nuclear families with a primary breadwinner, even if they were supported by agricultural work from the rest of the family.[78] The shift may not have happened overnight, but the dominant family forms in the region were undoubtedly affected by these changes in working life. What is more, the tensions such changes might have aroused are part of the subject of Marichoun's story. In both the narrative about the 'rotten werewolf' and the other narrative she told about the man watching two talking dogs eating carrion, the guilty party was no shepherd, or farmer. They were not even the social outcasts who had most often been suspected of lycanthropy in the early-modern period, such as beggars, rag pickers, or soldiers.[79] Instead, the men suspected of being werewolves in Marichoun's stories were semi-outsiders of another kind, men who lived in the rural community but did not do agricultural work. In the story of the 'rotten werewolf', the guilty party was an innkeeper, and in the other story, a local carpenter turned out to be the shapeshifter. The protagonist of the story swore never to use his services again.[80]

---

[78] Dupuy, *Le Pin de la discorde*, 212–13.
[79] Meurger, 'L'homme loup et son témoin', 156–7; Oates, 'Metamorphosis and Lycanthropy in Franche-Comté', 326.
[80] NFA, 2 MI 29/11, f.88.

Such men presented a challenge to the integrity of the extended household even before the changes associated with forestation swelled the ranks of the wage-earning population. Songs such as 'All Artisans Are Thieves' (Coirault 6416[81]) suggest that artisans had long been the focus of simmering tensions. Discussing another song about the tensions between artisans and farmers, the Gascon folklorist Justin Cénac-Moncaut commented on 'the preference girls have always had for artisans, who are better off than simple farmers'.[82] They provided ideal avatars for the concerns Marichoun expressed about the boundaries of the household, since, like the wage earners, their interests were independent of the extended family. This was a tension that affected the moorlands particularly acutely in the nineteenth century, as many working men were forced into new forms of employment which paid wages, rather than working for their family. This helps to explain why Marichoun's artisanal werewolves, representatives of the breakdown of old agricultural working systems, were by no means typical of the suspected werewolves in other parts of France. While there were individual stories 2of legal functionaries, priests, tailors, and butchers who were suspected of shapeshifting, the vast majority of werewolves elsewhere were plain workers, farmers, or hired hands.[83] In this sense, as in others, Marichoun's stories are at once unusual, and yet seem deeply connected to the standard themes of werewolf stories across France.

Marichoun's concerns about changing boundaries, families, and households were deeply personal: the extended family was also a distant memory for Marichoun herself. When she married her husband Jean Lescarret in 1852, neither the bride or groom was wealthy. Although they had enough possessions to draw up a marriage contract, it listed possessions worth just a couple of hundred francs, including the wood that Jean owned and intended to make into a bed and a table. The newly married couple may not have come from the poorest strata of the working population, but they belonged to a class more vulnerable to the disintegration of the bonds of family and community. Survival was about the survival of the household, whose boundaries took on an overwhelming symbolic significance.

And yet by the time she met Arnaudin in the 1870s, Marichoun was widowed and living on her own in a small house in Labouheyre.[84] When she insisted to the folklorist that she remembered the story from her own experience, she was situating her narrative about confused boundaries in a very real set of lived experiences. This close connection to Marichoun's own life makes her story unusual in the context of the 126 other werewolf narratives, many of which talked about werewolves as if they

---

[81] Coirault refers to the song 'type' as catalogued in *RCFTO*.

[82] Justin Cénac-Moncaut, *Littérature populaire de la Gascogne, contes, mystères, chansons historiques, satiriques, sentimentales, rondeaux recueillis dans l'Astarac, le Pardiac, le Béarn et le Bigorre* (Paris, 1868), 310.

[83] I have counted seventeen examples, while the other, more specialized occupations only account for one story each.

[84] The 1872 census was still held by the archives in Labouheyre when I visited in 2012.

were a distant memory. Imprecise and uncertain, the werewolf was real to Marichoun. But its reality was not what historians might assume. It had little to do with wolves, or folk Catholicism, or even witchcraft. Instead, the werewolf was a way to talk about, and to embody, the uncertainty of redrawn boundaries, and especially the redrawn boundaries of the household. Marichoun could do this by drawing on the wider tradition of werewolf belief, but the ways that she did it were specific to her own situation. Like other legend tellers Marichoun's stories all tended to deal in similar themes, building a picture of a particular vision of the world.[85] Most recounted key relationships with family members, such as a brother who had recourse to an unwitching specialist. It is this interplay between Marichoun's own experiences and the cultural tradition that is the key to understanding her werewolf.

Conclusion

Rural people were not as credulous as outsiders liked to claim. Their supernatural beliefs were shot through with doubt and indifference, and the individuals, like Marichoun or the beggar woman Nannette Lévesque, most likely to talk in vivid terms about werewolves were women exploring the specific ruptures to household and personal boundaries. These women may have been unusual, but their stories make sense as part of shared, local bodily cultures, of the kind explored in Chapter 4. Werewolves were not the wild, extreme, violent, and dramatic figures of Hollywood or the early-modern trials, but were instead a way to discuss, think, and argue about everyday domestic uncertainties of household boundaries, community, and animals. For an individual like Marichoun, the most meaningful way to think about the period between her childhood in an extended family of rural labourers and the relative solitude of her old age was in terms of the sensitivity of the boundaries of the body itself. Although her story, and her personal investment in the reality of the werewolf, may be unusual, her repertoire of other stories suggest that she was a recognized storyteller, whose narratives had meaning to her wider community. Other individuals, such as the men and women whose lives Chapter 6 focuses on, lived the changes to local society in different ways, but enough of them could sympathize with Marichoun's experiences that her story was worth hearing. The pity for the historian is that a folklorist like Arnaudin was not interested enough in the performative nature of storytelling to record how Marichoun told the story to an audience, and how the audience responded. But a different folk genre—singing—provides a more rounded view of this community, representing a folk tradition that aspired to harmony and consensus, often presenting the shared views of singers. It is to this shared culture of making love that Chapter 6 turns.

[85] Timothy R. Tangherlini, *Danish Folktales, Legends, and Other Stories* (Copenhagen, 2014).

6

Singing Love

Many of the working women in Arnaudin's photographs were dressed as if they were in mourning. Their dark clothing looks much like that worn in societies that emphasize chastity and strict social codes, such as the nearby Mediterranean cultures of 'honour and shame', where women's sexual behaviour has been subject to moralistic community regulation.[1] Alain Corbin has suggested that the spread of sombre clothing for women affected many different parts of nineteenth-century France.[2] But the songs the women of the moorlands sang reveal that they longed to wear brighter colours. A song entitled *When I Was Fifteen or Sixteen*, for instance, ends with the death of the heroine's tiny husband. She knows she should dress in mourning, but declares that instead 'the red tempted me'.[3] This temptation is not just an aesthetic choice, but a reference to social tensions around sexuality.[4] It draws its power from the colour symbolism of local folk culture, where red was associated with sexuality and drinking, and was the traditional colour of brides on their wedding day, or pretty girls.[5] When the singers Arnaudin met, most of whom were women, sang songs such as this about their preference for red, they were not just talking of clothing: they were making coded references to the pleasures of youth and sexuality, pleasures they associated with the historical, as well as individual, or remembered past.

These songs suggest that, from the point of view of the singers at least, the sexual culture of the moorlands was moving in the opposite direction to the 'first sexual revolution' that Anne-Marie Sohn has identified during the Third Republic (1870–1940).[6] Far from seeing increasingly free sexual relations, as Sohn

---

[1] On 'honour and shame, see, for instance: Anton Blok, 'Rams and Billy-Goats: A Key to the Mediterranean Code of Honour', *Man*, xvi (new series, 1981), 427–40; David D. Gilmore, *Honor and Shame and the Unity of the Mediterranean* (Washington, DC, 1987); Jean G. Péristiany, ed., *Honour and Shame: The Values of Mediterranean Society* (Chicago, 1966).

[2] Alain Corbin, '"Le Sexe en deuil" et l'histoire des femmes au XIXᵉ siècle', in *Le Temps, le desir, l'horreur: Essais sur le dix-neuvième* (Paris, 1998), 91–105.

[3] See *When I Was Fifteen or Sixteen* as well as the following song, *I Have Hired an Oaf*, which has a similar ending where the girl 'preferred the red'. *OC*, iii, 207–8, 208–11.

[4] Barre Toelken and Roger de van Renwick both point out that sober clothing was the norm in nineteenth-century European village life. Coloured clothes in folk songs therefore suggest coded meanings. Toelken, *Morning Dew and Roses*, 39–40.

[5] For the association of red and debauchery, see: *OC*, vii, 256. For a song that associates red with drinking, see: *OC*, iii, 301–2. For songs associating red with prettiness and drinking, see: *OC*, iv, 438–41, 595–7.

[6] Sohn, *Du Premier baiser à l'alcôve*. As I suggested in the Introduction, this is a question of what the singers themselves believed. The Arnaudin collection does not provide enough longitudinal material to prove how the culture was changing, but it can reveal the changes that people discussed.

Body and Tradition in Nineteenth-Century France: Félix Arnaudin and the Moorlands of Gascony, 1870–1914.
William G. Pooley, Oxford University Press (2019). © William G. Pooley.
DOI: 10.1093/oso/9780198847502.001.0001

suggested, the songs fit better with Bernard Traimond's picture of growing social control of sexuality in the moorlands.[7] Historians have not been very interested in rural cultures of love making for their own sake, preferring to think of 'peasant' families in terms of their material interests, rather than their emotional under-pinnings.[8] When historians have studied rural courtship, it has been easier to address questions of collective *mentalités* than to pursue how these ways of thinking and feeling were taken on by a variety of historical individuals. The singers in Arnaudin's manuscripts offer historians a more fine-grained cultural approach, that explores how individuals negotiated shared understandings of sexual cultures.

The demographic evidence suggests a complete revolution in rural courting, and nowhere was it more pronounced than in the south-west of France.[9] In 1821, the Landes was one of the most fertile departments, with a high birth and marriage rate, and a very high rate of illegitimacy. By 1920, the marriage, birth, and illegitimacy rates had all collapsed. A lower proportion of the population were getting married each year, and married couples were having fewer children. The illegitimacy rate had declined even faster than the marital fertility rate, taking the Landes from one of the largest producers of illegitimate children in France to an area that appeared to be among the chastest.[10] These two different declines in fertility can be attributed to the combined factors of the changing labour demands of agricultural work, greater life expectancies, and the spread of contraception, but what these social explanations do not reveal is who chose to limit fertility, how they justified these choices, and who resisted.[11] Rather than the steady sexual liberation of the Third Republic, the songs Arnaudin collected expressed a widely shared sense of regret and anxiety about making love among women who felt that their freedoms had been eroded.

Songs are a unique meeting point between individual feelings and desires, and wider social expectations. Singers recognized this in moments of surprising self-awareness. In a memorable example, one of the folklorist Achille Millien's singers in the Nièvre recited a version of Coirault 2325 *Pregnant Although She Didn't Feel It* which addressed the link between national politics and personal love making. It included the lines 'He lifted my skirt, he went straight in ... The Republic orders us to make more children. Oh! It's to replace those who have died [in the fighting].'[12] Arnaudin may not have collected any material that drew such explicit links

---

[7] Traimond, 'La Sociabilité Rurale Landaise', 227.

[8] The most sensitive historians have long been critical of this artificial division between 'interest' and 'emotion'. See: Hans Medick and David Warren Sabean, eds, *Interest and Emotion: Essays on the Study of Family and Kinship* (Cambridge, 1984).

[9] Jean-Philippe Bardet and Hervé Le Bras, 'La Chute de la fécondité', in *Histoire de la population française*, ed. Jacques Dupâquier (3 vols, Paris, 1988), iii, 351–401.

[10] See: G. Callon, 'Le Mouvement de la population dans les Landes au cours de la période 1821–1920', *Bulletin de la Société de Borda* (1931), 1–28.

[11] Bardet and Le Bras, 'La Chute de la fécondité', 364–78.   [12] *RCFTO*, i, 271.

between national demographic challenges and personal feelings, but the songs he recorded do provide an unrivalled insight into the shared culture of making love in the moorlands, which can help historians to understand how the demographic shift was experienced and contested.

The Shared Culture of Love

'Laws,' one nineteenth-century folklorist pointed out, 'may be imposed on the unwilling, but not songs.'[13] It is in this sense that singing together represents one of the most basic forms of community consensus, a way for groups to agree standard views on emotionally charged topics.[14] The problems and desires the songs of the moorlands explore were those that were most important to the majority of people at the time. The 'cantometric' research into the relationship between songs and culture led by Alan Lomax in the 1960s found that 'Song and dance style . . . symbolize and summarize attitudes and ways of handling situations upon which there is the highest level of community consensus'.[15] Tonal harmony reflects cultural harmony, and to sing and dance is to move in rhythm with the social order. This fits well with the evidence concerning singing in the moorlands. Arnaudin often collected his songs from groups of singers, whether mother and daughter pairs, or simply groups of neighbours who came together to sing for him.

For this reason, songs do not often speak directly in the individual voice. And there are other reasons why they are opaque statements of personal intentions: their symbolism, and the vagueness of their narratives and moral stances. Ideas and words seep from song to song, giving many of the different texts the same aesthetic of flowers, herbs, May mornings, shepherdesses, and soldiers laying their heads on the young girls' laps.[16] Their meanings depended on shared understandings, performances in contexts where singers knew one another, and could read between the lines of which songs someone chose to sing, and how they sang them. More than any other topic, folk songs concentrate on making love. Early folklorists were struck by the 'quite shameless delight and interest' that folk songs demonstrate in the details of 'fornication and pregnancy', and, above all, the temptations and frustrations of courtship.[17] Sex was never a taboo of rural society.[18]

---

[13] Evelyn Lilian Martinengo-Cesaresco, *Essays in the Study of Folk-Songs* (London, 1886), xiv.

[14] This is central to Toelken's book on folk song metaphors. See: Toelken, *Morning Dew and Roses*, 28, 46, among others.

[15] Alan Lomax, *Folk Song Style and Culture* (Washington, DC, 1968), 15.

[16] This insight dates back at least as far as Tristram Coffin's work on ballads. See: Tristram P. Coffin, '"Mary Hamilton" and the Anglo-American Ballad as an Art Form', *Journal of American Folklore*, lxx (1957), 208–14.

[17] James Reeves, ed., *The Idiom of the People: English Traditional Verse* (London, 1958), 8.

[18] Martine Segalen, *Love and Power in the Peasant Family: Rural France in the Nineteenth Century* (Chicago, 1983), 129–31.

Nowhere was this truer than in the moorlands. The catalogue of French folk songs begun by Patrice Coirault, and finished by Georges Delarue, Yvette Fédéroff, and Simone Wallon, reveals the distribution of song types through the French-speaking world.[19] Many of the songs Arnaudin collected were what folklorists call 'ecotypes', specific variations that were limited to this geographical area. The resistance to black, for instance, was quite specific to the moorlands. Songs similar to the ones Arnaudin collected which mention women choosing red over black clothing were found by five other folklorists in the south-west of France, but only one version from nearby Ariège made any mention of the temptations of red clothing.[20] The red and the black were cultural symbols that took on specific resonance in the context of the progressive sexual repression of the nineteenth-century moorlands.

Far from being completely unchanging, these songs of love were responding to the upheavals in local society. It is true that the constraints of the genre—rhyme, rhythm, and tune—encourage conservatism in folk singing.[21] Some of the songs sung by Arnaudin's singers in the late nineteenth century can be traced back to the early-modern period.[22] The songs preserved a rarefied vocabulary of social relations—nobles, kings, and barons—and clothing which was no longer related to everyday life. Yet this apparent timelessness was also combined with adaptations. Some, such as the references to the republican politics of post-revolutionary France, were obvious innovations, while others, such as changing attitudes to making love, are harder to plot.[23] The sheer size of Arnaudin's collection, and the fact he recorded songs from many different people of different ages, provide an answer to this problem. With such a large amount of material, it is possible to explore generational shifts in singing. Arnaudin's manuscripts contain 3,620 different song texts, which correspond to 420 different songs in his complete works. These texts were collected from 517 singers, and his notes confirm that these singers learned their songs over their lifetime. Older singers represent older strata of local singing cultures: on a number of occasions, Arnaudin recorded

---

[19] *RCFTO.*

[20] There is scope for some confusion over song titles between Arnaudin's Gascon and the French titles listed in the national catalogue, not least since a great many of the songs Arnaudin collected have very similar, or even identical titles, even when the song is completely different. The only sure way to identify which song is being discussed is to refer back to the catalogue, but I have also provided my own translations of the song titles from the catalogue and from Arnaudin's notes. For this song, see no. 5606, *The Little Husband Who Drowned. RCFTO*, i, 215–16; Louis Lambert, *Chants et chansons populaires du Languedoc* 2 vols (Leipzig, 1906), ii, 282–4.

[21] Toelken suggests songs are more conservative than, for instance, legends and jokes, and certainly rumours and puns. *The Dynamics of Folklore*, 41.

[22] A sixteenth-century book entitled *S'ensuyvent plusieurs belles chansons nouvelles... et plusieurs autres qui sont en nombre cinquante et troys*, for instance, featured at least two songs Arnaudin collected. See: Brian Jeffery, ed., *Chanson Verse of the Early Renaissance* (2 vols, London, 1971), i, 149–50.

[23] For examples of references to Revolutionary and republican politics in the songs Arnaudin collected, see: *OC*, iv, 60–1, 536–8.

songs that his singers learned fifty or more years earlier. And there is little evidence from folklorists that elderly singers substantially change their songs over their lifetime.[24] The differences between what young and old singers sang help historians to make sense of the changing sexual culture of the region.

'They Eat the Jam, and Blame the Rats'

Most of Arnaudin's singers were women, and what these women liked to sing about was carefree love, before or outside marriage. A song that Arnaudin collected from Babé Plantié, entitled *The Other Day, as I Walked on the Road to Talera*, is typical:

> On my way I met,
>> The wife of a lawyer...
>> I asked her gently:
>> 'Madam, will you let me stay the night?'
>> 'Yes, yes, of course, my good fellow,
>> You will sleep next to me.'
>> When midnight struck,
>> The lawyer came home.
>> He knocked on the door:
>> 'Madam, will you let me in?'
>> 'How can I let you in?
>> I have the baby in my arms.'
>> This is how women behave,
>> When their husbands are away.
>> They eat the jam,
>> And blame the rats.[25]

Babé's song, like many others Arnaudin collected, has little interest in female sexual honour. The songs of the moorlands are both more flippant and more explicit in terms of sex than many of the songs collected in other parts of France, and they present a much more forceful female voice. This is especially true of the older singers, whose songs are filled with nostalgia for a period when sexual relations were more carefree. Arnaudin commented on one song that people used to say, 'If twenty bastards weren't born [in the village of Sabres in] any given year, it was considered a poor year.'[26] His father, born in 1816, claimed that

---

[24] I could find no research by a folklorist who has explored this question. Many agree, however, as I point out above, that songs are inherently more conservative than some other genres.

[25] *OC*, iv, 362–4.   [26] *OC*, iii, 386.

'Back in the days, no-one paid any attention to what went on. Fathers did not even bother to keep their daughters under watch.' Young women, Arnaudin's father remembered, were free to experiment sexually on their way home from the dances, or working in the fields.[27] As one of the characters in Edmond About's novel of life in the moorlands put it: 'as the young men and women are together from morning to evening, in some lost corner of the moorlands, far away from their family and everyone else, surrounded only by sheep, you can imagine what went on, and accidents were common'.[28] Attitudes to the illegitimate children born of these 'accidents' were disapproving, but not rigid. The carpenter Michel Colin reflected on the fate of an unmarried mother by referring to an anecdote about another woman he had known called le Tchitchique de Boré:

> The poor girl . . . she has been left hanging on the hook. Well, she only has to make an announcement in the town square like that woman from Escource (Tchitchique de Boré). She'd had a bastard. But she was a smart girl, she sold buns and chestnuts. 'You haven't given me many chestnuts, Tchitchique,' people said to her. 'Oh, I don't know how to count that high,' she would say . . . Someone married her.[29]

Fig. 6.1 Portrait of three women, most likely singers. The physical resemblance suggests they might represent three generations of the same family. Courtesy of the Musée d'Aquitaine

---

[27] NFA, 2 MI 29/21, f.170.   [28] About, *Maître Pierre*, 43–4.   [29] *OC*, viii, 582–3.

Several of Arnaudin's female informants had illegitimate children and then later married.

This relaxed attitude was reflected in the songs. Few dwelt on the honour of young women, while songs that were widely known in other parts of France which emphasized chastity were not sung in the moorlands. Arnaudin found no record, for instance, of the popular song *A Kiss to Remember Me By* (Coirault 407), which ends with the cry: 'What use are a thousand écus if I have lost my honour?'.[30] The sentiment expressed in *Take a Sweet Kiss from My Mouth* (Coirault 716) was similarly alien to the sexual culture of the moorlands, and unknown to Arnaudin's singers. After her father refuses to marry her, the girl tells her lover: 'Come, my love, fortify yourself, take a sweet kiss from my mouth. But do not touch anything else on my pale, rosy breasts, where love reigns: honour forbids it.'[31] The differences between the version of *The Girl Who Had Strolled out Too Often* (Coirault 801) collected by Jean-François Bladé in the Gers and the version collected by Arnaudin are revealing.[32] The girl in the version from the Gers is inconsolable about her lost honour, while the heroine in the moorlands appears happy to be paid off.[33] She says she will tell her parents she earned the money sewing, in an allusion to an everyday activity that was symbolically associated with the sexuality of women's bodies.[34] Honour was not as important to the singers of the moorlands as it was in other parts of France.[35] Even the local songs known as *charivaris*, which were composed and sung to shame sexual and marital transgressions, are light in references to proper behaviour. Just one of those found by Arnaudin in the moorlands mentions 'honour', while another refers more euphemistically to a 'mess'.[36]

Instead, the songs of the moorlands are bawdier and more daring than songs collected elsewhere in France. Several appear in the section of the Coirault catalogue devoted to 'Smut', and some are even labelled 'Obscene', including *The Girl Who Wanted to Shave Her Cunt* (Coirault 12005) and *The Miller Cuckolded by the Monk* (Coirault 12008).[37] Arnaudin's notes make it clear that many more of the songs had obscene connotations that might not be obvious to outsiders. He worried about whether it was appropriate to publish them, and how.[38] Comparisons with other versions from elsewhere again show how daring the songs from the moorlands were. The version of *The Old Man Who Made His Wife Spin* (Coirault 5715) which Charles Guillon collected in the Ain was much

---

[30] Neither was the popular song no. 3412 *Virginity Cannot Be Returned Like Borrowed Money* known in the moorlands. See *RCFTO*, i, 64, 353.

[31] *RCFTO*, i, 89.   [32] *RCFTO*, i, 93.

[33] Jean-François Bladé, *Poésies populaires de la Gascogne* (3 vols, Paris, 1882), ii, 242–7.

[34] *OC*, iv, 496–7. On sex and sewing, see Chapter 7.

[35] For other examples of songs dwelling on honour which were popular throughout France but unknown in the moorlands, see, for example, *I Will Catch You* (no. 722), *The Beauty Who Played Dead to Guard Her Honour* (no. 1307), and *Painted Horses* (no. 1908). *RCFTO*, i, 91–2, 141, 232.

[36] *OC*, iv, 760–1, 762–4.   [37] *RCFTO*, iii, 221–31.

[38] See, for instance, his extensive notes: NFA, 2 MI 29/17, ff.61–2, 2 MI 29/5, ff.442–54, 458–60, 529.

more coy than the version Arnaudin recorded.[39] In the version from the Ain, a young girl complains to her elderly husband after their first night together that she cannot get out of bed because she has hardly slept.[40] The version from the moorlands is more direct: the girl refuses to get up because her husband has not consummated the marriage.[41]

Not All of the Cows on the Moor Belong to the Same Farmer (Coirault 5721) provides an example that demonstrates just how different this situation was from elsewhere in France.[42] In most versions of this song, women are compared to the sheep or cattle of the moorlands and to the castles of France. In this analogy, they are possessions which cannot all be owned by one man. But the song from the moorlands does not liken women to possessions, preferring to use an analogy that gives women more independence than sheep or buildings:

> All the birds that take flight,
>   Are not for the same hunter,
>   Young girls are the same,
>   They are not all for one lover.[43]

Arnaudin's oldest singers were more likely to sing in similar terms of independent women. The older singers sang songs that dealt flippantly with sex before marriage, such as *I Rose Early in the Morning, Before the Sun Came Up*, where a young girl is whisked away by a knight, who then pays to sleep with her on the moor.[44] Singers born at the start of the nineteenth century, like Marie Daugey, veuve Cassagne (1819–1905), sang songs declaring resistance to parents' attempts to marry girls for wealth: 'damn the money, if it comes at the price of pleasure'.[45] As Marie Pomade, known as Trézine, femme Duviella (b. 1819) put it in one song: 'Daddy, when I'm dead, I won't need these things'.[46] This freedom was not without its darker side. In this view of the recent past, love had been free, because life was cheap, and everyone was poor. Young men and women could marry who they wanted, because after all, as Marie Dupiau, known as Tchignoye dou Cla (b. 1827) sang, 'We will be miserable, like everyone is'.[47]

Where the heroines of folk songs in other parts of France tend to plead with their mothers that they were young once, too, the mothers in the songs of the

---

[39] *RCFTO*, ii, 227.

[40] Charles Guillon, *Chansons populaires de l'Ain* (Paris, 1883), 491–2.

[41] *OC*, iv, 575–7.   [42] *RCFTO*, ii, 230.

[43] *OC*, iv, 576. The only other version to mention the analogy of the birds also used the analogy of the sheep. See: Jean Poueigh, *Chansons populaires des Pyrénées françaises* (2 vols, Paris, 1926), i, 449.

[44] *OC*, iv, 271–85. This is related to no. 7211 *Love and the Silver Thread*, but the song from the moorlands has a more complex plot: *RCFTO*, ii, 395.

[45] *OC*, iv, 400; this is the very popular no. 5703 *To The Devil with Riches III*: *RCFTO*, ii, 221–2.

[46] *OC*, iv, 403–4.

[47] *OC*, iii, 168. This is the popular no. 1012 *It Is Time for Me to Marry*: *RCFTO*, i, 112–13.

moorlands hardly need persuading, instead openly admitting that in their youth they, too, were 'naughty'.[48] The version of *The Old Man Who Would Only Sleep* (Coirault 5704) from the moorlands is unique among French versions in that the mother actually suggests to her daughter that the solution to her marriage problems is to commit adultery.[49] The mother tells her:

> Make him a cuckold, my daughter,
>> Since your father is one, too...
>> In the time that your father has worn the horns,
>> He has worn through seven berets.[50]

Perhaps the clearest expression of this rebellious feminine identity comes from the song which Arnaudin called 'without a doubt the most popular [of all the songs] that are sung and danced to this day in the moorlands'.[51] The song he called *Long Live the Women of Sabres!* was catalogued by Coirault as *The Women Who Liked Wine*.[52]

> Long live the women of Sabres!
> To enjoy wine.
> They go to mass...
> Not because they are pious.
> From there to the inn...
> To have a party.
> One has brought some sausage...
> Another some ribs.
> One has a pint of beer...
> They are drunk.
> They go from room to room...
> To find the horse-dealers.
> Their husbands go looking for them...
> With thwacks of their sticks.
> 'What are you doing here, you wretch?...
> Off we go! To the house.
> The children are crying...
> They want to suckle.'
> 'Let them cry...
> You don't have any who are crying.'

---

[48] See, for example: *OC*, iv, 252–7; compare to the other versions of no. 4521 *The Shepherd Who Takes the Shepherdess to the Woods*: *RCFTO*, ii, 93–4.
[49] *RCFTO*, ii, 222–3.   [50] *OC*, iv, 412–13.   [51] *OC*, iii, 367.
[52] No. 11017: *RCFTO*, iii, 184.

'Whose are they, you wretch?...
If they aren't mine?'
'One is the vicar's...
The other the priest's.
The priest is a good man...
He recognizes his children.'[53]

This song is not unique to the moorlands, but the version Arnaudin recorded is the longest version, and features the most transgressive details. The version collected by Justin Cénac-Moncaut further east, for instance, does not include the closing section where the wife gets her revenge by revealing that all of her children are cuckoos in the nest.[54] Not only was *Long Live the Women of Sabres!* the most popular song in the region according to Arnaudin, but he also collected a whole series of other songs which Coirault catalogued in a section entitled 'Women and Girls Getting Drunk and Feasting'.[55]

Even more unusually for the French singing tradition, the songs of the moorlands discussed contraception. Most French versions of *The Herb of Love* (Coirault 206) deal with an aphrodisiac plant, but the version Arnaudin collected in the moorlands is strikingly different.[56] When three young Germans come across a beautiful miller's wife, they hatch a plan to seduce her: they will tell her they have discovered a herb that has contraceptive properties.

The miller's wife said,
'So then, we can come to an agreement.'
A little time passed,
And she said, 'They tricked me!'
Let them be damned,
Both the herb and the lover!
They have ruined my figure,
For nine months or a year.[57]

There is only one other reference to contraception in the index of the Coirault catalogue, and it is to a song also known in the moorlands, *The Fountain that Restores Virginity* (Coirault 320).[58] The willingness to sing about a topic as taboo as this is the most extreme example of wider tendencies in the songs of the moorlands, which allowed women a greater sexual licence than in other parts of France.

---

[53] *OC*, iii, 364–8.   [54] Cénac-Moncaut, *Littérature populaire de la Gascogne*, 335–6.
[55] *RCFTO*, iii, 181–5.   [56] *RCFTO*, i, 45.   [57] *OC*, iv, 151–4.   [58] *RCFTO*, i, 57.

The Rise of Gossip

Where the songs sung by older women depict a permissive culture of love, the ones popular among Arnaudin's younger singers place more emphasis on gossip and jealousy. Far from being a period when adultery became a private concern, it became a more sensitive issue than ever in the late nineteenth-century moorlands.[59] 'These days,' one of Arnaudin's singers lamented, 'you can't do anything if you don't want people to know.'[60] The genre of shaming songs or *charivaris* seemed as popular as ever in the moorlands, where their function as communal regulations of sexual behaviour fitted with the growing moralism of local culture. Arnaudin's friend Jules Sart told him that a song called *In Canenx There Is a Man* was recently composed, and the song called *My God! What a Mess* must have detailed recent events as well, since the naughty young girl is packed off to a thermal bath to hide the fact she has got pregnant before marriage.[61] Locals worried more about gossip at the end of the nineteenth century than they had at the beginning. This would make sense, given what historians know about the relationship between social differentiation and sexual morality. In societies with strict social hierarchies, extra-marital sex is policed more stringently.[62] The moorlands at the start of the nineteenth century may not have been an egalitarian society, but the effects of the sale of the moorlands and forestation certainly made life less equal. While many of Arnaudin's family friends were making vast fortunes, other local men and women lost their livelihoods, or were effectively proletarianized by new working arrangements. For every manual worker who managed to secure a salary, as Henri Vidal, the subject of the final chapter of this book did, there were many more sharecroppers like Babé Plantié and Jean Saubesty, who found themselves working under increasingly exploitative conditions into their old age.

These changes in working conditions had consequences for family planning. Under the old agro-pastoral sharecropping system, poverty placed no constraint on sexuality. The most successful families were those who had plenty of children, since they could be put to work young as shepherds. Once they reached their teens, they swelled the family workforce and saved the head of household from hiring outside help. In this way, children were an asset, an indispensable part of surviving the marginal economy of pastoralism. Fertile and promiscuous young women might not seem such a bad thing, and one contemporary even wrote that the economy depended on what local people called the 'little women', unfortunate girls who provided labour and babies, but did not secure themselves husbands.

---

[59] Anne-Marie Sohn argues that adultery's power to scandalize was declining in this period: 'The Golden Age of Male Adultery: The Third Republic', *Journal of Social History*, 28, no. 3 (1 April 1995), 469–90.

[60] *OC*, vi, 435.   [61] *OC*, iv, 758, 762–4.   [62] Segalen, *Love and Power*, 20–1.

With the triumph of forestation and the new availability of work on the railways and roads, however, local men found themselves earning a fixed salary. Men like Henri Vidal, and many of Arnaudin's other informants sought out the stability of employee status, and women preferred to marry postmen, road builders, and other employees.[63] In this new situation, more children were just more mouths to feed.

The relationship between the songs and the singers' own lives confirms that these new social relations placed increasing pressure on female sexuality. Mariouquete Labeyrie (b. 1861), for instance, had a particular preoccupation with the consequences of pre-marital sex, which makes sense, given her precarious status as a day labourer before her marriage. Among the twenty-three songs she sang, there were at least three rare songs that worried about sex before marriage. *Marceline the Beautiful* was a song only known by one other singer:

> Marceline the beautiful,
> Went to do the washing.
> There was a young man,
> Who saw her go.
> M[arceline] looked around,
> She looked in every direction.
> There was no-one in sight,
> Except this handsome young man.
> Marceline was not scared,
> At midday,
> There was no-one.[64]

Unfortunately for Marceline, an old woman is actually spying on the young lovers and she runs to tell Marceline's mother. Another song with a similar, but more spiritual warning about pre-marital sex was *Young Girl of Sorrow*, which was only sung by Mariouqete and one other singer in Arnaudin's collection.[65] Mariouquete was also one of only six singers to sing *When Marguerite Goes to the Woods*.[66] Although her version is less explicit about what Marguerite does with her baby, it plays on similar themes to the version sung by Marie Deyzieux, known as Valérie (b. 1854) and Anne Dubourg, known as 'la Dubourque', veuve Lantrès (b. 1841):

---

[63] The Gascon word for these 'little women' is 'hemnotes'. See, Guérin, 'Paysan-Résinier de Lévignacq (Landes)', 384–5.

[64] The song is not catalogued in *RCFTO*. See: *OC*, iv, 769–71. Mariouquete's version is not reproduced in the complete works. NFA, 2 MI 29/4, f.15.

[65] The song was not catalogued in *RCFTO*. See: *OC*, iv, 698–700.

[66] The song was not catalogued in *RCFTO*. *OC*, iv, 705.

When Marguerite goes to the woods,
To the woods, to the woods, all alone,
When she was in the middle of the woods,
She was seized by birth pains.
She cried out to the sky: 'Virgin Mary!'
Her mother heard her:
'Daughter, pick up your creature,
One day she will be happy.'
The poor girl did not understand,
She took her child and killed it,
She threw it in the street.
The police arrived.
They took her, they led her away,
They put her on the scaffold.
When she was on the scaffold,
She cried out to the sky: 'Virgin Mary!
Give my ring to my mother.
The necklace I have on,
Give it to my mother,
So that she remembers her poor daughter.'[67]

The songs Mariouquete sang are related to growing concern about the consequences of pre-marital sex, and growing concern with marrying, not just according to the heart's wishes, but at all. The responsibility for caring for children who were no longer the household asset they had once been fell squarely on women, especially if they had not managed to secure a marriage.[68] This explains why a song like *I Rose Early in the Morning, in the Cool Morning* about untrustworthy fiancés was so much more popular among the female singers born from the 1840s onwards. The song tells of a young girl who goes off to find her lover in the army. When she finds him, he asks:

'Who is this shepherd,
Who has laid her apron over my forehead?'
'I am no shepherd,
I am your fiancée.'
'If you are my fiancée,
I never loved you.'
'Lover, if it weren't for your deceptions,
I would be married.'[69]

[67] *OC*, iv, 703–4.
[68] Pregnancy, rather than the venereal disease that has so fascinated historians of this period, remained the biggest fear in illicit relationships. See: Sohn, *Du Premier baiser à l'alcôve*, 114.
[69] *OC*, iv, 258–70.

The girls of the moorlands whose only wealth was in the labour they could perform for others increasingly worried about the risk of becoming the 'little women' tossed around by economic uncertainty and unreliable suitors.[70]

But the increasing stratification of society affected wealthier women, as well. Where property and inheritances are at stake, families tend to place tighter controls on women.[71] Marguerite Dupin-Brigailles, known as Justine, femme Bouniord (1829–1905), was unusually well off for Arnaudin's singers. She came from a family of smallholders, and married another landowner, Jean Bouniord. Where sharecroppers had little concern about inheritances, families like the Dupin-Brigailles and Bouniords had an interest in preserving their holdings intact. Heiresses were under more pressure to conform both to parental wishes and to avoid having any illegitimate children who might threaten the family line. Of the thirty-two songs Justine sang, a few speak to this pressure. For example, she sang *I Am Going to Take off My Boots*, the classic moorland song of conflicts between parents and children over marriages.[72] She also sang the fairly popular song *Early in Morning, Our Ploughman Pierre Rises*.[73] In the only other version of this song recorded in France, the conflict is between a master, his servant, and the ploughman:

> Our good ploughman,
> Rises early in the morning.
> He takes his oxen, his cows,
> He leaves for the meadow to watch them.
> The cows are full.
> The oxen haven't eaten.
> The ploughman comes back,
> To shut them in.
> The cows went in.
> The oxen wander off.
> He calls the maid,
> To come and help.
> Their master watches them,
> Through the hole in the sink.
> 'So then, so then, maid,
> You love the ploughman.
> When you make the soup,
> It goes to the ploughman first.

---

[70] The song does not appear in *RCFTO*.   [71] Sohn, *Du Premier baiser à l'alcôve*, 229–31.
[72] The song does not appear in *RCFTO*. *OC*, iv, 228–31.
[73] *OC*, iv, 190–3; NFA, 2 MI 29/3, f.62.

> The ploughman gets a fork,
> The master, a spoon.
> The ploughman gets a napkin,
> The master a dirty rag.
> The ploughman gets a white plate,
> The master, a bowl.'[74]

But in the version Justine and other singers sang in the moorlands, the conflict is not between servants and masters, but between a daughter, her father, and the ploughman. When she was an eligible young woman, Justine's parents would have worried about her carrying on with the ploughman in a similar way:

> The ploughman called to Jeanne:
> 'Come and help me harness the oxen.'
> As he tied the first strap,
> He wanted to talk to her.
> As he tied the second,
> He tried again.
> Her father was watching,
> Through the hole in the sink.
> 'So then, so then, Jeanne,
> You have been making love to the ploughman.'
> 'Certainly not, father,
> He has been making love to me.'[75]

Even more interestingly, Justine modified *In My Father's Garden*. In many other versions of this song, the young girl invites her lover to come back when her father is away. In Justine's version, she invites him to come home for dinner to ask her father for her hand in marriage.[76] Justine's own experiences led her to put more emphasis on the discussion of marriage partners than many of the sharecropper singers did, and this difference is a result of the intensification of social pressures as the society of the moorlands changed with forestation.

These social changes also encouraged Arnaudin's singers to think differently about marriage. They became increasingly worried about jealousy. Jeanne Garbay known as Néte de Penalh (b. 1859) was one of only two singers to sing a song called *Father, Marry Me Off*. It began, as so many local songs did, with a daughter pleading with her father to marry her this year. The daughter asks to be given to a

---

[74] This is no. 6315 *The Master Who Envies the Ploughman*: *RCFTO*, ii, 308; Bladé, *Poésies populaires de la Gascogne*, iii, 360.

[75] In the version sang by Anne Joie, the ploughman goes so far as to kiss the girl. *OC*, iv, 191–3.

[76] *OC*, iv, 93–4.

young man who knows how to build a house, a house with four corners and a little window. The window, she reveals, is for men to come and visit her. Néte ended with a couple of violent and quite unique lines that the only other singer who knew this song, Jeanne Gellibert, femme Maurin (b. 1864), did not include:

> Let all those who are jealous be put in an oven
> With straw and fire around them.
> Let all those who are jealous burn.[77]

Jealousy was not completely novel in the singing tradition, but the emphasis and concern that younger singers such as Néte expressed around it suggest it was growing in importance.[78] A younger singer such as the fishmonger Martin Magnes, for instance, added three verses taken from another song to *In the Beautiful Village of Passage d'Agen* to make the song about jealousy.[79] Marie Courréguelongue (b. 1860) was the only identifiable singer of *I Got Up One Fine Morning*, a song that clearly demonstrates the distance between laughing at adultery, which had always been common in the songs, and taking it seriously. The refrains of her bitter song laments: 'Oh! how my heart sighs, Oh! how my heart hurts.'[80]

These concerns over the policing of sexual behaviour are cultural concerns, and it would be a mistake to take them at face value, as expressions of social experiences. It would be too simple to accept the picture of a golden age of sexual freedom some time before the 1840s that was curtailed by increasingly repressive social norms after the forestation of the moorlands. Instead, the cultural changes in family life and courting had paradoxical effects. Women expressed clear resentment of untrustworthy, exploitative, and jealous men—especially husbands—and yet also talked of a closer bond to their partner. The resentment is obvious in songs such as *I Want to Choose* (Coirault 4905). This south-western French song was normally sung from a man's point of view.[81] It tells of how he wants to choose a wife who will conform to his needs. If she does not, he will beat her. Arnaudin collected five versions of this misogynistic song, but he also collected six versions of a similar song with a very different conclusion. The husband confronts his wife:

> I said: 'Good evening, my beauty,
> What are you doing?'
> 'I am sewing a shirt,
> It is for my friend.'
> 'You will sew one for me,

---

[77] *OC*, iv, 217–18 This song is not in *RCFTO*.

[78] For examples of songs that mention jealousy that were popular with singers of all ages, see: *OC*, iii, 199; *OC*, iv, 658–62.

[79] *OC*, iv, 68–71. This song is not in *RCFTO*.   [80] *OC*, iv, 573.   [81] *RCFTO*, ii, 139.

I will be your friend.
Let it not be hemp,
But soft cotton.'
The mattress of hessian,
The bed sheets of tow.
Coarse tow of oakum,
To scratch the husband.
The bed canopy of straw,
The fire has caught it,
The husband has burned.[82]

At least one of Arnaudin's singers suggested that this rebellious ending was an innovation, by singing the last few verses hesitantly, to a different tune.[83] As singers placed more and more emphasis on gossip and jealousy, the tenor of relations between men and their wives became more strained.

Even as these relations grew more strained, they also grew more open to idealization. The song *Girls, Don't Love Men So Much* (Coirault 5405) was among the most popular of those Arnaudin collected, and it was slightly more popular among the younger singers than most songs.[84] It warned girls not to rush into marriage, since their husbands will gamble and drink, and beat them. But the message of the song is ambiguous. Marriage might not be all it is made out to be to young girls, but the song ends with the husband affirming that he 'loves no other more than you'.[85] Marriage was becoming both more fraught and more tender. A subtle choice of words in this song reveals one obvious way in which the meaning of the bond of marriage was different across the generations. Where Arnaudin's older informants used the formal *bous* between the husband and wife, younger singers preferred the more modern, even egalitarian *tu*. The increasing pressure that was being felt in the marital bond was not the survival of 'peasant' patriarchalism and the need to protect the material interests of the farm. It was a corollary of gender complementarity, and the intensification of the marital bond. For women, that meant the triumph of the black, and a longing for the red.

Conclusion

The shared culture of love expressed in the songs of the moorlands was changing with the changing social structures of work and family. But the songs of women like Justine Dupin-Brigailles and Mariouquéte Labeyrie are reminders that this

---

[82] *OC*, iv, 74–6, 76–9.   [83] *OC*, iv, 78.
[84] *OC*, iii, 362–4. This is *The Husband Who Gambled*, a song largely confined to the south and west of France. See: *RCFTO*, ii, 189–90.
[85] *OC*, iii, 363.

influence flows both ways. Individuals reacted to social changes in different ways that could represent unusual cultural improvisations. Arnaudin did his best to exclude these innovations from the songs he collected, noting bitterly of Néte de Penalh, the woman who introduced radical jealousy into her version of *Father, Marry Me Off* that she 'changes everything on a whim'.[86] But these changes are important to historians, because they are a reminder of how working people, and especially women, used the songs to express agency, as well as conformity.

The short life of Anne Loubeyre, known as Anna de Hourrègues (1887–1907) provides a good example. Where other singers sang *How Is Your Flock, Shepherd?* (Coirault 206) as a vague song about minding sheep, Anna's version, *Have You Seen the Flock, Shepherd?* is an optimistic love story. When the young girl's lover leaves for the army, she discovers she is pregnant. He tells her not to worry: he will write. In contrast to most folk songs, he actually does, and even gets permission from his captain to have her come and join them: 'We will make her a cook, She will accompany you to battle'.[87] Things did not work out so well for Anna in real life. She died aged just twenty, before Arnaudin had even finished the first volume of his folk songs. But the way her song combined optimism with the tragedy of her own life could be emblematic for heterosexual culture in the moorlands. On the one hand, there is a forceful female agency to the song. In the Coirault catalogue, the song is called *The Abandoned Army Cook*, and fits into a widely known tradition of men leaving their mistresses to join the army.[88] Anna's song is more radical: the young woman takes control of her own destiny, succeeding in getting the man she wants. But singing was clearly out of step with social reality on this count. The forceful women of the songs of the moorlands were facing new challenges at the end of the nineteenth century, and the demographic record suggests that they were losing their struggle against the black. If they were well off, this meant a closer control of their love life, and if they were poor, it meant greater penalties for flouting the rules of marriage. This predominantly rural society was moving in a different direction to the urban sexual revolution of the Third Republic studied by Anne-Marie Sohn: for most women, sexuality was policed ever more carefully, at the expense of what they commemorated as a joyous tradition of carefree love.[89]

---

[86] NFA, 2 MI 29/1, f.44.   [87] *OC*, iv, 538–9.
[88] See: David M. Hopkin, *Soldier and Peasant in French Popular Culture, 1766–1870* (Royal History Society, 2003).
[89] Sohn, *Du Premier baiser à l'alcôve*.

7

Silence and Chastity

Although traditional songs present a kind of communal consensus, it is possible to identify individual voices within the shared culture of singing. Just as the local tradition of singing in the moorlands can be distinguished from other cultures of song in rural France, it is possible to pick out singers within Arnaudin's notes who sang against the chorus. While many of the women who sang for Arnaudin used songs to explore the illicit topics of sexuality and drinking, one of his favourite singers named Catherine Gentes (1848–1906) preferred more chaste materials, actively omitting references to sex and making love. After Babé Plantié, Catherine was Arnaudin's richest source of traditional songs, yet her repertoire is marked by this absence: wherever possible, Catherine left out the bawdier verses that were so popular with many of the women of the moorlands. These absences are evident from the way Félix actively recorded the songs and verses she did not know.[1] He wrote 'Cath. Gentes: unknown' or 'Cath. Gentes: nothing' on songs or couplets. This method was not systematic, nor did Arnaudin apply it to all of his singers, only using it for his favourite, and most prolific singers. His interest in both Catherine's unsung songs and those of Babé Plantié suggests that he treated them in some way as his most trustworthy informants. He often placed versions of particular songs sung by Catherine and Babé at the head of his notes, signalling that they were standard, reliable performances. If, on the other hand, they did not know a song, this was surprising, or noteworthy for Arnaudin.

Catherine provided seventy-seven different tunes or texts, while another eleven were 'unknown' to her.[2] To know a rare song suggests an individual has a different idea from other singers of what is beautiful or true. To not know a popular song suggests a similar idiosyncrasy. And silence, anthropologists, folklorists, and historians have all found, is not the same thing as absence of meaning.[3] 'Like

---

[1] He may have got the idea from a questionnaire sent to him on behalf of the (London) Society for Psychical Research by L. Marillier. However, this letter dates from 1889, and my impression is that he had already adopted this habit before then. Since he did not consistently date his fieldnotes, it is hard to prove. *OC*, v, 118.

[2] Catherine sang many more songs for the second volume of Arnaudin's projected folk-song collection, which he left unfinished at his death. The editors of the recent complete works gave Catherine's versions pride of place, and almost all of them appear in full. This may be because she was so faithful to Gascon, or because Arnaudin himself often placed her versions at the top of his sheets, and wrote them out in full. When checking a song with other informants, he tended to abbreviate, noting only the differences from his fullest version.

[3] Richard Bauman, *Let Your Words Be Few: Symbolism of Speaking and Silence among Seventeenth-Century Quakers* (Cambridge, 1983); Keith H. Basso, '"To Give up on Words": Silence in Western

Body and Tradition in Nineteenth-Century France: Félix Arnaudin and the Moorlands of Gascony, 1870–1914.
William G. Pooley, Oxford University Press (2019). © William G. Pooley.
DOI: 10.1093/oso/9780198847502.001.0001

the zero in mathematics, [silence] is an absence with a function.'[4] Because singing is an aesthetic activity, something that people do because they think it is beautiful and meaningful, Catherine's failure to sing specific songs on request suggests she did not find these particular ones important or relevant to her life.[5] There is a logic to the songs Catherine never learned, or refused to repeat, and this logic has everything to do with her own life and her bodily identities.

Catherine's Silences

Above all, Catherine remained silent about sex. Of the seventy-seven songs she sang for Arnaudin, just four contained direct references to pre-marital sex. On the other hand, of the eleven songs which Arnaudin recorded her as not singing, six dealt with the same topic. The most popular song Catherine was unaware of was *I Have a Little Brother* (Coirault 320). In Babé's version, as in many others, a brother returning from the war questions his sister's chastity: 'My sister, you have not been faithful'.[6] When the young woman asks how he knows, he lists the signs of her clothing that give her away: her shoes show that she is no longer light on her feet, her stockings are no longer white, her skirt fits poorly, and her apron barely reaches around her belly. Catherine was also unfamiliar with the similarly popular *My Lord! My Beautiful Cows*. In Babé's version, the song is told from the point of view of a man recently married:

> The evening of our wedding
> Together we went to bed.
> I put my hand on her belly
> And felt the child move.
> I turned my back to her
> And began to cry.[7]

Other songs Catherine was unaware of were slightly less popular, but also openly dealt with sexuality. *I Would Like to Sing You a Song*, which Arnaudin collected from nine singers, told the story of a valet caught having sex with the mistress.

Apache Culture', *Southwestern Journal of Anthropology*, xxvi (1970), 213–30; Hopkin, *Voices of the People*, 79–108.

---

  [4] William Samarin, 'Language of Silence', *Practical Anthropology*, xii (1965), 115.
  [5] For the importance of aesthetics and the status of 'art' as a keyword for the study of folklore, see: Gerald Pocius, 'Art', in *Eight Words for the Study of Expressive Culture*, ed. Burt Feintuch (Urbana, 2003), 42–68.
  [6] *OC*, iv, 142–8. See *The Fountain that Restores Virginity*, a south-western ecotype discussed in Chapter 6. *RCFTO*, i, 57.
  [7] *OC*, iv, 351–6. The song is not in *RCFTO*.

In his rage, the master wants to kill him, but his maid suggests revenge in kind instead.[8] *There's a Place in Heaven* (Coirault 8112) is a lament about how parents should correct the—presumably sexual—follies of their children before it is too late.[9] Arnaudin collected seven versions. *I Got Up Early in the Morning, the Very Early Morning* (Coirault 2417), a song where a 'thorn' from an encounter in the garden cannot be removed for nine months, was known by just five singers.[10] So was *My Father and Mother* (Coirault 4521), where a mother allows a young girl to meet with her lover because: 'When mama was younger, She was worse than me.'[11] The versions of this song from the moorlands were typically more direct about this sexual license than versions from elsewhere in France.[12] Catherine also ignored some rare songs that dealt with sex, such as another song entitled *My Father and My Mother* (Coirault 6219), which was known by only three singers.[13] What all of these songs have in common is a lenient attitude to extra-marital sexuality. Catherine's inability or unwillingness either to learn or remember these songs reveals her attitudes to sex and marriage.

The songs that Catherine did not know help to understand those she did. *On the Pretty Bridge of Avignon* (Coirault 1829) is a good example.[14] Only three singers sang this song, so it was probably not a great surprise to Arnaudin that Catherine did not know it.[15] But one reason he might have thought her ignorance of this song worth noting is because she did know a very similar song which she called *On the Bridge of Lyon* (Coirault 1710).[16] Both feature a woman on a bridge who resists the entreaties of young men. But in the case of the song Catherine did not sing, the young woman rebuffs her admirers by saying: 'I am no virgin, I have three children living'.[17] Catherine's song, on the other hand, describes a different situation. The young woman resists her lover for fifteen years, because she is already married to another man. The day she gives in, her husband returns.[18] Her preference for the bridge of Lyon over the bridge of Avignon fits into wider patterns in her song repertoire, patterns of de-emphasizing sexuality, rejecting courtship, and using absent partners as a justification for chastity.

It is not that Catherine never sang of making love. In common with many other singers in the moorlands, she sang lyrics, songs that evoke a romantic mood,

---

[8] *OC*, iv, 341–6. The song is not in *RCFTO*.

[9] *OC*, iv, 729–32. This is *The Tree of Paradise*: *RCFTO*, iii, 21.

[10] *OC*, iv, 248–51. The song from the moorlands is an example of 2417A *What Boys Do after Marriage*, but it does not, in fact, continue to describe what men are like after they are married. *RCFTO*, i, 280.

[11] *OC*, iv, 252–7.

[12] *The Shepherd Who Takes the Shepherdess to the Woods*: *RCFTO*, ii, 95.

[13] *OC*, iv, 309–10. This song, *The Gloves Made from the Scraps of a Petticoat*, was much more popular elsewhere in France. *RCFTO*, ii, 295–6.

[14] *The Recovered Comb. RCFTO*, i, 222.   [15] *OC*, iv, 117–18.

[16] *OC*, iv, 122–3. *The Boat Which Brings News of a Lover*: *RCFTO*, i, 199.

[17] *OC*, iv, 118.   [18] See NFA, 2 MI 29/1, f.622.

rather than telling a story, as a ballad does.[19] But these songs were not only vague in how they dealt with love, they were also very popular with all singers in the moorlands. *The Young Girls of Jouan-Hau*, for instance, was known by fifteen other singers, and *As I Passed the Bridge at Pau* (related to Coirault 4717) was known by another twelve.[20] Catherine even sang four songs that openly discuss pre-marital sex, but these also tended to be very widely known. A song she knew as *Jan de la Réole Had Three Daughters* (Coirault 1115) was called *There Is a Miller in Clarac* by many of the eighteen other singers who provided versions for Arnaudin.[21] In all of these versions, a concerned father calls out the doctor to investigate his daughter's mysterious illness. The doctor's advice to the father is simple: 'Father, marry her this evening, By the morning she will be fine'.[22] The only thing wrong with her is that she has become pregnant before marrying.

A couple of the songs concerning pre-marital sex that Catherine knew were slightly rarer, although none were uncommon. *The Mother and Her Daughter* (Coirault 2315) and *The Girls of La Réole* (Coirault 2301.1) were known by eight and seven other singers, respectively.[23] The first song was a conversation where a mother gives advice to her wayward daughter, while the second features the memorable lines:

> I haven't gone to bed with any man,
> Nor slept with any either.
> Except a school teacher,
> Who came a few times.[24]

I Got Up Early, Before the Sun Had Risen (Coirault 7211), on the other hand, was one of the most popular songs in the region at the time. Arnaudin collected thirty other versions, but Catherine's took pride of place in his notes.[25] In the song, a knight appears to carry a girl back to her homeland in which war is raging. On their journey they sleep together on the moors with nothing but a thread of silver between them. Soon afterwards, they are forced to petition the parlement for permission to marry. This was a rare example of Catherine singing a song that clearly explored pre-marital sexuality. It seems likely that she knew it because it was so popular in the moorlands.[26]

---

[19] The distinction between 'lyrics' and 'ballads', which have a more narrative structure, is made, for instance, in: Toelken, *Morning Dew and Roses*, 14.

[20] *OC*, iv, 427, 445–6. *The Younger Daughter Married before the Elder: RCFTO*, ii, 123–4.

[21] *OC*, iv, 168–73; *The Doctor and the Love-Sick Girl: RCFTO*, ii, 123–4.

[22] *OC*, iv, 169.

[23] *OC*, iv, 246–7, 302–3. *The Girls Who Wear Their Corsets Loose* and *The Mother, the Daughter, and the Merchant*, neither of which were common outside the moorlands. *RCFTO*, ii, 262–3, 267.

[24] *OC*, iv, 247.   [25] *OC*, iv, 71–285, see NFA, 2 MI 29/3, f.165.

[26] *Love and the Silver Thread* was not very popular elsewhere, and the version from the moorlands was more developed and complicated than the other French versions. *RCFTO*, ii, 395.

The songs Catherine sung about courting were similarly popular, but her repertoire focused on ones that dealt with the ambiguities of the process. *Good Evening, Master of the House* (Coirault 4717) was known by thirteen other singers. Although it is about a young girl being asked for her hand, the song is structured around a contrast with her older, less lucky sister: 'The big sister sitting by the fireside, Cries and sighs'.[27] Nine other singers provided versions of *On the Bridge of Toulouse, Saint John's Eve* (Coirault 4517), a song which leads from a meeting between two dancers to a conversation about marriage.[28] In Babé Plantié's, as in most other versions, the woman tells her suitor her wedding will not be this year, leading him to reply: 'Be quiet, my sweetheart, It will be tomorrow'.[29] Catherine characteristically omitted this ending, giving the woman the final, negative say. She had less interest than other singers in the marriage outcome.

Catherine had a marked tendency to sing songs where marriages were frustrated, delayed, or rejected. Some of these, such as songs about girls refusing marriage, were fairly well known. *On the Banks of a Stream* (Coirault 1905), for instance, is about a girl who rejects the proposals of some passing soldiers, and was sung by eight other singers.[30] Another song sung by eight other singers in the moorlands, *Do Not Go, Beautiful* (Coirault 6206) features a girl who turns down all of the army, the captains, the king's brother, and the king himself, because she does not want to marry a warrior.[31] Often, in Catherine's songs, an absent husband or lover provided the pretext for women to refuse the advances of other men. Some of these songs were not specific to Catherine, but were popular throughout the moorlands. *Any Young Girl Who Is in Love*, for instance, was sung by fourteen other singers, and *Landeridi, in My Father's Garden* (Coirault 1502) was sung by thirteen.[32] But some of these songs of frustrated marriages were rarer. *The Other Day as I Was Walking* was known in seven other versions, and *I Made Myself a Bunch of Flowers* (Coirault 114) was known by just one other singer in the moorlands.[33]

Catherine also sung of more eclectic excuses. *In the Town of Salles There Is* (Coirault 1803), a song sung by five other singers, tells of a woman who rejects a suitor because his hands are not as clean as her lover's are.[34] *In Saint-Léger There Are Four Beautiful Young Girls* was much more popular with the singers in the moorlands. In the versions Arnaudin recorded from Catherine and from sixteen other singers, the marriage-delaying conclusion is the same as the narrator of the

[27] *OC*, iv, 3–4.

[28] *The Gloves to Be Worn Three Times a Year*: RCFTO, ii, 91–2.   [29] *OC*, iv, 25.

[30] *OC*, iv, 465–7. *The Lover Put Off by Tears*. This was one of the most popular songs in French oral tradition. RCFTO, i, 229–31.

[31] *OC*, iv, 470–1. *The Soldier Preferred to the King*: RCFTO, ii, 290.

[32] *OC*, iv, 473–4, 498–9. *The Dutchmen's Prisoner*: RCFTO, i, 173–4. *Any Young Girl Who Is in Love* was not catalogued in RCFTO.

[33] *OC*, iv, 64–5, 113–15. See *The Bouquet of Pretty Flowers*: RCFTO, i, 38.

[34] *OC*, iv, 166–7; *The Dyer Whose Hands Were Not Clean*: RCFTO, i, 212.

song orders: 'Leave that one, Pierre, That one is my sister.'[35] Other songs that Catherine sang which indefinitely postponed marriage, on the other hand, were considerably rarer. *The Girls of La Rochelle* (Coirault 1113), for instance, was sung by just two other singers.[36]

> I am not getting married yet,
>> Not yet this year.
>> Not yet this year.
> Another year I might be dead.[37]

Arnaudin noted that Babé, who knew almost half of the songs he collected, did not know it.

Another rare song Catherine sang also seems to express cynicism about marriage prospects. *When the Shepherdess Goes to the Fields* (Coirault 102) was only sung by three other singers in the moorlands.[38] Unusually for Arnaudin's collection, which concentrates on female singing repertoires, two of the singers who sang this were men, Jean Castaignède, known as lou Clerjé (1832–92), and Martin Magnes. The only other woman to sing the song was another unmarried singer, Marie Duvignac (1834–1909), known as le Samioune. The message of the song is pessimistic about marriage:

> They will want the handsome men.
> If they want them, they shall have them ...
> But perhaps not the ones they want ...
> They will have what they can get.[39]

In other examples, Catherine sung songs that other singers sang, but omitted the endings, as if she was not as bothered about marriage either way. Nineteen other singers sang *I Got Up Early, in the Cool Morning*, a song which typically ends with the girl expressing disappointment with her soldier-fiancé, as in Babé's version: 'My love, if it weren't for your deceptions, I would be married'.[40]

Catherine left off these final stanzas. She also omitted the verses about persuading an older husband to have sex from the song *My Father Is Marrying Me Off, Ho Ramonet* (Coirault 5703), which was sung by twelve other singers.[41] Perhaps the best example of this kind of omission by Catherine is her version of

---

[35] *OC*, iv, 155–9. The song was not catalogued in *RCFTO*.

[36] *OC*, iv, 454–5; *What Use Is Beauty? RCFTO*, i, 122–3.

[37] *OC*, iv, 454–5; NFA, 2 MI 29/5, f.221.

[38] *The White Duck* was very popular outside the moorlands. The song from the moorlands is not exactly the same, but seems to be an ecotype. *RCFTO*, i, 32–3.

[39] *OC*, iv, 220–2.

[40] *OC*, iv, 258–70. The song was not catalogued in *RCFTO*.

[41] *OC*, iv, 398–404. *To the Devil with Wealth III: RCFTO*, ii, 221–2.

The Other Day as I Was Walking, a song sung by fifteen other singers. Babé's version was typical in describing a shepherdess who offers a passer-by bread, wine, ham, chicken, and pigeons, and finally a place in her bed.[42] Catherine's shepherdess provides the food for the stranger, but does not share her bed.[43]

Although most of the songs of the moorlands took little interest in the preservation of feminine honour, there was at least one song that was popular in the region that talked about the defence of virginity. Fourteen singers apart from Catherine knew *When the King Went Out* (Coirault 3809), but Catherine was the only singer Arnaudin met who sang two different versions.[44] The fact that she sang the same words to two different jaunty tunes indicates that she found the words, with their vitriolic denial of sexual experience, rather than just the melody, especially meaningful:

> 'Your sister told me
> You are not a virgin,
> You are not a virgin.'
> 'My sister lied to you,
> The false wretch!
> The false wretch!
> Between me and my sister,
> You will see a great war,
> You will see a great war.'[45]

But it is a song known in its full version by Catherine alone which provides the strongest evidence of her feelings about courting and marriage. Marie Dumartin, known as Louise, femme Dupart (1841–88), and Jeanne Lescarret, known as Janéte dou Baqué, femme Dupart (1837–1927), knew a few lines of *Little One, Do You Want to Come to the Woods*. Babé knew parts of it, but seemed to confuse it with another song. It was not known outside of the moorlands. Catherine's version is the only one that is fully developed, and is about a suitor who invites his sweetheart to pick flowers in the woods, a well-known metaphor for making love. The woman declines in French, on the grounds that her suitor should make her a present of:

> 'Some kind of ring or jewels,
> Or something more beautiful.
> Or some kind of engagement ring,
> So that we may be married.'

[42] OC, iv, 370–5. The song was not catalogued in *RCFTO*.   [43] OC, iv, 373–4.
[44] *The Shepherdess and the King of England*: RCFTO, ii, 24–5.   [45] OC, iv, 504–5, 506.

Now it is the man's turn to refuse, first speaking in Gascon, but slipping into French:

> 'My lord, girl, you are mistaken
>> To ask for things so boldly.
> [In French:] Any girl who takes, must give,
> She has given up her heart.'

The girl defends herself against what her suitor is suggesting:

> 'I have taken, and I have given,
> [But] I did not give up my body.
> I have taken, and I have some left,
> I am no fallen woman.'[46]

With that the girl calls off the engagement, and the song ends. Compared to many of the other dancing songs Catherine sang, the tune she sang this song to—the same one she used for *In This Canton There Is a Young Man*—is noticeably plaintive, as if to lend more force to her statement: 'I did not give up my body'.[47]

Catherine's choices in singing relate the unusual life she lived. She never married, nor is there any evidence that she had any illegitimate children, unlike most of the other informants from whom Arnaudin collected folklore. Of the individuals whose archival identity is close to certain, 268 were married, leaving just twenty who might have remained unwed. Catherine is one of the clearest cases, since her death certificate from 1906 confirms she had never married. Most of the other unmarried informants Arnaudin contacted had extra-marital sexual relations. This is hard to prove for the twelve unmarried men, but Arnaudin's own diaries made it clear that he himself had relationships with at least two different partners, neither of which he married. Of the sixteen unmarried women from whom Arnaudin collected folklore, four had illegitimate children, and Catherine Bertrande (b. 1860) probably did as well. Marie Darlanne never had any children, but Arnaudin's diary details the long romance she had with him. Another two of the unmarried female informants were too young for marriage.[48] This means that out of 216 clearly identified female informants, Catherine was one of just eight

---

[46]   The Gascon is hard to translate, as Catherine uses words with the same root to describe 'giving up' her body, and being a 'fallen' woman. 'Jou que n'éy près, que n'éy balhat,/N'éy pa moun cos abandounat./Jou que n'éy près, que n'éy encare,/Ne suy pa "u" filhe abandounade.' *OC*, iv, 450.

[47]   For the tunes, see: 'Association d'étude, de promotion et d'enseignement des musiques tradition-nelles des pays de France: "Arnaudin—Chants populaires de la Grande-Lande 2"', https://web.archive.org/web/20130712040203/http://www.aepem.com/Arnaudin2.php. *In This Canton There Is a Young Man* was not catalogued in *RCFTO*.

[48]   Marilys Ducourneau (b. 1893) may have married after Arnaudin collected songs from her (probably before 1912). Anna Loubeyre (1887–1907) died aged just twenty.

adult women who neither married nor had children. This is no proof that Catherine never had any kind of sexual experiences with other people. That certainty is beyond what the historian can establish. But it is also important that Catherine's cultural preferences in terms of singing help to make sense of what the official archive suggests about her romantic and sexual experiences.

Catholicism

There is little evidence that Catherine's reticence about sex comes from embarrassment or prudishness. Other young female singers sometimes had qualms about singing obscene songs to Arnaudin. One refused to finish a song: 'it is so rude at the end that she will not give it to me', and another told him a lullaby he had asked for was actually obscene.[49] But there is no hint from the manuscripts that Catherine absolutely refused to sing verses that contained innuendo. She did, in fact, sometimes sing songs that discussed sex. Over the scale of her whole repertoire, she simply shows her preference for downplaying the importance of making love, by either forgetting, or leaving out discussions of courtship. Nor does the evidence from her songs suggest that her piety encouraged her to remain celibate. She was not, on the available evidence, one among the many women who rallied to the Catholic Church in the nineteenth century, as the men of their families grew laxer.[50]

It is true that songs are not statements of belief, but the evidence her songs provide about her cultural choices do not lend much weight to the idea that her interest in celibacy was connected in any way to the religious revival of the nineteenth century.[51] Catherine did sing some religious songs, such as *When Jesus-Christ Was Just a Child* (Coirault 8805), which was only sung by four other singers in the moorlands and briefly described the sufferings of Jesus.[52] She also sang *Up There in the Heavens*, which included the message: 'We all come from God, We deserve to go and see him'.[53] It was only sung by one other singer in

[49] NFA, 2 MI 29/4, f.20, 2 MI 29/20, f.37.

[50] On the 'feminization' of religion, see, for instance: Richard Burton, *Holy Tears, Holy Blood: Women, Catholicism, and the Culture of Suffering in France, 1840–1970* (Ithaca, 2004); Ralph Gibson, 'Female Religious Orders in Nineteenth-Century France', in Frank Tallett and Nicholas Atkin, eds, *Catholicism in Britain and France since 1789* (London, 1996), 105–13; Harris, *Lourdes*; Raymond Jonas, *France and the Cult of the Sacred Heart: An Epic Tale for Modern Times* (Berkeley, 2000); James McMillan, 'Religion and Gender in Modern France: Some Reflections', in Frank Tallett and Nicholas Atkin, eds, *Religion, Society, and Politics in France since 1789* (London, 1991), 55–66; Jean Faury, *Cléricalisme et anticléricalisme dans le Tarn (1848–1900)* (Toulouse, 1980), 273–8; Ralph Gibson, 'Why Republicans and Catholics Could Not Stand Each Other in the Nineteenth Century', in Frank Tallett and Nicholas Atkin, eds, *Religion, Society, and Politics in France since 1789* (London, 1991), 117–19.

[51] Hopkin, *Voices of the People*, 236; Ellen Badone, 'Breton Folklore of Anticlericalism', in Ellen Badone, ed., *Religious Orthodoxy and Popular Faith in European Society* (Princeton, 1990), 140–60.

[52] OC, iv, 725–6. This is the extremely popular *The Passion of Jesus Christ*: RCFTO, iii, 52–3.

[53] OC, iv, 735.

the moorlands and does not appear in Coirault's catalogue of French folk songs. But in general, Catherine's songs display a lack of interest in Catholicism, as well as some open criticisms of piety. Her version of *On the Bridge of Lyon* (Coirault 1710) did not include the lines sung by other singers that referred to God and the Virgin Mary.[54] Catherine sung a version of *The Girls of La Rochelle* (Coirault 2301.1), a song that seven other singers sang for Arnaudin. All of these different versions were critical of the wayward young girls of La Rochelle, but Catherine was the only singer to include the following couplets, which focused on outward displays of piety in the context of courting:

> Poor young men who want to marry.
> Take care not to be deceived.
> Do not trust those girls
> Who go to the priest so often.[55]

There is no study of Catholicism in the moorlands in the nineteenth century, perhaps because it occupies such a moderate position in the geography of piety and anti-clericalism. It was neither firmly within the belt of devout regions that stretched from the Massif Central into the Pyrenees, nor did it belong to the de-Christianized regions around this heartland of piety. Parents were still fairly conscientious about having their children baptised, yet the local clergy were given to complaining that the region was among the most ungodly.[56] Many of the priests of the moorlands felt a similar shock to that expressed by the *curé* of Commensacq in 1889 when he realized that his flock did not invest the rituals he performed with orthodox Catholic meanings. Overjoyed by the enthusiasm of his parishioners for ringing the church bells after baptisms, it took him some time to realize that this enthusiasm stemmed from the belief that the bells could prevent the newborn child from being deaf or unable to speak.[57]

Few of Arnaudin's informants provided much in the way of religious folklore. Simon Loubère (1831–1908) was a rare storyteller, in that his preferred narratives dealt with religious themes. He told Arnaudin versions of ATU 752A *Christ and St Peter in the Barn*, ATU 753 *Christ and the Smith*, and ATU 1182 *The Level Bushel*, stories more associated with devout parts of France, such as the Massif Central or Brittany.[58] Mariane de Mariolan, who told Arnaudin a story about a local lord murdered in the eighteenth century during a dispute over a pine

---

[54] *OC*, iv, 122–3. *The Ship Bringing News of a Lover: RCFTO*, i, 199.
[55] *OC*, iv, 346–51.
[56] François-André Isambert and Jean-Paul Terrenoire, *Atlas de la pratique religieuse des catholiques en France* (Paris, 1980), 34, 36, 40; Gérard Cholvy and Yves Marie Hilaire, *Histoire religieuse de la France* (3 vols, Toulouse, 1985–8), ii, 46.
[57] ADL 1000 J 65, 'Monographie Paroissiale: Commensacq' (1889), 20.
[58] *OC*, i, 211, 211–13, 363.

plantation, had a pious side as well. She told him another legend about a group of local dancers who ignored a priest passing by to bless a dying man on a Sunday.[59] The dancers were punished by being turned 'as black as pure soot'.[60] Although Mariane was very long-lived and Arnaudin's single most important narrator, she sang him no songs. Perhaps her legend, with its criticism of traditional singing and dancing, explains why.

There are scattered bits of evidence that Catholicism continued to pervade everyday life in the moorlands in the nineteenth century. It was, for instance, no coincidence that the riot later known as the 'Revolution of Sabres' in 1863 broke out on Easter Monday. The *curé*, M. Pédégert, was the only person who could restore order once violence had erupted.[61] It is harder to find strong evidence of quotidian devotion in the moorlands. The informants Arnaudin found who expressed pious sentiments were not only rare, but the relation between their piety and the lives they led was often ambiguous. One of his most apparently devout informants, Magdelaine Lescarret, known as Babelic (1828–1901), sung a particularly gruesome religious song called *What Have You Done to Me*:

> What have you done to me!
> I am without hope,
> Me who so enjoyed,
> The pleasures of dancing.
> He has banished me to *tihéu* [?],
> From on high down to Lucifer,
> Jump from the top of the sky,
> To the depths of hell.
> Pleasures which deceived me,
> Pleasures which are so brief,
> Pain which will last,
> All of eternity,
> Without ever seeing God,
> Without ever feeling his pity.
> My heart is full of fire,
> One foot is attached to a chain,
> The other is attacked by a serpent.
> The demon, the toad,
> Do not give me a moment's rest,
> Night or day.

---

[59] This is motif Q386, although the story is not listed in the French national catalogue. See: Thompson, *Motif-Index of Folk-Literature*. See also: Alessandro Arcangeli, 'Dance and Punishment', *Dance Research: Journal of the Society for Dance Research*, x (1992), 30–42.

[60] *OC*, i, 218–19. See NFA, 2 MI 29/11, f.646.

[61] Pierre Leshauris, 'La Révolution de Sabres (1863)', *Bulletin de la Société de Borda* (1979), 395, 397.

> And all of us who are damned,
> We will soon repent,
> The drum and the fife,
> Have changed their tune.
> In hell, in hell,
> We will burn night and day.[62]

It is hard to know in what tone Babelic sang this song, given that the bodily mortification it expresses connects awkwardly to her own life, which betrays more than a little familiarity with the drum and the fife. In 1898, aged seventy, she was in trouble with the police for running an illegal cabaret.[63] This must have been the same cabaret she rented, and later owned with her husband.[64] After his death, Babelic found herself in an unusual living arrangement, sharing a house with two people, neither of whom were direct family relations.[65] It was at this stage in her life that she got in trouble over her license. Perhaps her religious singing was ironic, or perhaps Babelic had always struggled with a conflict between devotion and deviance.[66]

In general, Arnaudin found it very hard to collect any religious folklore at all. When he tried to find evidence for the religious prayers collected by the abbé Dumartin just a few years before in the village of Commensacq, he drew a blank: 'Found nothing. No-one remembers anything.'[67] Arnaudin told the folklorist Paul Sébillot that there was no popular Christian imagery in the moorlands.[68] Statues of the Virgin Mary were so rare that the few devout Catholics that did live there would pay pedlars to let them kiss their images.[69] Cooroou, a miller from Richet, apparently told Arnaudin that during the Revolution people did not find it hard to make do without priests: 'There wasn't any confession with the priests. [They] used to confess to an old chestnut tree.'[70] This was not simply because Arnaudin was unsympathetic to Catholicism. His diary shows that he went to church fairly regularly, at least in his thirties.[71] It is true that he was suspicious of local priests, but this was largely because he resented their attempts to collect folklore, attempts which he castigated for being both amateur and inaccurate: 'tidying the materials is instinctive for priests'.[72] There is other evidence that the moorlands were not

---

[62] *OC*, iv, 700–1. The song is not in *RCFTO*.
[63] Traimond, 'La sociabilité rurale landaise', 148.   [64] NFA, 2 MI 29/1, f.28.
[65] ADL E DEPOT 333/1 F 2.
[66] For a similar argument about sexuality and devotion in the life of the singer and storyteller Nannette Lévesque, see: Pooley, 'Independent Women and Independent Body Parts'.
[67] NFA, 2 MI 29/20, f.113.   [68] *OC*, v, 63–4.
[69] *OC*, vii, 281.   [70] NFA, 2 MI 29/14, f.495.
[71] See the entries for 1 December 1861, 29 December 1861, 16 November 1862. He did not mention going later in life, but the diary became much less detailed as he grew older. *OC*, viii, 26, 29, 48. Guy Latry suggests he had remained fairly close to the Church his whole life. Latry, 'Miroirs voilés', 150.
[72] NFA, 2 MI 29/25, f.160.

particularly devout.[73] Some nineteenth-century authors maintained that the region had never been effectively converted to Catholicism.[74] When it came to spending the money that the local councils had earned from selling the common moors, the villages of the central moorlands took a very different approach to those in the Gironde. While the Gironde spent 1,417,492 francs on churches and just 646,919 francs on schools, the department of the Landes spent more on schools (989,453 francs) and much less on churches (974,011).[75]

The reports written by the village curés of the moorlands for the diocese in 1889 confirm that, in general, the clergy despaired of the piety of their flocks, but that indifference and anti-clericalism varied on a micro-geographical scale.[76] It is interesting to note from these reports that the village of Trensacq, for instance, was not as affected by conflicts between the secular authorities and the Church as many of the other villages, since this was where Simon Loubère, who told Arnaudin the series of religious tales, lived.[77] There were other villages that were similarly devout, such as Garein and Le Sen, whose inhabitants—at least according to a local cleric—were almost unanimous in asking for a priest to be established in their area in 1905.[78] According to the priests themselves, this micro-geography of devotion and anti-clericalism was largely explained by the actions and memories of specific priests and village councillors. In the tumultuous period at the start of the nineteenth century Trensacq had been fortunate, the curé wrote, since a cart driver had found a priest at the fair in Liposthey and brought him back to the village.[79] In the village of Sabres, what religion the locals still possessed could be traced to the missionary zeal of the curé Pédemagnan between 1839 and 1841.[80] Commensacq, the village where Catherine lived her whole life, had not been so fortunate from a religious point of view, according to the curé, the abbé Dumartin.[81] Arnaudin himself thought that the abbé Dumartin was rather credulous, and it is also hard to understand how villages as close together as Trensacq and Commensacq could differ so much in their religious devotion given how mobile the sharecropping population was.[82] But there is nothing in the religious micro-geography of the moorlands to suggest that Catherine lived in an especially devout

---

[73] Roger Magraw includes the 'south-west' in his list of regions that were de-Christianized in the nineteenth century. See: Roger Magraw, 'Rural Anticlericalism in Nineteenth-Century France', in *Disciplines of Faith: Studies in Religion, Politics, and Patriarchy*, eds. Jim Samuel Obelkevich, Lyndal Roper, and Ralph Samuel (London, 1987), 351.

[74] Cholvy and Hilaire, *Histoire Religieuse de la France contemporaine*, ii, 86.

[75] Sargos, *Contribution*, 568.

[76] Magraw suggests a number of reasons why this might have been the case, from the influence of monasteries on local communities before the Revolution to the deep memory of the Wars of Religion. Magraw, 'Rural Anticlericalism', 352.

[77] ADL 1000 J 65, 'Monographie Paroissiale: Trensacq' (1889), 3.

[78] ADL 1000 J 65, 'Monographie Paroissiale: Labrit' (1905).

[79] ADL 1000 J 65, 'Monographie Paroissiale: Trensacq', 10.

[80] ADL 1000 J 65, 'Monographie Paroissiale: Sabres' (1889).

[81] 'Monographie Paroissiale: Commensacq', 36.   [82] NFA, 2 MI 29/17, f.160.

area, and that this explains her singing. The reasons for her choices were, I think, more personal than this.

Sewing and Limping

Catherine limped.

It is hard to say how serious her limp was, and Arnaudin made no mention of it in the notes he wrote about her, but it was important enough to be recorded by the census in 1872.[83] The culture of the moorlands was not kind when it came to disabilities. A disability was not seen as an aspect of an individual, but rather as their identity, so that people talked not of men and women who limped, but 'cripples'.[84] People with disabilities were the target of many jokes and were paradoxically thought to excel at things which their disabilities affected. One proverb suggested that 'Singing should be left to stammerers, And dancing to those who limp', linking two of the most common physical impairments to the combined activities of singing and dancing.[85] Arnaudin noted that: 'It is widely believed that those who stammer are excellent singers, and those who limp excellent dancers'.[86] This idea was also evoked in the final verses of Pierre Sournet's (1847–1919) version of *On the Bridge of Toulouse, Saint John's Eve* (Coirault 4517). Catherine characteristically left these verses out:

> The men and women with limps
> Will dance at the dance.
> The men and women who stammer
> Will sing at the dance.[87]

The association that singers made between limping and dancing was sexually suggestive. No matter what the folklorists sometimes tried to pretend about the innocence of rural singing, the Church was right about the close symbolic relationship between dancing and sex. Early nineteenth-century ethnographic accounts of the moorlands presented village dances as primitive match-making ceremonies where men unceremoniously chose a bride and immediately presented her to their parents.[88] Arnaudin's understanding of the links between singing, dancing, and sex eighty years later was subtler. An anonymous note he recorded remembered a wedding by mentioning both singing, and sexual experience: 'When...and...married—what fun we had!—Jani de Tanot was there, the

---

[83] ADL E DEPOT 85/1 F 1, 'Recensement de La Population: Commensacq' (1872).
[84] The Gascon word was 'tort' (masculine) or 'torte' (feminine).   [85] *OC*, ii, 123.
[86] *OC*, ii, 123. See also the rhyme on 373–4.   [87] *OC*, iv, 27.
[88] Caila, 'Recherches sur les moeurs des habitants des Landes de Bordeaux'.

poor thing! She knew a thing or two! And she knew how to sing!'[89] When suggesting a young woman 'knew a thing or two', the knowledge in question was undoubtedly sexual.[90]

This folk culture associating limping with dancing also sexually marked the bodies of women who limped. Their buttocks, which played such an important role in the sexual and phenomenological anatomy of the rural body explored in Chapter 4, were more pronounced than most people's: 'A woman with a limp is cleaner than any other, With one buttock, she cleans the other'.[91] Nonsense rhymes reinforced the association between limping and the buttocks:

> 'Cripple, where have you come from
> With your fat bottom?'
> 'I've come from Tartas,
> Stick your nose up it.'
> 'And from Tartas to Rion,
> Stick your own up there!'[92]

Both of these examples of folk speech about limping are about women, and both use ideas about the way a limp changes a woman's bottom, making it 'fat' or making it rub: to be a woman with a limp meant to be a symbol of sexual excess. Catherine lived with these everyday associations linking limping to dancing, sex, and buttocks. Because of her physical disability, Catherine was both expected to have a particular affinity to dancing and music and was simultaneously reduced to her sexual body. I think this provides a better explanation than religion does for why she systematically excluded references to sexuality from her songs and emphasized that her body was not 'abandoned'.

As if this were not enough, there was another important way in which Catherine's body was marked as sexual. Catherine worked as a seamstress. Indeed, she may have been destined for this work, given that her parents gave her the same name as the patron saint of seamstresses. This was an occupation associated with sexual licence. Seamstresses were more intimately involved with a range of other bodies than many rural labourers, touching and measuring them, and entering into private spaces normally reserved for only the closest family. In rural cultures, as in the industrial cities of the nineteenth century, this intimacy and mobility were grounds to suspect all seamstresses of being fallen women. But, unlike in the city, in folk cultures this marginal sexual status also came with a certain amount of authority. The ethnologist Yvonne Verdier has pointed out the special role of the seamstress in French rural society as an educator who taught young girls 'the law of the female body'.[93] In the Burgundian example Verdier studied, this special role

---

[89] OC, vii, 519.   [90] Verdier, Façons de dire, façons de faire, 159–258, especially 204.
[91] OC, ii, 252.   [92] OC, ii, 401.   [93] Verdier, Façons de dire, façons de faire, 188.

was expressed in the symbolic associations between clothing, pins, sewing, the body, and menstruation. *La marquette* was an embroidery that young girls were expected to master with the seamstress, but its name also connoted the marking of the young girl's body by menstruation.[94] The girls sang as they worked with the seamstress.[95] There is some evidence of similar associations in the songs of the moorlands. The song *A! Mama, Are You Pleased* (Coirault 902), for instance, is sung from the point of view of a young girl. She asks her mother if she is pleased with her progress in a range of areas, beginning with sewing, and ending with courting and sexuality.[96] The same cultural connections Verdier found between singing, sewing, and sex were important in the moorlands.

Perhaps, like twentieth-century seamstresses, Catherine was even responsible for dressing brides on their wedding days.[97] Whatever the case, Arnaudin's notes on wedding songs provide ample evidence of the importance of clothing and of dressing the bride for this most important occasion: 'Look at the bride from every angle, To see if there is anything wrong [with her outfit]'.[98] According to van Gennep, these wedding-day songs are one of most striking and original aspects of the folklore of the south-west.[99] Other activities during the day made reference to sewing and cloth work, and Babé told Arnaudin: 'In the old days, the bride would wear a pair of [sewing] scissors on her belt'.[100] Whether or not Catherine's role dressing local brides was formalized, her skills as a seamstress gave her authority in this domain. As Verdier pointed out, this authority is not without its ironies. Seamstresses may have been experts when it came to marriage, but this sexual expertise was itself the reason why they could not marry. In the moorlands, professional sewing was considered incompatible with married life. As the proverb held, 'Married seamstress, Blunt needle'.[101] Needles and pins were a language that played on associations with clothing and sex, pricking and bleeding, and a language that was governed by the ambiguous figure of the village seamstress.[102] In this sense, Catherine's unmarried status might have been considered appropriate by the people who knew her, since it fitted with what they thought of seamstresses.

The connection between seamstresses and singing is clear from the interest Arnaudin took in collecting songs from women who worked in tailoring.[103] This is not simply a quirk of his fieldwork methodology. It is true that by activating

---

[94] Ibid., 177–86.   [95] Ibid., 179.

[96] *OC*, iii, 232–3. *The Perfect Girl*. In fact, the Coirault catalogue only refers to the version Arnaudin collected. *RCFTO*, i, 96.

[97] Verdier, *Façons de dire, façons de faire*, 246–51.   [98] *OC*, iv, 746–7.

[99] Gennep, *Le Folklore français*, i, 313, 334; Césaire Daugé, *Le mariage et la famille en Gascogne d'après les proverbes et les chansons* (3 vols, Paris, 1916), i, 59–66.

[100] *OC*, vii, 582.   [101] *OC*, ii, 129.

[102] Anne Monjaret, 'De l'épingle à l'aiguille: L'éducation des jeunes filles au fil des contes', *L'Homme*, no. 173 (1 March 2005), 119–47.

[103] In the 1861 census, just 0.5 per cent of the local population worked as seamstresses, yet more like 2.6 per cent of Arnaudin's singers were seamstresses (8 out of 286).

a network of women and men in the cloth trades, Arnaudin was able to collect songs long distance. Two of his seamstress-singers lived in Hostens, in the neighbouring department of the Gironde. It seems clear that he met Catherine Goujon (1829–1913) and Jeanne Pruzeau (b. 1866), known as le Pruzoline, through the Raba-Triscos family, whose daughter Jeanne Raba, known as Anaïs, femme Triscos (b. 1859), was also a seamstress. Another one of his seamstress-singers, Marie Dulucq, even collected songs for him, and sent them to him in letters.[104] But the reason why it was easy for Arnaudin to tap into this network of seamstresses was because the cloth trades were an important conduit for song culture. He noted, for instance, that Catherine learned one song from a tailor named Cousteau in Belhade, and while most of his singers learned songs from family members, Catherine had also learned another song from a man who came from a different village, and whose family originated in the fairly distant town of Mont-de-Marsan.[105] More than many of the other singers, Catherine's work connected her to exactly the kind of trans-regional networks that made folk traditions dynamic and adaptive.

Conclusion

The temptation when writing about folk cultures is to emphasize cultural harmony and unity, to find the big story, such as the triumph of black described in Chapter 6, or the common features of rural ideas about the body explored in Chapter 4. Given what historians know about the importance of silence in nineteenth-century rural France, it is important to question how individuals might refuse the common assumptions of the culture around them, for good reasons.[106]

Catherine's silence on sexuality was not typical, and neither was her experience of being a seamstress with a limp. Her life was not one that went with the flow of the history of the body in this region. The demographic revolution had little to do with her childlessness, her work was not dependent on the environmental changes of the second half of the nineteenth century, and there is little in her life or songs that suggests she had strong feelings about the tensions over work and exploitation discussed in Chapter 8. Yet Catherine's singing was in dialogue with local understandings of the body, understandings that focused on comely buttocks and legs, and that discussed women's bodies almost exclusively through the idiom of sexuality. Her repertoire of sometimes unusual songs, and her choice not to sing verses and songs that drew attention to her own sexuality are similar to

---

[104] NFA, 2 MI 29/31, f.717.   [105] NFA, 2 MI 29/2, ff.287, 322.
[106] Corbin, *The Life of an Unknown*, 66; Hopkin, *Voices of the People*, 79–108.

the case of Carlo Ginzburg's heretical early-modern miller, Domenico 'Menocchio' Scandella.[107] Like Menocchio, and like the storyteller Henri Vidal in Chapter 8, Catherine is what Ginzburg has called a 'normal exception', someone whose transgressive or unusual life and actions draw attention to the often unspoken norms that people around them considered important.[108] What mattered was not necessarily the conflict over Church and State that has been such a central concern of historians of nineteenth-century France. It was not necessarily even the momentous shift in sexual cultures that Anne-Marie Sohn has so powerfully explored.[109] For an individual like Catherine, it could be as personal as her occupation and her physical disability.

---

[107] Carlo Ginzburg, *The Cheese and the Worms: The Cosmos of a Sixteenth-Century Miller*, trans. John Tedeschi and Anne Tedeschi (Baltimore, 1992).

[108] Carlo Ginzburg and Carlo Poni, 'The Name and the Game: Unequal Exchange and the Historiographical Marketplace', in *Microhistory and the Lost Peoples of Europe*, ed. Edward Muir and Guido Ruggiero, trans. Erin Branch (Baltimore, 1991), 8.

[109] Sohn, *Du Premier baiser à l'alcôve*.

8

Exploited Bodies

In 1878, a young joiner named Henri Vidal (1850–1919) from the village of
Trensacq told Arnaudin a story about a fox in conflict with a 'ploughman' over
food, housing, and agricultural tools and favours. He entitled it 'Mr Lamarque and
Mrs Senguinët'. Henri's tale might look typical of the animal stories that are
known in many different parts of the world going back as far as ancient Greece.
It would be easy for historians to assume that this was an almost timeless allegory
of the kind where animals talk and incarnate human moral characteristics,
perhaps an example of a story from *Aesop's Fables,* or the *Roman de Renart,*
preserved among the French peasantry, who still found its simple moral lesson
relevant.[1] Yet Henri's story is neither as simple nor as universal as the image of the
cunning fox might encourage readers to assume. Both in flavour and in structure,
it is related to well-known fables of the fox, but it is also noticeably different. The
tale is about his own life, and it was not only a window into what life was like for
the working population, but also a kind of manifesto, a criticism of the existing
social order and a desperate account of an underdog's attempt to escape domination. His tale does not belong to the last vestiges of early-modern 'peasant'
culture, but to the throes of modern social relations that rocked the former
moorlands in the second half of the nineteenth century.

In Henri's story, the fox is a kind of hapless anti-hero whose first mistake is to
be caught in a farmer's trap on his way home from stealing a chicken.[2] When the
farmer finds him, the fox is desperate, and promises never to steal, or allow any of
his family to steal any more food from the farmer. In exchange, the farmer
suggests a new place for the fox to build his den. Sadly, it soon turns out that
the farmer has tricked the fox. His new home floods in the winter and the fox and
his wife are almost killed. From this point on, the fox does his best to please and
ingratiate himself with the farmer, but to no avail. His idea is to steal a new form of
plough from a neighbouring region and give it to the farmer. At first, the farmer
seems grateful, offering the fox two chickens as a reward. But when the fox goes
to collect his prize, the farmer sets his dogs on him. In revenge, the fox decides to
steal the plough back. Once again, the farmer outwits him. He pays a donkey

---

[1] The oldest recorded animal tale probably comes from the writings of the poet Archilocus around
650 BCE. See: Hans-Jörg Uther, 'The Fox in World Literature: Reflections on a "Fictional Animal"',
Asian Folklore Studies, lxv (2006), 133.

[2] The story is found in: NFA, 2 MI 29/11, ff.436–43. More precisely, the fox has stolen a cockerel or
capon.

Body and Tradition in Nineteenth-Century France: Félix Arnaudin and the Moorlands of Gascony, 1870–1914.
William G. Pooley, Oxford University Press (2019). © William G. Pooley.
DOI: 10.1093/oso/9780198847502.001.0001

to pretend to be dead outside of the fox's den. The fox and his wife cannot believe their luck: the donkey's carcass would provide enough food for the winter. But when they try to use the yoke to pull the donkey inside, he jumps up and drags the fox back to the farmer and his dogs, who savagely attack him. The fox miraculously survives, and limps home to tell his wife that it is time to move on. The story ends with an abrupt formula: after they have packed their bags and set out on the road, the fox and his wife drown. There is no moral to the story.

Foxes and Sharecroppers

The key to understanding Henri's story is when it was told. Chapter 1 described how social tensions in the moorlands were exacerbated by the 1857 law, and how the rapid changes to the environment were both repressed and intensified by the system of sharecropping.[3] The year of 1878, when Henri told this story, is squarely in the period when the everyday deference of the labouring population was only rarely punctured by violent outbursts. It would be almost thirty years until the first resin collectors' syndicate was formed in 1906, and workers began to express their grievances openly. On 31 December 1858, the prefect of the Landes wrote to the minister of the interior: 'The state of subservience sharecroppers are in relative to the landowner, who they call "master", makes these landowners veritable oligarchs, capable of ordering their dependents to do what they want, and to vote according to orders.'[4] Sociologists and economists have pointed out that sharecropping is particularly well suited to areas where class domination is extreme but direct supervision of labour would be impractical because the agriculture is already so marginal.[5] The poor, sandy soil of the moorlands, which required abundant fertilization, and back-breaking hoeing and weeding, fitted this labour system perfectly. Where wage earners might shirk, sharecroppers have no temptation.[6] If their harvest fails, they will starve. A figure of Gascon speech that Arnaudin recorded sums up the dilemma by suggesting that working slowly 'feeds your own misery'.[7] The system institutes a kind of 'self-supervision' whereby the head of the sharecropping household must assume the psychological and physical strain of meeting both the demands of the elements and the landlord.[8] What this creates is 'a "web of dependency" incorporating both economic

---

[3] See pp. 10–20.   [4] Cailluyer, *Regards sur l'histoire sociale des Landes*, 31–2.
[5] R. Pearce, 'Sharecropping: Towards a Marxist View', in *Sharecropping and Sharecroppers*, ed. T.J. Byres (London, 1983), 53.
[6] José Maria-Caballeros, 'Sharecropping as an Efficient System: Further Answers to an Old Puzzle', in *Sharecropping and Sharecroppers*, ed. T.J. Byres (London, 1983), 107–18.
[7] *OC*, vi, 15.
[8] The idea of self-supervision comes from: Amit Bhaduri, 'Cropsharing as a Labour Process', in *Sharecropping and Sharecroppers*, ed. T.J. Byres (London, 1983), 85–93.

and non-economic structures of subordination'.[9] Instead of simply paying him rent, the sharecropper's fortunes are personally tied to the figure of the sometimes benevolent, and sometimes inexplicably violent and unreasonable landlord. Émile Guillaumin's fictionalized account of the life of a sharecropper in nineteenth-century Allier, written from his own experiences, suggests that all landlords are difficult, in different ways, from brutality and greed, to oily joviality, and apparently well-meaning interference in the management of the farm.[10] These problems of familiarity and contempt are exactly the problems that Henri's fox faces in his relationship with the farmer in the story.

Animals have always made good allegories for human social relationships, and perhaps never more so than in an agricultural system where they were the source of one of the key tensions between landlord and tenant. As one of the sharecroppers in Guillaumin's *La Vie d'un Simple* complained: 'we are slaves to our beasts... we care for these animals as if they were good Christian people'.[11] In fact, it is striking that when the simmering resentment of the sharecroppers did turn violent in the moorlands, as in the so-called 'Revolution of Sabres' in 1863, the language that angry workers drew on was the language of animals. The crisis was sparked by rumours that local landlords were planning to decrease the share that they paid to their resin collectors. Sixty years later, a local weaver named Pierre Sourbès remembered how one flashpoint unleashed a serious social disturbance. According to Sourbès, a local landowner called de Capet carelessly remarked that the resin collectors were so stupid that they should be fed chopped straw. Later that day, an angry crowd seized him, marched him outside, sat him down on a chair, and turned his own idea against him.[12] This incident fits a wider pattern of nineteenth-century rural men and women who expressed resentment against exploitation by imagining social relations in terms of relationships between humans and animals. The 'peasants' who murdered noble landowners in the Corbières in 1830 and in Dordogne in 1870 made similar comparisons between human–animal relations and social tensions, drawing on imagery that had been an important part of the revolutionary climate of the 1790s. Alain Corbin has suggested that the symbolisms of animal–human relationships formed part of a submerged language of social relations, especially in rural contexts, a language which only emerged at exceptional moments of crisis.[13]

Arnaudin himself believed that the moorlands were like a museum of cultural traditions, and the folklorist Marie-Louise Tenèze later echoed this view,

---

[9] Adrienne Cooper, 'Sharecroppers and Landlords in Bengal, 1930–50: The Dependency Web and Its Implications', in *Sharecropping and Sharecroppers*, ed. T.J. Byres (London, 1983), 226–55.
[10] Guillaumin, *La Vie d'un Simple*, 70–1, 84–6, 149–51.   [11] Ibid., p. 226.
[12] The incident is recounted in: Leshauris, 'La Révolution de Sabres (1863)'.
[13] On the Dordogne, see: Alain Corbin, *The Village of Cannibals: Rage and Murder in France, 1870*, trans. Arthur Goldhammer (Cambridge, MA, 1992), 9–10, 75; on the Corbières, see: McPhee, *Revolution and Environment*, 213–15.

suggesting that something about the dancing and fables Arnaudin recorded owed more to the medieval world than the nineteenth century.[14] It is true that the language men like Henri used to talk about social conflict has deep historical roots, but this is not the same thing as saying Henri's story is simply an echo of the medieval *Roman de Renart*. The oral versions of stories found in the *Roman* that have been collected since the start of the nineteenth century are often more fully developed, and sometimes more coherent than the medieval poems.[15] They have a flavour all of their own, a flavour that develops out of the ways storytellers adapted them, whether consciously or not, to fit the contexts of their own lives.[16] Most obviously, Henri's story could be likened to James C. Scott's description of animal tales among American slaves as expressions of a 'hidden transcript' criticizing domination from below. 'At one level these are nothing but innocent stories about animals; at another level they appear to celebrate the cunning wiles and vengeful spirit of the weak as they triumph over the strong'.[17] Animal stories, and especially fox stories, have long been used as 'allusions' to historical events and problems, deployed for 'social and moral criticism'.[18] Unlike the fantasy world of the folk tale, where lowly heroes turn out to be princes and princesses in disguise, or at least capable of winning a spouse whose worldly riches match the protagonist's moral virtues, animal tales are set in a fundamentally cynical and static universe.[19] There is no dizzying social rise here. Indeed, many of the stories of tricks and deceptions found across France and Europe can be chained together, to make longer narrative sequences, as if there is no final victory to be gained.[20] Where the magical tales close with a marriage, animal tales often end with the different parties going their different ways, or simply dying, as in Henri's tale.

There are problems with Scott's model, however. It both tends to romanticize the resistance of the underdog and underplay the pessimism of these animal tales.[21] Henri's fox makes use of as much cunning as he can, but there is no eventual triumph. The fox's relationship to the farmer is a hopeless battle, and the only sensible solution is to move on. Right from the start, this is a moral universe structured around the breakdown of trust, deception, and betrayal.[22] To behave like a fox might have been a colloquial phrase for being cunning, but the fox in Henri's story, like other foxes from the tradition, is not always as successful as his cunning reputation might suggest.[23] The fox is often a victim, 'outfoxed', as the

---

[14] NFA, 2 MI 29/12, f.101; *CPF*, ii, 96.   [15] *CPF*, ii, 89–98.

[16] Tenèze, 'Aperçu sur les contes d'animaux'.

[17] James C. Scott, *Domination and the Arts of Resistance: Hidden Transcripts* (New Haven, 1990), 19, 162–6.

[18] Uther, 'The Fox in World Literature', 136.

[19] This interpretation of 'fairy tales' is a summary of the canonical work of Bengt Holbek: *Interpretation of Fairy Tales: Danish Folklore in a European Perspective* (Helsinki, 1987).

[20] *CPF*, ii, 55–6.   [21] Abu-Lughod, 'The Romance of Resistance'.

[22] This is a point made in: *CPF*, ii, 54.   [23] *OC*, vii, 245.

title of one of Aesop's fables suggests.[24] Out of the eight stories concerning foxes that Arnaudin collected, just two see the fox emerge victorious. When he comes up against blackbirds, dogs, squirrels, partridges, eagles, and humans his cunning serves him very poorly.[25] The fox does not seem to have been very successful in nearby regions either. Out of the five tales of the fox collected by another south-western French folklorist, Jean-François Bladé, the fox only triumphs in one.[26] This is a grim, violent, and strangely realist universe.[27] If anything, the fox is a symbol of failed resistance. And, like the sporadic violence of the sharecroppers, it might make sense to think of the fox as an unusual example. Other local people were just as likely to talk of donkeys. To understand the special interest of Henri's story of the rebellious fox, it is necessary to first think about these beasts of burden, and the men and women who likened themselves to humble donkeys.

The Loyalty of Donkeys

Arnaudin collected stories from fifty-nine narrators, although he kept notes about many more whose narratives he never got around to recording. In a similar pattern to the general picture of his informants explored in Chapter 3, the majority of these storytellers lived most of their lives in the second half of the nineteenth century and died early in the twentieth. All saw the transformation of the moorlands and the resulting social problems, and many lived to see the dramatic labour movements of the early twentieth century. Arnaudin's best sources for stories tended to be long-lived working women, such as Mariane de Mariolan, who told twenty, Babé Plantié, who told sixteen, and Beroun Poudens, who told eleven. Shepherds were also important narrators, so Jean Saubesty, known as 'the Boss', told nineteen stories and Jean Destruhaut (b. 1833) told nine stories. These men and women were often poor and poorly educated. Twenty of the narrators, including Babé, Beroun, and 'the Boss', were unable to sign their own wedding certificates. Farming was the commonest occupation, and twenty-one of the individuals were called farmers at least once in their life.

When it comes to working out what class these narrators belong to, the problem is not simply inadequate sources, or a lack of information about their

---

[24] *Aesop's Fables*, ed. Stanley Handford (4th edn, London, 1994), 14; for other authors who have commented on the fox's frequent failures, see: Haim Schwarzbaum, *The Mishle Shu'alim (fox Fables) of Rabbi Berechiah Ha-Nakdan: A Study in Comparative Folklore and Fable Lore* (Kiron, 1979); Uther, 'The Fox in World Literature', 147–9; Brian Juan O'Neill, 'Social Conflict in the Galician Folktale', *Cahiers de Littérature Orale*, xiv (1984), 24. In fact, the fox's reputation is so poor that Ralph Boggs entitled his section in his index of Spanish folk tales 'Fox Not Clever'. Ralph Steele Boggs, *Index of Spanish Folktales* (Helsinki, 1930).

[25] *OC*, i, 510–85. Manuscript versions of some, but not all, of these stories can be found in ADL 2 MI 29/11. Some of the texts not found in the manuscripts were published by Arnaudin in 1886.

[26] Bladé, *Contes populaires de la Gascogne*.

[27] *CPF*, ii, 79; Scott, *Domination and the Arts of Resistance*, 163.

lives, frustrating as these puzzles can be. It has to do both with how individuals were moving through social categories, and how they themselves acted to construct them. Several of these storytellers were experiencing the process of proletarianization first-hand, as previously skilled work was replaced with increasingly exploitative and unskilled work. Several were sinking down the social scale. Dominique Vidal, known as 'Menicot' (1838–1901), who told Arnaudin some bawdy stories, was working for the folklorist in the 1870s.[28] But by 1883 he was sick, and dependent on the charity of the local council.[29] Antoine Garbay, known as 'the Tinker' (1836–1911), a sometime farmer, shepherd, and itinerant tinsmith, was rich enough in 1862 to repay his parents a loan of 1,080 francs, but he died a pauper almost fifty years later in 1911.[30]

These harsh lives found their echo in the grim tales of beasts competing against one another, and against humans. With their vivid depictions of a world of constant hunger and violence, the unsanitized animal tales of nineteenth-century oral culture offered opportunities for storytellers to metaphorically explore the difficult conditions of their own existence. It is perhaps no coincidence that on the scale of France as a whole, the regions where sharecropping was widely practised coincide with the regions where animal tales were most popular, with some stories only known in the south-west, the heartland of sharecropping in the nineteenth century.[31] Arnaudin claimed that the tale of 'The Fox and the Wolf', for instance, was matched in popularity in the moorlands by just a few other tales.[32] This popularity has something to do with the ways that animal tales can be used to discuss sharecropping, a system that puts heavy weight on the relations between landlords and tenants, and heads of household and their families. In other stories from Jean-François Bladé's collection in nearby Gascony, the fox actually takes on shareholdings with other animals.[33]

For many of the storytellers Arnaudin encountered, these animal tales rationalized a brutal social system, and may even have functioned as a way of subtly bargaining with employers and rivals. Some narrators used their stories to carve out identities as reliable and dependable workers. Babé Plantié and her husband 'The Boss' make good examples. Just before Henri told his fox story, around 1875, Jean and Babé moved to the hamlet of Monge in Labouheyre to take up the sixth different shareholding they had farmed since their marriage in 1844.[34] Their employers were the Arnaudin family. This special relationship may explain how

---

[28] The nickname is a traditional contraction of 'Dominique'.
[29] ADL E DEPOT 134/1 D 5, 'Archive Communale: Labouheyre'.   [30] ADL 4 E 307/41.
[31] *CPF*, ii, 103. For an example of a story only known in the south-west, see for example: *CPF*, ii, 472. For examples that Arnaudin collected that were rare elsewhere in Europe, see for example ATU 103C, *CPF*, ii, 351–2, as well as the unclassified episodes, *CPF*, ii, 470–567. There is a map of the prevalence of sharecropping in: Xavier de Planhol, *Géographie historique de la France* (Paris, 1988), 154.
[32] *OC*, i, 524.
[33] Jean-François Bladé, *Contes populaires de la Gascogne* (new edn, Pau, 2008 [1886]), 466–7, 487–8.
[34] NFA, 2 MI 29/24, f.417.

Fig. 8.1 Babé Plantié (right) and Jean Saubesty (left), with their son, daughter-in-law, and grandchildren, courtesy of the Musée d'Aquitaine

Arnaudin was able to collect so much material from the husband and wife, including several stories that were very rare in the French tradition. Babé, in particular, seems to have had a fraught relationship with her employer, the folklorist. She was his most important informant, yet because of the tensions between them, Arnaudin wanted to relegate her to a less prominent place in his published works.[35] Perhaps it should not be surprising, then, that the animal stories that Babé and Jean told the folklorist revolve around the tensions between sharecroppers and employers.

Many of the stories they told were among the most popular animal tales known in France, and these tended to be stories emphasizing that, despite the brutality of the world, animals have much to gain by collaborating with one another, with the powerful protecting the powerless wherever possible. 'The Halfchick Tale' (ATU 716), which Jean told, for instance, was an example of a story so popular in France that the French name is often used in international catalogues to identify the story.[36] The tale deals with the challenges that the half-chick hero faces. When the half-chick finds some money, a passer-by tricks him out of it. He is only able to regain the money by calling on the help of other animal friends.[37] A story like this

---

[35] NFA, 2 MI 29 1, f.14.   [36] *CPF*, ii, 684–5.
[37] *OC*, i, 185–9; NFA, 2 MI 29/11, f.512–15.

uses the animal world to encourage solidarity among humans. Other stories they told present similar messages. Both Jean and Babé told versions of another extremely popular French tale, 'The Wolf and the Seven Young Kids' (ATU 123).[38] There are eighty-eight versions of this story in the French catalogue.[39] The story focuses on the family solidarity of the goat kids outwitting the wolf who intends to eat them while their mother is away, just as 'The Halfchick Tale' focused on community solidarity.

The less well-known animal tales that Babé and Jean told also fit into a model that emphasized social cohesion. Babé told a story called 'The Pig and the Donkey' that was not classified in the Aarne-Thompson international tale-type system used to catalogue traditional narratives.[40] This short story sees a new pig arrive in a mill. The pig soon takes on airs with the old donkey who works there, pointing out that he is better fed, and does not have to work, or endure beatings. The donkey tries to warn him, saying that he has been there many years, and seen many different pigs, but the pig pays no attention. Sure enough, sometime later, the pig is killed and eaten. There is only one other record of this tale in France, aside from medieval sources.[41] Babé's version is one of the few records to suggest that the conservative message of this story was relevant to the working population in this period. Working hard and enduring beatings may be difficult, but that, her story suggests, is how life is, and those who expect to eat well and laze around might be in for a surprise. It is hard to say how much telling this story was simply a way for Babé to rationalize a life of toil, and how much she used it as veiled criticism of her employer, Arnaudin, and his conspicuously indolent lifestyle.

A rare tale that Jean told makes the message of these stories even clearer. 'The Donkey, the Wolf and the Lion' (ATU 103C) tells the story of how a donkey bests the other, more threatening animals, using only his wits.[42] This story is only known in one other oral French version, collected by Frédéric Ortoli in the quite different context of Corsica.[43] Jean's tale is in many ways similar to the one collected by Ortoli. By making the hero of the tale a donkey, both narrators can talk about 'peasant' virtues of determination, cunning, and playing dumb in order to outwit those who are apparently stronger than them. The donkey outdoes the lion in various tests, sometimes using his natural strength, for instance kicking down a wall, but more often pretending his weaknesses are strengths in themselves. When he struggles to swim across a pond, he tells the lion it is because he was fishing.

In the tale collected by Ortoli, the donkey is so successful that he ends up the king of the lions. The message seems to be that 'peasant' cunning can triumph over even the most powerful adversary. But Jean's tale establishes, from the very

[38] *OC*, i, 547–53; NFA, 2 MI 29/11, ff.419–25, 429–30.
[39] And this does not include four unpublished versions in Arnaudin's manuscripts.
[40] *OC*, i, 587; NFA, 2 MI 29/11, f.137.   [41] *CPF*, ii, 487.
[42] *OC*, i, 541–7; NFA, 2 MI 29/11, ff.501–8.
[43] J.B. Frédéric Ortoli, *Les Contes populaires de l'île de Corse* (Paris, 1883), 133–7.

outset, an entirely different message to the one collected in Corsica. While the Corsican tale sees the donkey choosing to set off on an adventure, Jean's donkey is kicked out of his home because he has grown too old to work. Both tales are about a violent world that requires wit and exhausting labour, but the Corsican tale offers a challenge to this world, suggesting that even a donkey can overcome the lions if he is cunning enough. Jean's tale, on the other hand, looks much more like a way for an old, tired man to persuade his employer that he is not only a faithful donkey, but that his talents are beyond what you might expect. The tale both evokes sympathy, and needles its primary audience, Arnaudin, to treat his elderly employee well.

Talking about donkeys allowed Jean and Babé to play dumb, and to present themselves as faithful, sturdy workers to a man whose opinion governed their livelihoods. Like the subjects in James C. Scott's work on 'hidden transcripts', the two sharecroppers made 'creative use of the stereotypes intended to stigmatize them', the long tradition among elites and ethnographers of depicting the population of the moorlands as mere beasts.[44] When Jean Thore described the locals of the moorlands in 1810, he claimed 'little set them apart from the animals whose skins they had borrowed'. These kinds of insult could provoke sharp responses from the sharecroppers. When offered potatoes to improve their poor diet, the 'peasants' of Saint-Magne asked if the reformers thought they were pigs. Other locals, it seems, had learned to use outsiders' assumptions to their own advantage. Jacques Arago's first impression was that the oxen of the moorlands were 'less stupid than their masters'. Over time, he realized, however, that: 'Treating the locals as idiots and brutes has taught them prudence, cunning, and wiliness. They have learnt from experience, and have made their supposed weakness their greatest strength.'[45]

Henri and the Fox

Henri Vidal's life took a different direction to Arnaudin's sharecroppers, Jean and Babé. Henri was born to a family of fairly lowly artisans and sharecroppers in the isolated village of Trensacq, but his life was destined to take a slightly different course. When he married his first wife, Catherine Labile, in 1872 he was a humble joiner, and she was simply called a farm wife. Joinery was not well paid, and it was hard work. Joiners appear at least once in local folklore as the embodiment of the crudeness of manual labour.[46] But, following Catherine's death in 1887, Henri

---

[44] Scott, *Domination and the Arts of Resistance*, 133.
[45] All three examples come from: Sargos, *Histoire de la forêt landaise*, 60, 86, 83.
[46] In the song *In the Town of Salles There Is* a young girl rejects the advances of a joiner because his hands are too rough: *OC*, iv, 166–7. Arnaudin recorded six versions, including his own, so the song was relatively well known.

remarried into a slightly different social world. His second wife, Léonie Lagoffun, was a local teacher, and by this point, he himself had become a white-collar worker, and a relatively wealthy one at that.[47] In his marriage contract, the former joiner brought 1255 francs worth of personal possessions, including three beds with linen, three nightstands, two pinewood chests, mirrors, and a library worth 50 francs on its own.[48] There were clues in between that he was not going to remain a manual worker. At one point, he even went into business with Arnaudin himself, selling pit props made from local timber.[49] Where Babé and Jean worked for the folklorist, Henri worked with him. By the time he died in 1919, Henri was living in Labouheyre, part of an urban, commercial, and industrial culture, instead of the village world of his youth. This was nothing less than a reinvention of Henri's self.

This unusual biography was reflected in Henri's unusual story: there is no obvious parallel written—or indeed oral—version. The editors of Arnaudin's tales suggest the story bears some relationship to the international folk-tale type ATU 155 'Ingratitude is the World's Reward', a story well represented in French oral tradition by fifteen different recordings.[50] Jean-François Bladé collected a fairly typical version of this tale from one of his favourite narrators, a woman named Pauline Lacaze. In Pauline's story, a man discovers a wolf dangling from a tree, who begs him to set him free. The man has his doubts: won't the wolf just eat him as soon as he is liberated? The wolf promises not to, but once he is on the ground he changes his mind. The man understandably thinks this is unfair, and reflects that the proverb is true: 'ingratitude is the world's reward', or '*de bien faire, mal arrive*'. Before the wolf can eat him, however, they agree to submit their dispute to judgement by a third party. First they meet a dog, who replies that his answer will not be much use. Having served his master faithfully all his life, he has been turned out on his ear now that he is too old. He concludes that the proverb is true: '*de bien faire, mal arrive*'. They then meet a mare, who says the same thing. Finally, they meet a fox, who asks how the wolf was originally hanging. The wolf puts himself back in place, and the man and the fox leave him dangling there. As a reward for helping him, the man promises the fox a nice pair of fattened chickens. When he opens the bag, however, instead of the promised chickens, two dogs jump out and kill the fox. As they say, '*de bien faire, mal arrive*'.[51]

Although Henri's story shares the same dark vision of rural competition as the story 'Ingratitude is the World's Reward', it is inflected with a slightly different meaning in his unusual tale, and this meaning also contrasts with Jean and Babé's tales of faithful donkeys. In fact, in Henri's story, the donkey behaves more like the

---

[47] See ADL 1 MIEC 134/5, 22 August 1890.
[48] ADL 3 E 52/116, Jean Vidal and Léonie Lagoffun marriage contract, 22 August 1890.
[49] See the letter from Arnaudin to Bombaut, 10 September 1901: *OC*, v, 243.
[50] Uther, *The Types of International Folktales*, i, 107–8.
[51] Bladé, *Contes populaires de la Gascogne*, 462–4.

detested bailiff who worked for the landlord, enforcing his rules on the share-croppers.[52] While the fox exhausts himself struggling with the farmer, the donkey uses the simple ruse of pretending to be dead in order to trick the fox into bringing out the plough. In return, the donkey is allowed to eat as many oats as it wants. In Henri's story, it is the donkey's idea to get the plough back. Like the untrustworthy bailiff so despised by the sharecroppers of the moorlands, he is pre-empting the landlord's desires to ingratiate himself. Once the farmer agrees to give the donkey oats for his service, the donkey promptly gorges himself and falls asleep, giving the farmer good cause not to trust him. Furious, the farmer beats him. The donkey may be relatively well off in this system of exploitation, but only at the cost of doing whatever his master wants. In Henri's tale this position is not to be envied.

The idiosyncrasies of Henri's story point to the personal meanings of his tale. It not only reflects the social structure of local life, but Henri's own shifting place within it. Rather than simply calling his hero and his wife foxes, Henri's tale gives them human names, 'Mr. Lamarque' and 'Mrs. Senguinët', rooting the story in quotidian social encounters with real people. It takes place in a realistic world of everyday labour and personal relationships specific to the agricultural system of the moorlands.[53] Something about these fantastical fox tales helps us think about very real bodily and emotional exploitation. Henri's story concerns the kinds of tension that often arose between landlords and agricultural tenants in a system of sharecropping. His foxes might live in a den and get chased by dogs, but they can also talk, and their ideal diet for the winter is soup.[54] The areas of conflict between the foxes and the farmer in Henri's story—housing, food, tools, and responsibilities—are precisely the areas of conflict in sharecropping regions.

As in sharecropping, where labourers and landowners argued over agricultural products that were necessary for survival, a key source of tension in the story is food. The whole chain of events is set off by Mr Lamarque's attempt to steal a chicken to feed his wife, and the foxes remain ravenous throughout the story, 'exhausted by hunger'.[55] Sharecroppers and their landlords often argued over petty thefts like this, whether of food or other items. Arnaudin himself kept assiduous notes about the various tools and materials he suspected his own sharecroppers of pilfering.[56] Another source of conflict common to sharecropping and the story is housing. Because sharecroppers do not own their houses, they are constantly at risk of losing the shelter over their heads. The foxes of Henri's story suffer from the same problem, and are at the mercy of someone else when it comes

---

[52] See: Dupuy, *Le Pin de la discorde*, 281.
[53] Although an obvious omission is resin farming, which is not mentioned at all.
[54] See: NFA, 2 MI 29/11, f.442.   [55] NFA, 2 MI 29/11, f.438.
[56] NFA, 2 MI 29/20, f.122. On the importance of tools, see for instance Guillaumin, *La Vie d'un simple*, 24.

to this most basic need. Like sharecroppers in search of a better situation, the foxes change house regularly and frequently, three times in this short story.[57]

Along with the uncertainty over the most basic necessities of food and housing, Henri's story is permeated with a sense of a body under threat.[58] The farmer beats the unfortunate fox whenever he is given a chance. He also sets his dogs on him, and the fox is forced to spend most of the story running around, the hounds on his heels. There is a palpable sense of physical exhaustion, as well as a thematic concern with tools, and manual labour. The fox's theft of a new form of plough from a different region relates to the real technological changes in ploughing that occurred in the nineteenth century, as ards were unevenly replaced by lighter and more reliable ploughs.[59] This was not simply a new tool for the same job, but a change in bodily dispositions and a labour-saving device. In Henri's story, the farmer is clearly delighted with his new improved technology, which allows him to plough his field faster. But as well as speaking of this historical transition, the significance of the plough in the story is as a technology of social differentiation. A man without his own plough and team would be unable to take on a share-holding, and would instead have to work as a hired hand.[60]

When Henri told this tale in 1878, many people in the region would have been more concerned than ever about the perennial problems of housing, labour, changing agricultural technologies, and social differentiation. Because of the increasing forestation of the moorlands, agriculture was in flux. Social divisions became more marked across the former moorlands after the sale of the commons in the 1860s, as the richest families came to dominate local business and agriculture, while the poorest risked proletarianization. Like the Tuscan example studied by Desmond Gill, sharecropping in the moorlands uncomfortably co-existed with new forms of wage labour. Instead of providing an economic alternative, these new forms of labour were often the desperate recourse of those whose sharehold-ings could not feed their families.[61] In particular, men in both the moorlands and Tuscany took jobs on public works, building roads and railways, and these modern proletarians were increasingly important informants for Arnaudin's folklore collections.[62] The 1880s was the 'decisive period' of proletarianization in France as a whole, and in the south-west in particular, as declining resin prices fell hardest on the sharecroppers.[63]

---

[57] Dupuy, Le Pin de la discorde, 194.

[58] Scott suggests that this body under threat occupies 'a large space in the hidden transcripts' of the victims of serfdom and slavery. See: Domination and the Arts of Resistance, 23.

[59] Robert Specklin, 'Les Progrès techniques', in Histoire de la France rurale, eds. Georges Duby and Gabriel Wallon (new edn, 4 vols, Paris, 1992), iii, 181.

[60] Dupuy, Le Pin de la discorde, 110–12.

[61] Desmond Gill, 'Tuscan Sharecropping in United Italy: The Myth of Class Collaboration Destroyed', in Sharecropping and Sharecroppers, ed. T.J. Byres (London, 1983), 146–69.

[62] The railway workers provide Noiriel with one of his key examples of proletarianization in the workforce. See: Gerard Noiriel, Les Ouvriers dans la société française (Paris, 2002), 92–7.

[63] Ibid., 83; Sargos, Histoire de la forêt landaise, 508–9.

Special emotional pressures accompanied these social changes because of the ways that sharecropping was framed as a personal relationship between the father of a household and a landowner. Sharecropping was, above all, about an informal system of trust.[64] Similarly, Henri's story is not simply organized around trickery, which is what the pre-eminent folklorist Marie-Louise Tenèze calls the defining feature of this genre.[65] Instead, like sharecropping, it is organized around oral agreements, promises, and rewards. The farmer's repeated failure to deliver on oral promises is the kind of deception that every sharecropper would worry about, dependent as they were on their landlords not only for employment, but also housing. At five different points, the fox and the farmer explicitly evoke 'favours', and it is hard not to see these obligations in terms of the kinds of service sharecroppers were routinely expected to provide for their landlords, such as carting and maintenance work.[66] This is a social universe where the surface level of benevolent, patriarchal discourse is constantly disrupted by violence and dishonesty. Not only are all of the fox's efforts in vain, but the closing rhyming formula abruptly kills the fox and his wife: 'They packed their bags, and crossing a river they drowned'.[67] The general negative trend in fox tales in the modern period identified by Hans-Jörg Uther towards the fox being duped more often is evidence from the folklore archives of a growing consciousness of proletarianization and exploitation in the nineteenth century.[68] Henri's story, from this point of view, is one among many examples emphasizing the growing problems of rural social relations, especially under sharecropping systems.

Finding out what the sharecroppers themselves thought of this social control is fraught with problems, since talking about resentments openly would have been too risky for these men and women. Someone like Henri, however, who had both experience of exploitation and the ability to escape the sharecropping system in his own lifetime, gives a rare insight into the 'emotional labour' sharecropping involved.[69] There is more than a passing resemblance between the logic of Henri's fox, losing his temper with his wife when she asks him about the progress of his plans, and the logic of the working-class men Richard Sennett and Jonathan Cobb interviewed in Boston in the second half of the twentieth century: 'Sacrifice... legitimates a person's view of himself as an individual, with a right to feel anger', but it also leads to men who 'are both angry and ambivalent about their right

[64] For the same point, see: Elizabeth Griffiths and Mark Overton, *Farming to Halves: The Hidden History of Sharefarming in England from Medieval to Modern Times* (Basingstoke, 2009), 194.
[65] *CPF*, ii, 54.   [66] Dupuy, *Le Pin de la discorde*, 87–104, 121–2.
[67] The words are hard to make out exactly: 'Que [picau?] ses cliques é ses claques, en traversan uu [baiat?] aqui se soun negats'. NFA, 2 MI 29/11, f.443.
[68] Uther, 'The Fox in World Literature', 147.
[69] Arlie Russell Hochschild, *The Managed Heart: Commercialization of Human Feeling* (Berkeley, 1983).

to be angry'.[70] The fox is at once the hero of the tale, and yet remarkably unsuccessful and frustrated, unable to express his emotions even to his wife. Yet we know, from incidents like the ritualistic assault on de Capet in 1863, that aggression seethed under the calm surface of these workers' faces. When Mr Lamarque's wife asks him what the problem is half-way through Henri's tale, he snaps back: 'Let's not talk about it'.

This phrase goes to the heart of how tales perform emotions. Arnaudin wrote that 'rustic storytellers do not beat around the bush', but this characteristic directness has an unexpected result.[71] Rather than spelling out how characters feel, narrators such as Henri, Jean, and Babé performed stories in order to elicit feelings from an audience. The stories themselves create feelings, as well as reflecting them. This helps explain why in its original manuscript form, Henri's story is more telegraphic than the published version. It is lighter in details, motivations, and stage directions, and less coherently stitched together with linking phrases and explanations. Much of the speech is direct, and sometimes the logic of characters' actions and the development of the story are very hard to work out. These might be problems for twenty-first-century readers, but they would have posed fewer issues when Henri was performing the story, using gestures, intonation, and insinuation to make the narrative come alive. Many of the elements that seem somehow condensed or opaque would have been clearer to an audience who shared the same assumptions, and for whom a storyteller like Henri acted out the dialogue and action. Like real life, the characters of Henri's tale do not self-narrate their emotional states: they perform them. The fox does not say that he 'despairs', and his wife does not have to say out loud that she doubts him. Neither does the farmer spell out what the real motives of his actions are. Yet underlying all of these narrative developments, there are inexplicit emotions: Henri's.

While most of the metaphors of local speech focused on domestic animals, harnesses, straw, and beasts of burden, foxes make a slightly different case. As with poaching, it is clear that there were social tensions around the hunting of foxes, which was becoming a leisure activity for the middle class.[72] It seems unlikely that many agricultural workers would have had much sympathy for real foxes, yet their plights shared similarities. Like the sharecroppers and the hands, foxes lived a necessarily mobile lifestyle. They might survive off of their wits, but more than a few foxes, not to mention sharecroppers, met tragic ends. Foxes furnished a real-life example of agents put in a difficult situation by the system of farming, and what made them good anti-heroes for tales such as Henri's has something to do

---

[70] Richard Sennett and Jonathan Cobb, *The Hidden Injuries of Class* (new edn, New York, 1993), 140, 79.

[71] *OC*, v, 133.

[72] On poaching, see: Lescarret, *La Vie dans la Grande-Lande*, 263; and Dupuy, *Le Pin de la discorde*, 280; on fox hunting as a leisure pursuit, the best source is Arnaudin's own diary. See: *OC*, viii, *passim*.

with the ways they might express a desire for agency and freedom in mobility, even as this agency is recognized to be illusory.

The most compelling reason to argue in favour of reading anger between the lines of Henri's tale is the course his own life took. Henri left his first occupation as a relatively humble artisan, who would have worked with and lived among sharecroppers who were his friends and family, and this choice expressed a rejection of the social system of sharecropping. The fox in his story actively tries to reshape his emotional relations with the farmer, trying first trust, and then open war, before giving up. He also tries to reshape his bodily exploitation. The plough which proves the crux of the story is not simply a technological innovation, but one that historians have suggested made an immense difference to body postures in the countryside, as the new technology allowed labourers to work with a more upright stance.[73] Here is a narrative that explicitly invokes changes to working practices of a fundamental importance to the rural obsession with verticality.[74] On the most basic level, a body that allows a subject to look his social superior squarely in the eye is a different kind of political possibility from a body ground down both in discourse and in material terms. One way for the most politically inarticulate populations to make some kind of intervention in the course of their own lives is through a revolution of bodily practices.[75] Seizing the new plough is a gesture towards such a revolution.

There is much from Henri's story and his life to suggest that men like him were not the 'generally resigned creatures' 'peasants' are sometimes assumed to be.[76] Mr Lamarque may be ultimately unsuccessful, but he is nothing if not determined. The deal he strikes with the farmer at the beginning may not turn out that well for him, but at the time it is life-saving. Throughout, he demonstrates intelligence and resourcefulness, as when he decides to use the plough to pull the donkey into his den. He is inquisitive and has a desire to see the world, and he is endowed with an ability to seize opportunities, such as the plough. Throughout all of this there is a kind of dogged optimism. At the end of the story, he tells his wife, 'Despite all these misfortunes, I still had one piece of incredible good fortune. I pulled the yoke so hard that it broke.' Yet the fox's optimism is tinged with realism: 'I won't always have such luck. We should move somewhere else.'[77] The fox in Henri's story is not stupid. He knows to be suspicious of the farmer when he offers him a pair of chickens, but he has no choice but to risk his chances. And when the farmer does show his true colours, the fox attempts to get some kind of revenge. Henri's tale is an explanation for the otherwise skeletal story of his life. It reveals a man

---

[73] Specklin, 'Les progrès techniques', 181.
[74] See Chapter 4, and: Pellegrin, 'Corps du commun, usages communs du corps', 127.
[75] Connerton, *How Societies Remember*, 10; For an example, see Ruth Harris' argument about the bodily revolt of nineteenth-century women in the case of possession at Morzine: 'Possession on the Borders'.
[76] Singer, *Village Notables in Nineteenth-Century France*, 4.   [77] NFA, 2 MI 29/11, f.443.

struggling with the burdens of an unfair social system, and it is a glimpse of the future development of his life as someone who used his wits to free himself from the most oppressive aspects of this system.[78] Emotions, historians have empha-sized, are not knee-jerk reactions to situations, they are also strategies, whether conscious or not, interventions into social life.[79] Anger is not simply a product of structures of oppression, it is also a strategy, however hopeless, to overcome this oppression.

Most obviously, Henri's story is a story for his family. The tale is partly about the strain of a system of agricultural labour where the power of the landlord is mediated through the institutions of the family. The few written sharecropping contracts that survive typically included injunctions to the sharecropper 'to maintain everything as a good patriarch and sharecropper should'.[80] The share-cropper answers both to the needs of their family and the demands of a landlord.[81] Mr Lamarque enacts these conflicts with his wife, Mrs Senguinët. Her only active role in the story is to question him about what has gone wrong, why he has returned yet again exhausted and bruised. His normal reply is: 'Let's not talk about it'. Later, she questions whether he will really earn the reward he thinks he deserves from the farmer. Her husband ignores her, and when she is proved right, he lies to her to save his honour. This pressure on his masculinity, his ability to provide for and protect his family, does not just come at the cost of his hungry, battered, and exhausted body. In the multiple ways he tries to react, to manage his wife's expectations, to regain the upper hand, it is clear that this is a psychological strain, an everyday bodily struggle.

This struggle was not unique to Henri's life, and the themes his story explores are in dialogue with a tradition. In a sense, the story was not even 'his' anyway. When he told Arnaudin the tale in 1878, he told him he had previously heard it himself from a man named 'Dudon'. In fact, Henri attributed six of the nine tales he told to the folklorist to other storytellers, who he often emphasized were old, sedentary, and illiterate.[82] This is by no means to say that Henri was simply a conduit for other storytellers. There is no indication that he wrote the stories down and gave them to Arnaudin. Instead, he must have listened to other storytellers and retold the tales to Arnaudin. As many folklorists have noticed, no matter how faithful narrators claim to be to their source, they change myriad details and sometimes even the outcomes of the story.[83] The changes narrators make, whether consciously or otherwise, shape the stories to fit their own personal

---

[78] Scott, *Domination and the Arts of Resistance*, 16.

[79] Barbara Rosenwein, 'Controlling Paradigms', in *Anger's Past: The Social Uses of an Emotion in the Middle Ages*, ed. Barbara Rosenwein (Ithaca, 1998), 236–7; Fay Bound, '"An Angry and Malicious Mind?" Narratives of Slander at the Church Courts of York, c.1660–c.1760', *History Workshop Journal*, lvi (2003), 61.

[80] Dupuy, *Le Pin de la discorde*, 89, 92.   [81] Gill, 'Tuscan Sharecropping in United Italy'.

[82] NFA, 2 MI 29/11, ff.330–7, 395–8, 436–43, 445–8, 475–81, 553–7.

[83] Dégh, *Folktales and Society*, 168.

tastes and biographies.[84] What is more, of Henri's nine stories, six were animal tales or at least featured animals prominently. Given that Henri relayed tales from at least four different narrators, this strongly suggests that the affinity for animal tales came from Henri, rather than his sources. After all, Henri's tale is unique in the French oral tradition. What it shares with other local tales is an atmosphere of violence and oppression, the aesthetic of misery. But it differs in its forceful striving against this oppression, the hopeless efforts of the fox to please the farmer. Henri may not have been typical of local narrators, but perhaps he could be considered important precisely because he was not typical, in the same way that micro-historians talk of a 'normal exception'.[85]

This is not to say that his experience was unparalleled. Arnaudin collected stories from other men who had lived similar lives. Jules Sart was a local clerk, and also seems to have told some stories of his own and relayed others. The man Arnaudin referred to simply as 'Maumen', who told him several legends and jokes, must have been one of the two brothers living next door to the Arnaudin family in Labouheyre in the 1880s. The elder brother Jean (b. 1846) had a job as an intermediary between local industry and the railway, while his younger brother (b. 1848) also worked for the railways. It is tempting to see Henri's tale as a glimpse not simply of an individual's future, but that of a whole group, the men who chose to reject the paternalism and seething hatred of sharecropping in exchange for a salary, the men whose transition to wage earning was not the tragedy of proletarianization or the disintegration of family life feared by Marichoun Lescarret with her stories of the werewolf, but a liberation. Henri's tale helps to understand both his own future and the future of the moorlands, as a naked and pessimistic picture of the social situation of sharecropping, but one that contained the emotional seeds of changes to come.

Conclusion

Animal tales provided workers like Jean, Babé, and Henri with different ways to express their feelings towards landowners, employers, friends, and family. As a genre that was especially well suited to sharecropping regions in France, animal tales flourished in the moorlands. But even more than a static picture of the grinding labour and exploitation of sharecropping, Henri, Jean, and Babé's stories reveal strategies that real people used to negotiate their situations. Inciting pity or solidarity was a survival technique for men and women like Jean and Babé, but a younger generation, like Henri, turned their feelings to new ends. The

---

[84] Mark Konstantinovich Azadovskii, *A Siberian Tale Teller* (Austin, 1974); Hopkin, 'Storytelling, Fairytales and Autobiography'; Pooley, 'Independent Women and Independent Body Parts'.
[85] Ginzburg and Poni, 'The Name and the Game', 8.

performance was not over at the end of the story: the dissatisfaction Henri expressed set him on a new course in life.

In the 1870s Henri's tale was a warning of the previously unheard rage and pain of the exploited. It was less of an injunction to be obeyed than a code to be deciphered, less expressive of how the world already is, and more suggestive of how it should change. It is true that Henri was somewhat unusual in exploring these darker possibilities in his tales in a period when other individuals were still committed to a 'moral economy', a traditional way of doing things that the assault on de Capet, for instance, was designed to protect. But he was not the only person in the region who came to feel that if he could not change the world at least he could change himself. His muted anger was symptomatic of the feelings that would erupt with the syndicalist movement at the start of the twentieth century. In this way, the oral tradition of animal tales could both act as a brake on class consciousness, as in Jean and Babé's tales, or as a safety valve, as in Henri's. What historians need to find out is much more about who used these stories to convey which message, how individual narrators crafted emotional cultures that shaped their own life possibilities.

9

Conclusion

Historicizing the body poses particular problems to historians, especially when they aspire to write about the experiences and culture of the working population. This book has argued that folklore collections offer some of the most important materials for writing this history, and folklore methods provide the ways to interpret these materials. The traditions recorded by Félix Arnaudin depict a harsh and often violent rural bodily culture whose focus lay below the waist. But they also demonstrate the flexibility and creativity of this rural bodily culture, and its historical changeability. I have drawn attention to two big shifts in experience and thinking about the body. The first was a shift towards the exploitative labour conditions of the period when sharecropping co-existed with resin farming, a shift discussed through the example of the animal tales told by Henri Vidal and Babé Plantié and Jean Saubesty. The second general shift was towards an ever closer policing of women's bodies and sexual choices, evident in the songs Arnaudin collected. But the different individuals whose lives this book has explored talked about these shifts in different ways, because they experienced and negotiated them in different ways. Other chapters of the book situated specific individuals in these wider changes, showing how a storyteller like Marichoun Bouzats experienced the threat to the coherence of the family represented by changing forms of work and cooperation as a threat to bodily integrity itself. In a similar way, Catherine Gentes' refusal of a given sexual identity makes sense in her own life, situated as it was in a changing culture of making love.

This is above all a story of cultural changes, but these interrelated modifications of bodily expectations and feelings are not immaterial. They represent real physical changes, and to call them cultural is only to say that the focus of interpretation is on what these changes meant and how people symbolically refashioned and decoded their own experiences. To understand these changes, it is therefore necessary to understand the physical changes to the environment that have so often drawn historians to the moorlands, even if the conclusions drawn are not direct contributions to environmental history. The Arnaudin collection has little to say about this, or about electoral politics, or even the divides between monarchists, republicans, and bonapartists, or conservatives, liberals, and socialists, or Catholics and secularists. The changes rural people experienced and discussed do not necessarily correspond to the categories

Body and Tradition in Nineteenth-Century France: Félix Arnaudin and the Moorlands of Gascony, 1870–1914.
William G. Pooley, Oxford University Press (2019). © William G. Pooley.
DOI: 10.1093/oso/9780198847502.001.0001

historians know best. But old and quaint as folk traditions can appear, they are nonetheless changing.[1]

Stars and Exemplars

This argument depends on the folklore methods outlined at the start of the book. The focus on performance calls for research into the contexts, actors, and audiences involved in the transmission and recording of folk traditions, methods that will be familiar to all social and cultural historians. This begins with Arnaudin himself. Chapter 2 suggested that, like many of the nineteenth-century folklorists, he was a liminal figure. Neither very wealthy nor poor, he lived a resolutely provincial life, hardly leaving the town where he was born, yet was connected to an international correspondence network of other folklorists. Some of his informants may have been his social inferiors, or even employees, but some were at least his equal, and the relationships he struck up are hard to characterize as simple exploitation or domination. The folklorist did favours for his singers and storytellers, and in turn they provided what they knew. Rather than some outsider learning about this material for the first time, Arnaudin himself was a native speaker of the patois, and knew the songs and stories he had grown up with.

For these reasons, his manuscripts can be treated like a kind of privileged insight into local tradition, from within. They have many advantages over published folklore collections, of which the most obvious is what I have called the 'mess' they often contain. Rather than neat, final versions of a song or story, they contain contradictions, paratextual information, omissions, and multiple versions. Arnaudin not only noted what singers and storytellers performed, but sometimes what they said about their performances, and when they refused, or claimed to be unable to provide material. These texts have the advantage of representing a living tradition, folklore in action, as it was performed and adapted. Whether widely shared or deeply personal, what this material has in common is its creativity.[2] The wit of everyday speech, just like the skill evident in a long story, invites interpretation. Folk speech often speaks in codes and stereotypes. Its metaphors—such as the comparison between the human body and the pine tree— are widely shared, and deeply felt, ingrained into how people understood their most basic experiences.

This culture is both shared and personal. Different genres represent different degrees of consensus and improvisation. The dictionary notes, with their references to proverbial wisdom, or the songs sung together, provide some of the

---

[1] See for instance, Marie-Louise Tenèze's conviction that the animal tales and dancing of the moorlands were somehow 'medieval'. 'Aperçu Sur Les Contes d'animaux'.
[2] Pocius, 'Art'.

strongest evidence of community consensus.[3] But other genres are more polemical. Marichoun's legends invited discussion, even disagreement and disbelief, and the meanings of the animal tales told by Henri, Babé, and Jean only make sense when they are compared to one another, to reveal fundamentally different attitudes to work and the social order.[4] And even the most consensus-based genres leave space for individual choices, whether they are just the choice to not sing a song, or to change a few words, or to place a different emphasis. Such small choices add up to individual aesthetics.

The point is not that any given individual is typical. Rather it is that what folklorists have sometimes called 'stars'—culturally significant individuals, those who were known as important performers, even if only among a small group of friends, neighbours, and family—crafted their own performances in a way that created a repertoire of exemplars, or possible ways of behaving. For Henri, this was an identity centred on a refusal to accept an unfair social contract, and a determination to repudiate exploitation. For Marichoun, this was a fear of the dissolution of the family and the household. For Jean and Babé, it was an identity as loyal and obedient workers. For Babelic Lescarret and Mariane de Mariolan, piety was a defining characteristic. Mariouquete Labeyrie's identity was shaped around poverty, while Justine Bouniord's was focused on her relative affluence.

There are two possible misapprehensions about this argument to address. First, the value of these 'exemplars' is not simply that they are unusual. In a banal sense, every individual is different. But the value of thinking about how individuals defined themselves in exemplary ways is that in doing so they set the parameters for how other people might think about their own identities and experiences. The historian has some right to imagine the implied audience to these performances, and to think about how these star performers might have given a range of different people different ways to think about their own lives. Catherine Gentes, the seamstress discussed in Chapter 7 who omitted romantic themes from the songs she sang, makes a good example. The importance of her singing repertoire is not just that it was unusual, but that it throws added light on the generally licentious and bawdy repertoire sung by many other women. The fact that her omissions do not correspond to a particular interest in religion also suggest that this was not an important part of attitudes to love making in the moorlands.

The second possible misapprehension concerns determinism. A cultural exemplar such as that embodied by Catherine is not determined by the conditions these individuals lived in, but actively shaped in dialogue with the constraints of their lives. Catherine was not pre-destined to be averse to sexual themes because she

---

[3] Lomax, *Folk Song Style and Culture*; Wolfgang Mieder, *The Wisdom of Many: Essays on the Proverb* (New York, 1981).

[4] Dégh, *Legend and Belief*; Tangherlini, '"It Happened Not Too Far from Here...": A Survey of Legend Theory and Characterization', *Western Folklore*, 49, no. 4 (October 1990), 371–90.

was doubly marked as sexually available, being both a seamstress and having a limp. If anything, the traditions of the moorlands suggest exactly the opposite. The importance of Catherine's choices is that they were in dialogue with her occupation and her physical embodiment, but not determined by either. A history of cultures of the body tries to make sense of what real bodies meant to people, and how they used them, revealing the symbolic agency of individuals, rather than how they conformed to pre-determined conditions. But this in itself draws attention to the ways that individuals could shape their own exemplary identities.

Changing Cultures of the Body

Arnaudin's folklore collections do not lend themselves to thinking directly about the politicization of the French countryside. Nor do they have much to teach historians about the environmental reforms which most singers and storytellers passed over in silence. If historians take it on its own terms, the body is one of the central concerns of folk tradition. Chapter 4 argued that through metaphor and analogy, this is a body striving for symbolic unity and integrity, that makes sense as a series of interrelated parts, and not simply as fragments. Meaning was spread through the entire body, but the points of focus were not necessarily those of the 'modern' body discussed in the Introduction.[5] Great symbolic importance rested on the legs and buttocks, as well as the stomach. The violence associated with any talk of bodies helps to explain the cultural significance of 'teeth', but folk speech also focused on a range of delicate body parts, including the lips, and also the sensitive skin evoked by Marichoun's story of the werewolf. The shapeshifter is one example of a broader pattern of metaphors that drew links between bodily experiences and other concerns of everyday life, such as the integrity of the household. The importance of the pine tree to the local economy, and its ambivalent effects on rural life, made it a particularly rich analogy for a human body concerned above all with uprightness. Other symbolic correlations belong to the deep history of folk cultures, such as the enduring connections drawn between women's bodies, sewing, pins, and needles.[6]

Yet this was by no means an unchanging culture of the body, part of a coherent 'peasant' civilization swept away before, or during, World War One.[7] There are many small signs of cultural change in the Arnaudin collection, from the new metaphors discussed above, to the new vocabulary that appeared in the patois. It is much harder to prove that culture was changing in the ways that singers and

---

[5] Le Breton, *Anthropologie du corps et modernité*.

[6] Anne Monjaret, 'De l'épingle à l'aiguille: L'éducation des jeunes filles au fil des contes', *L'Homme*, 173 (1 March 2005); Verdier, *Façons de Dire*.

[7] This is the argument in: Segalen, *Love and Power*, 173–87; see also: Weber, *Peasants into Frenchmen*.

storytellers claimed in their songs and stories. Without such detailed folklore collections for the early nineteenth century, it can be hard to know if the growing strictness in sexual culture was real, or perceived. The evidence from other sources does support some conclusions about cultural change, however. Mentions of werewolf beliefs in criminal trials, for instance, were not uncommon in the period of Marichoun's youth in the mid-century. But by the time she told her personal story, it was unusual for werewolf beliefs to come up in court, which is why the case of the so-called 'werewolf' of Uttenheim became an international sensation.[8]

It should not surprise historians that rural culture was changing to adapt to new ways of life in the late nineteenth century, but it has proved difficult to escape the dichotomy of 'modernity' and 'tradition' championed by researchers in the second half of the twentieth century. Finding out who exactly the singers and storytellers were, what their occupations, wealth, education, and gender were, and how and where they transmitted traditions is fundamental to questioning this narrative of two opposed social systems or cultures. The fact that many of the 'folk' were also employees of the modern state or active and even relatively powerful participants in the forestation of the moorlands does not prove that their traditions were not really 'authentic': rather it proves that folklore exists in situations of contact fluidity, and not just within the isolation of some imagined traditional rural *veillée*.

The changes evident in this culture do not correspond neatly to what historians following Norbert Elias and Michel Foucault have written about civilization, interiorization, medicalization, and bio-power. They deal, instead, with many subtle shifts in bodily experiences, whether mentioned in passing—such as attitudes to fatness—or explored in detailed reflections—such as Mariane's story of the werewolf and the threat to the boundaries of the household. Bodily cultures have always been sites of tension and contest, but it is striking that the materials Arnaudin collected suggest intense conflicts over bodily autonomy. The unbridled body evident in much everyday speech, or the free sexuality of the folk songs, for instance, find their check in the growing fear of gossip that women also mentioned in their singing. The community of family and neighbours that Mariane's legend of the werewolf describes is specifically invoked to pass judgement on deviant bodily behaviours. Norms governed even posture itself, as verticality was interpreted as a moral language of laziness. But the two greatest changes in bodily experiences and attitudes evident in the Arnaudin collection are those discussed in Chapters 5 and 7. Although the body has probably always been a site of conflict, the overwhelming evidence from the animal tales and the songs is that conflicts over labour and sexual relations were intensifying in the period when Arnaudin recorded these traditions. Of course these changes are related to the changes the book has discussed, from the expansion of sharecropping to the draining of the

---

[8] It was not only reported in the French press, but as far afield as Australia, as well as being picked up by Montague Summers for his book *The Werewolf*. See: *Cairns Post* (10 February 1926).

moorlands and the planting of the forest. But from the point of view of many of the working men and women Arnaudin talked to, the changes in these two big spheres of everyday life were of most explicit importance.

The Moorlands and Beyond

If context is essential to decoding the interrelated symbolic meanings of folk cultures, then the advantages of a narrow geographical and chronological focus are clear. Understanding interrelated social, environmental, and cultural changes in even such a small and sparsely populated region is ambitious. This book has chosen to focus on the lives of specific individuals, showing how real people diverged from expectations or conformed to them, crafting their own identities in ways that would have made sense to the people they knew. In some ways, the moorlands makes an unusual example. What conflict there was between the state and local communities over the moorlands does not easily map onto a 'peasant' hunger for firewood and grazing lands. The top-down forestation project was not an attempt to protect or restore pre-existing woodlands, as it was in many of the highland areas of France.[9] Yet in other ways, the late nineteenth-century moorlands represents a dramatic caricature of changes that have been documented in many parts of France during this period: the rural exodus, the spread of centralized transport networks and literacy, and the increase in the standard of living.[10]

Historians have ventured to study the effects of these broad changes on rural culture, but have tended to come to two compatible conclusions. The first, discussed above, is the claim that this period saw the collapse of rural cultures, including cultures of the body. The second has been to study the spread of urban or 'modern' ideas about the body into the countryside, whether concerning hygiene, or disease, exercise, nutrition, or sexuality.[11] Studying folklore from within, and putting the cultural creativity of performers at the heart of understanding their attitudes to the body, produces a very different account of tensions within folk culture itself.

Some of these tensions may be particular, or particularly pronounced in the case of the moorlands. The transformation in nutrition and the increase in average heights of the moorlands were particularly dramatic, for instance.[12] Similarly, while sharecropping was present in several other parts of France, it was more common in the moorlands than anywhere else, and the materials Arnaudin

---

[9] For example: Whited, *Forests and Peasant Politics*.
[10] Weber, *Peasants into Frenchmen*.
[11] Thuillier, 'Pour une histoire de l'hygiène corporelle'; Guy Thuillier, *L'imaginaire quotidien au XIXe siècle* (Paris, 1985); Alain Corbin, 'Introduction', in *Histoire du corps*, eds. Jean-Jacques Courtine, Georges Vigarello, and Alain Corbin (3 vols, Paris: Seuil, 2006), ii, 7–10.
[12] Heyberger, *Santé et développement économique*, 85–6.

collected about this reflect the idiosyncrasy of the region. The relative unimport-
ance of Catholicism is also notable, as is the generally frank attitude to sexuality
and even contraception.[13]

In other ways, the moorlands clearly fit within cultural trends evident across
France. The triumph of black clothing and the fading belief in shapeshifters are
both consistent with how attitudes elsewhere within France were changing.[14]
A werewolf story only makes sense because of the knowledge that other people
have of the possibility of shapeshifting human beings. Any individual animal tale
draws part of its meaning from an audience knowing what animal tales in general
are like. Although scholarship on folk traditions such as animal tales or shapeshifters allows these local traditions to be placed within evolving global contexts,
the tools of comparison, such as the catalogues of tale or song types, make
comparisons with folk tradition within France more manageable.[15] What I hope
to have shown, in this small corner of a broader tapestry, is the cultural flexibility
of rural attitudes to the body, that were far from unchanging, but allowed
individuals and communities to adapt in different ways to changes that were
not always fully within their control.

[13] Alain Corbin, 'L'emprise de la religion', in *Histoire du Corps: 2 De la Révolution à la Grande
Guerre*, eds. Jean-Jacques Courtine, Georges Vigarello, and Alain Corbin, Vol. 2 (3 vols, Paris, 2006),
51–83.
[14] Corbin, 'Le sexe en deuil'.
[15] Uther, 'The Fox in World Literature'; Hutton, *The Witch*, 262–78.

Bibliography

Manuscript and Archival Sources

Archives départementales des Landes de Gascogne
'Affaires militaires', R/P, W.
'Archive Communale: Labouheyre', E DEPOT 134.
Arnaudin, Félix, 'Notes de Félix Arnaudin: Depôt du Parc Naturel Regional des Landes de Gascogne', 2 MI 29.
'État-civil', 1 MIEC.
'Monographie paroissiales', ADL 1000 J 65.
'Notaires', 3 E.
'Ponts et chaussées', S.
'Postes', PS 16 (unsorted documents).
'Recensements de la population', 6 M, 4 E.

Periodicals
Gazette des Tribunaux.
Revue des Eaux et Forêts.

Printed Primary Sources

About, Edmond, *Maître Pierre* (4th edn, Paris, 1862).
Aesop's Fables, ed. Stanley Handford (4th edn, London, 1994).
Arnaudin, Félix, *Chants populaires de la Grande-Lande et des régions voisines* (Paris, 1912).
Arnaudin, Félix, *Contes populaires recueillis dans la Grande-Lande, le Born, les Petites-Landes et le Marensin* (Paris, 1887).
Arnaudin, Félix, *Oeuvres complètes*, eds. J. Boisgontier, J.-Y. Boutet, B. Fénié, J.-J. Fénié, F. Lalanne, G. Latry, L. Mabru, J.-B. Marquette, and J. Miró (9 vols, Bordeaux, 1994–2007).
Arnaudin, Félix, 'Une Branche des Pic de la Mirandole dans les Landes', *Revue de Gascogne*, xiv (1873), 259–67.
Beauquier, Charles, *Blason populaire de Franche-Comté: Sobriquets, dictons, contes, etc.* (Paris, 1897).
Bladé, Jean-François, *Contes populaires de la Gascogne* (new edn, Pau, 2008).
Bladé, Jean-François, *Poésies populaires de la Gascogne* (3 vols, Paris, 1882).
Blanc, E., 'Les Landes, leur passé et leur avenir', *Revue des Eaux et Forêts* (1893), 401–27.
Bois, Louis Du, *Recherches archéologiques, historiques, biographiques et littéraires sur la Normandie* (Paris, 1843).
Boissier, Albert, *Carnets d'un folkloriste, 1910–1953* (2 vols, Saint-Didier-en-Velay, 1990).
Bon, Antoinette, 'Le Seigneur loup-garou. Légende de l'Auvergne', *Revue des Traditions Populaires*, v (1890), 216–18.

Caila, M. de, 'Recherches sur les moeurs des habitants des Landes de Bordeaux, dans la contrée connue ci-devant sous le nom du Captalat de Buch', in *Mémoires de l'Académie Celtique*, iv (1809), 70–82.

Carnoy, Henri, *Littérature orale de la Picardie* (Paris, 1883).

Cénac-Moncaut, Justin, *Littérature populaire de la Gascogne: contes, mystères, chansons historiques, satiriques, sentimentales, rondeaux recueillis dans l'Astarac, le Pardiac, le Béarn et le Bigorre* (Paris, 1868).

Chamberlain, A.F, 'Human Physiognomy and Physical Characteristics in Folk-Lore and Folk-Speech', *Journal of American Folklore*, vi (1893), 13–24.

Chapiseau, Félix, *Le Folk-lore de la Beauce et du Perche* (Paris, 1902).

Coissac, Georges-Michel, *Mon Limousin* (Marseille, 1978).

Cormeau, Henri, *Terroirs mauges: miettes d'une vie provinciale* (Paris, 2000).

Cosquin, Emmanuel, *Contes populaires de Lorraine comparés avec les contes des autres provinces de France et des pays étrangers* (Paris, 1886).

Cuisenier, Jean, *Récits et contes populaires de Normandie* (2 vols, Paris, 1979).

Daugé, Césaire, 'Félix Arnaudin: 1844–1921', *Bulletin de La Société de Borda* (1922), 1–5.

Daugé, Césaire, *Le mariage et la famille en Gascogne d'après les proverbes et les chansons* (3 vols, Paris, 1916).

Desbordes, Robert, *Les Syndicats résiniers dans les Landes* (Bordeaux, 1908).

Drouet, Dr, 'Le loup-garou en Limousin', *Revue d'ethnographie et de sociologie* (1911), 144–57.

Faré, Henri, ed., *Enquête sur les incendies de forêts dans la région des Landes de Gascogne* (Paris, 1873).

Foix, Vincent, *Sorcières et loups-garous dans les Landes* (new edn, Belin-Beliet, 1988).

Fraysse, Camille, 'Au Pays de Baugé', *Revue des Traditions Populaires*, xx (1905), 11–15.

Gaillard, Victor, 'L'habitant des Landes', in *Les Français peints par eux-mêmes: encyclopédie morale du 19e siècle* (Paris, 1841), ii, 413–20.

Gelin, Henri, *Légendes de sorcellerie* (Ligugé, 1898).

Gennep, Arnold van, *Le Folklore du Dauphiné, Isère. Étude descriptive et comparée de psychologie populaire* (2 vols, Paris, 1932).

Grasset Saint-Sauveur, Jacques, 'Les Landes de Bordeaux: Moeurs et usages de leurs habitants', in *Les Landes de Bordeaux: moeurs et usages de leurs habitants, suivi de Voyage dans le Département des Landes*, ed. Guy Latry (Pau, 2004), 49–67.

Guérin, Urbain, 'Paysan-résinier de Lévignacq (Landes)', *Les Ouvriers des deux mondes*, v (1884), 315–86.

Guillaumin, Émile, *La Vie d'un simple* (new edn, Paris, 1977 [1904]).

Guillon, Charles, *Chansons populaires de l'Ain* (Paris, 1883).

Hertz, Robert, 'Contes et dictons recueillis sur le front parmi les poilus de Mayenne et d'ailleurs, campagne de 1915', *Revue des Traditions Populaires*, xxxii (1917), 31–45, 74–91.

Jeffery, Brian, ed., *Chanson Verse of the Early Renaissance* (2 vols., London, 1971).

Joisten, Charles, Chanaud, Robert, and Joisten, Alice, 'Les Loups-garous en Savoie et Dauphiné', *Le Monde Alpin et Rhodanien*, i–iv (1992), 19–182.

Lambert, Louis, *Chants et chansons populaires du Languedoc* (2 vols, Leipzig, 1906).

Lavallée, Joseph, 'Voyage dans le Département des Landes', in *Les Landes de Bordeaux: moeurs et usages de leurs habitants, suivi de Voyage dans le Département des Landes*, ed. Guy Latry (Pau, 2004), 70–105.

Lavaud, Patrick, *Lo Medòc de boca a aurelha* (Bordeaux, 2011).

Lescarret, Jean-Baptiste, *Le Dernier pasteur des Landes: Étude de moeurs* (Bordeaux, 1858).

Letuaire, Pierre, *Les Cahiers de P. Letuaire, 1796–1884*, ed. L. Henseling (3 vols, Marseille, 1976).

MacPherson, James, *Fragments of Ancient Poetry* (Edinburgh, 1760).

Martinengo-Cesaresco, Evelyn Lilian, *Essays in the Study of Folk-Songs* (London, 1886).

Mauriac, François, *Thèrése Desqueyroux* (Paris, 1927).

Mensignac, Camille de, *Notice sur plusieurs coutumes, usages, préjugés, croyances, superstitions, médailles, prières, remèdes, dictons, proverbes, devinettes et chansons populaires du Département de la Gironde accompagnée d'un questionnaire* (Marseille, 1999).

Micha, Alfred, *L'Ourthe et l'Amblève* (Liège, 1919).

Nannette Lévesque, conteuse et chanteuse du pays des sources de la Loire, eds. Marie-Louise Tenèze and Georges Delarue (Paris, 2000).

Nynauld, Jean de, *De la Lycanthropie, transformation et extase des sorciers (1615)*, eds. Maxime Préaud and Nicole Jacques-Chaquin (Paris, 1990).

Ortoli, J.B. Frédéric, *Les Contes populaires de l'Ile de Corse* (Paris, 1883).

Otten, Charlotte, ed., *A Lycanthropy Reader: Werewolves in Western Culture* (Syracuse, 1986).

Pineau, Léon, 'Le Folklore de la Touraine: Le loup-garou', *Revue des Traditions Populaires*, xvii (1902), 579–80.

Poueigh, Jean, *Chansons populaires des Pyrénées françaises* (2 vols, Paris, 1926).

Queyrat, Louis, *Contribution à l'étude du parler de la Creuse. Le Patois de la région de Chavanat* (Guéret, 1924).

Sébillot, Paul, 'La Noblesse et le Tiers État', in *Le Folk-Lore de France*, vol. IV (1904).

Sébillot, Paul, 'Les Couturières', in *Légendes et curiosités des métiers* (new edn, Paris, 2000).

Seignolle, Claude, *Contes populaires de Guyenne* (2nd edn, Paris, 1971).

Sol, Eugène, *Le Vieux Quercy* (Aurillac, 1930).

Summers, Montague, *The Werewolf* (London, 1933).

Thore, Jean, *Promenade sur les côtes du Golfe de Gascogne ou aperçu topographique, physique et médical des côtes occidentales de ce même Golfe* (Bordeaux, 1810).

Toulgouat, Pierre, 'La vie d'autrefois d'après les souvenirs du "Bielhot de Sabres", dernier tisserand des Landes', *Bulletin de la Société de Borda* (1986), 183–220.

Trébucq, Sylvain, *La Chanson populaire et la vie rurale des pyrénées à la Vendée* (Bordeaux, 1912).

Verrier, A.-J. and Onillon, R., *Glossaire étymologique et historique des patois et des parlers de l'Anjou* (2 vols, Angers, 1908).

Villemarqué, Théodore Hersart de la, *Barzaz breiz: Chants populaires de la Bretagne* (new edn, Paris, 1883).

Printed Secondary Works

Abu-Lughod, Lila, 'The Romance of Resistance: Tracing Transformations of Power through Bedouin Women', *American Ethnologist*, xvii (1990), 41–55.

Agulhon, Maurice, *The Republic in the Village: The People of the Var from the French Revolution to the Second Republic* (Cambridge, 1982).

Aldhuy, Julien, 'Imaginaire géographique, idéologie territoriale et production régionale: Réflexions autour des Landes de Gascogne (XVIIIème–XIXème)', *Hegoa* (2006), http://halshs.archives-ouvertes.fr/halshs-00080645/.

Andries, Lise, 'Contes du loup', in Jean de Nynauld, *De la Lycanthropie, transformation et extase des sorciers (1615)*, eds. Maxime Préaud and Nicole Jacques-Chaquin (Paris, 1990), 197–217.

Arcangeli, Alessandro, 'Dance and Punishment', *Dance Research: Journal of the Society for Dance Research*, x (1992), 30–42.

Ariès, Philippe, *Centuries of Childhood: A Social History of Family Life* (London, 1965).

Aron, Jean-Paul, Dumont, Paul, and Le Roy Ladurie, Emmanuel, *Anthropologie du conscrit français d'après les comptes numériques et sommaires du recrutement de l'armée, 1819–1826* (Paris, 1972).

Arrouye, Jean, ed., *Jean-François Bladé, 1827–1900: Actes du Colloque de Lectoure, 20 et 21 octobre 1984* (Béziers, 1985).

Azadovskii, Mark Konstantinovich, *A Siberian Tale Teller* (Austin, 1974).

Badone, Ellen, 'Breton Folklore of Anticlericalism', in *Religious Orthodoxy and Popular Faith in European Society*, ed. Ellen Badone (Princeton, 1990), 140–60.

Bakhtin, Mikhail Mikhailovich, *Rabelais and His World*, trans. Hélène Iswolsky (Cambridge, MA, 1968).

Bardet, Jean-Philippe and Le Bras, Hervé, 'La Chute de la fécondité', in *Histoire de la population française*, ed. Jacques Dupâquier (3 vols, Paris, 1988), iii, 351–401.

Bardou, Pierre, 'Lou limajayre', in *Félix Arnaudin: imagier de la Grande Lande*, ed. Jacques Sargos (Bordeaux, 1993), 131–43.

Basso, Keith H., ' "To Give up on Words": Silence in Western Apache Culture', *Southwestern Journal of Anthropology*, xxvi (1970), 213–30.

Bauman, Richard, *Let Your Words Be Few: Symbolism of Speaking and Silence among Seventeenth-Century Quakers* (Cambridge, 1983).

Bauman, Richard, *Verbal Art as Performance* (Prospect Heights, 1977).

Bearman, Chris J., 'Cecil Sharp in Somerset: Some Reflections on the Work of David Harker', *Folklore*, cxiii (2002), 11–34.

Bearman, Chris J., 'Who Were the Folk? The Demography of Cecil Sharp's Somerset Folksingers', *Historical Journal*, xliii (2000), 751–75.

Beiner, Guy, *Remembering the Year of the French: Irish Folk History and Social Memory* (Madison, 2009).

Belmont, Nicole, *Paroles païennes, mythe et folklore: Des frères Grimm à P. Saintyves* (Paris, 1986).

Bendix, Regina, *In Search of Authenticity: The Formation of Folklore Studies* (Madison, 1997).

Benthall, Jonathan and Polhemus, Ted, eds, *The Body as a Medium of Expression: Essays Based on a Course of Lectures given at the Institute of Contemporary Arts, London* (London, 1975).

Beresford, Matthew, *The White Devil: The Werewolf in European Culture* (London, 2013).

Bhaduri, Amit, 'Cropsharing as a Labour Process', in *Sharecropping and Sharecroppers*, ed. T.J. Byres (London, 1983), 85–93.

Blécourt, Willem de, 'Monstrous Theories: Werewolves and the Abuse of History', *Preternature: Critical and Historical Studies on the Preternatural*, ii (2013), 188–212.

Bloch, Marc, *The Historian's Craft*, trans. Peter Putnam (New York, 1964).

Blok, Anton, 'Rams and Billy-Goats: A Key to the Mediterranean Code of Honour', *Man*, xvi (new series, 1981), 427–40.

Boggs, Ralph Steele, *Index of Spanish Folktales* (Helsinki, 1930).

Bottigheimer, Ruth B., 'Fairy Tales, Folk Narrative Research and History', *Social History*, xiv (1989), 343–57.

Boudon, Jacques-Olivier, *Le Plancher de Joachim: L'histoire Retrouvée d'un Village Français* (Paris, 2017).

Bound, Fay, '"An Angry and Malicious Mind?" Narratives of Slander at the Church Courts of York, c.1660–c.1760', *History Workshop Journal*, lvi (2003), 59–77.

Burke, Peter, *Popular Culture in Early Modern Europe* (New York, 1978).

Burke, Peter, *What Is Cultural History?* (2nd edn, Cambridge, 2008).

Burton, Richard, *Holy Tears, Holy Blood: Women, Catholicism, and the Culture of Suffering in France, 1840–1970* (Ithaca, 2004).

Butler, Judith, *Excitable Speech: A Politics of the Performative* (New York, 1997).

Butler, Judith, *Undoing Gender* (New York, 2004).

Bynum, Caroline, 'Why All the Fuss about the Body? A Medievalist's Perspective', *Critical Inquiry*, xxii (1995), 1–33.

Bynum, Caroline Walker, *Metamorphosis and Identity* (New York, 2001).

Cabanel, Patrick, 'La guerre des camisards centre histoire et mémoire: la perpétuelle réinvention du témoignage', *Dix-huitième siècle*, 39, no. 1 (1 July 2007), 211–27.

Cailluyer, Jean, *Regards sur l'histoire sociale des Landes* (Toulouse, 1983).

Callon, G., 'Le Mouvement de la population dans les Landes au cours de la période 1821–1920', *Bulletin de la Société de Borda* (1931), 1–28.

Certeau, Michel de, Julia, Dominique and Revel, Jacques, 'The Beauty of the Dead: Nisard', in *Heterologies: Discourse on the Other*, trans. Brian Massumi (Minneapolis, 1986), 119–36.

Cheesman, Tom, *The Shocking Ballad Picture Show: German Popular Literature and Cultural History* (Oxford, 1994).

Cholvy, Gérard and Hilaire, Yves Marie, *Histoire religieuse de la France contemporaine* (Toulouse, 1985).

Claverie, Elisabeth and Pierre Lamaison, *L'Impossible mariage: Violence et parenté en Gévaudan, XVIIe, XVIIIe et XIXe siècles* (Paris, 1982).

Clout, Hugh, *The Land of France, 1815–1914* (London, 1983).

Cocchiara, Giuseppe, *The History of Folklore in Europe* (Philadelphia, 1981).

Coffin, Tristram P., '"Mary Hamilton" and the Anglo-American Ballad as an Art Form', *Journal of American Folklore*, lxx (1957), 208–14.

Coirault, Patrice, Delarue, Georges, Fédoroff, Yvette, and Wallon, Simone, *Répertoire des chansons françaises de tradition orale* (3 vols, Paris, 1996).

Coleman, William, 'The People's Health: Medical Themes in Eighteenth-Century French Popular Literature', *Bulletin of the History of Medicine*, li (1977), 55–74.

Connerton, Paul, *How Societies Remember* (Cambridge, 1989).

Cooper, Adrienne, 'Sharecroppers and Landlords in Bengal, 1930–50: The Dependency Web and Its Implications', in *Sharecropping and Sharecroppers*, ed. T.J. Byres (London, 1983), 226–55.

Corbin, Alain, 'Douleurs, souffrances et misères du corps', in *Histoire du Corps*, eds. Jean-Jacques Courtine, Georges Vigarello, and Alain Corbin (3 vols, Paris, 2005–6), ii, 215–73.

Corbin, Alain, 'La Rencontre des corps', in *Histoire du corps*, eds. Jean-Jacques Courtine, Georges Vigarello, and Alain Corbin (3 vols, Paris, 2005–6), ii, 149–214.

Corbin, Alain, '"Le Sexe en deuil" et l'histoire des femmes au XIXᵉ siècle', in *Le Temps, le desir, l'horreur: Essais sur le dix-neuvième* (Paris, 1998), 91–105.

Corbin, Alain, 'L'emprise de la religion', in *Histoire du Corps: 2 De la Révolution à la Grande Guerre*, eds. Jean-Jacques Courtine, Georges Vigarello, and Alain Corbin, Vol. 2 (3 vols, Paris, 2006), 51–83.

Corbin, Alain, *The Life of an Unknown: The Rediscovered World of a Clog Maker in Nineteenth-Century France*, trans. Arthur Goldhammer (New York, 2001).

Corbin, Alain, *The Village of Cannibals: Rage and Murder in France, 1870*, trans. Arthur Goldhammer (Cambridge, MA, 1992).

Corbin, Alain, Courtine, Jean-Jacques, and Vigarello, Georges, eds, *Histoire du corps* (3 vols, Paris, 2005–6).

Cox Jensen, Oscar, The Travels of John Magee: Tracing the Geographies of Britain's Itinerant Print-Sellers, 1789–1815', *Cultural and Social History*, xi (2014).

Darnton, Robert, *The Great Cat Massacre and Other Episodes in French Cultural History* (New York, 1984).

Davis, Natalie Zemon, 'Proverbial Wisdom and Popular Error', in *Society and Culture in Early Modern France* (new edn, London, 1988), 227–67.

Dégh, Linda, *Folktales and Society: Story-Telling in a Hungarian Peasant Community* (Bloomington, 1969).

Dégh, Linda, *Legend and Belief: Dialectics of a Folklore Genre* (Bloomington, 2001).

Dégh, Linda and Vazsonyi, Andrew, 'The Memorate and the Proto-Memorate', *Journal of American Folklore*, 87 (1974), 225–39.

Delarue, Paul, 'Les Contes merveilleux de Perrault et la tradition populaire', *Bulletin Folklorique d'Île de France*, xiii (1951), 195–201, 221–8, 251–60, 283–91, 348–57, 511–17.

Delarue, Paul, Tenèze, Marie-Louise, and Bru, Josiane, *Le Conte populaire français: catalogue raisonné des versions de France et des pays de langue française d'outre-mer* (4 vols, Paris, 1957–2000).

Devlin, Judith, *The Superstitious Mind: French Peasants and the Supernatural in the Nineteenth Century* (New Haven, 1987).

Dorson, Richard Mercer, *Folklore and Fakelore: Essays toward a Discipline of Folk Studies* (Cambridge, MA, 1976).

Duby, Georges and Wallon, Gabriel, eds, *Histoire de la France rurale* (new edn, 4 vols, Paris, 1992).

Duden, Barbara, *The Woman Beneath the Skin: A Doctor's Patients in Eighteenth-Century Germany*, trans. Thomas Dunlap (Cambridge, MA, 1991).

Dupuy, Francis, *Le Pin de la discorde: Les rapports de métayage dans la Grande Lande* (Paris, 1996).

Efron, David, *Gesture, Race, and Culture; a Tentative Study of the Spatio-Temporal and 'Linguistic' Aspects of the Gestural Behavior of Eastern Jews and Southern Italians in New York City, Living under Similar as Well as Different Environmental Conditions* (The Hague, 1972).

Ellis, Bill, *Aliens, Ghosts, and Cults: Legends We Live* (Jackson, 2001).

Ellis, John, *One Fairy Story Too Many: The Brothers Grimm and Their Tales* (Chicago, 1983).

Faure, Olivier, 'Le Regard des médecins', in *Histoire du corps*, eds. Jean-Jacques Courtine, Georges Vigarello, and Alain Corbin (3 vols, Paris, 2005–6), ii, 15–50.

Faury, Jean, *Cléricalisme et anticléricalisme dans le Tarn (1848–1900)* (Toulouse, 1980).

Favret-Saada, Jeanne, *Deadly Words: Witchcraft in the Bocage*, trans. Catherine Cullen (Cambridge, 1980).

Festy, Octave, *Les Délits ruraux et leur répression sous la révolution et le consulat. Étude d'histoire économique* (Paris, 1956).

Flandrin, Jean Louis, *Familles: Parenté, maison, sexualité dans l'ancienne société* (Paris, 1976).

Forth, Christopher E., 'La Civilisation and Its Discontents: Modernity, Manhood and the Body in Early Third Republic', in *French Masculinities: History, Culture, and Politics*, eds. Christopher E. Forth and Bertrand Taithe (Basingstoke, 2007), 85–102.

Foster, George, 'Peasant Society and the Image of Limited Good', *American Anthropologist*, lxvii (1965), 293–315.

Foucault, Michel, *Discipline and Punish: The Birth of the Prison*, trans. Alan Sheridan (new edn, London, 1991).

Foucault, Michel, *The History of Sexuality*, trans. Robert Hurley (3 vols, 1998).

Fox, Adam, *Oral and Literate Culture in England, 1500–1700* (Oxford, 2000).

Furet, François and Ozouf, Jacques, *Reading and Writing: Literacy in France from Calvin to Jules Ferry* (Cambridge, 1982).

Gal, Susan, 'Lexical Innovation and Loss: The Use and Value of Restricted Hungarian', in *Investigating Obsolescence: Studies in Language Contraction and Death*, ed. Nancy C. Dorian (Cambridge, 1989), 313–31.

Gallagher, Catherine and Laqueur, Thomas, eds, *The Making of the Modern Body: Sexuality and Society in the Nineteenth Century* (Berkeley, 1987).

Garner, Alice, *A Shifting Shore: Locals, Outsiders, and the Transformation of a French Fishing Town, 1823–2000* (Ithaca, 2005).

Gennep, Arnold van, *Le Folklore français* (new edn, 4 vols, Paris, 1998–9).

Gennep, Arnold van, *Les Rites de passage* (Paris, 1908).

Gibson, Ralph, 'Female Religious Orders in Nineteenth-Century France', in *Catholicism in Britain and France since 1789*, eds. Frank Tallett and Nicholas Atkin (London, 1996), 105–13.

Gibson, Ralph, 'Why Republicans and Catholics Could Not Stand Each Other in the Nineteenth Century', in *Religion, Society, and Politics in France since 1789*, eds. Frank Tallett and Nicholas Atkin (London, 1991), 117–19.

Gill, Desmond, 'Tuscan Sharecropping in United Italy: The Myth of Class Collaboration Destroyed', in *Sharecropping and Sharecroppers*, ed. T.J. Byres (London, 1983), 146–69.

Gilmore, David D., *Honor and Shame and the Unity of the Mediterranean* (Washington, DC, 1987).

Ginzburg, Carlo, *The Cheese and the Worms: The Cosmos of a Sixteenth-Century Miller*, trans. John Tedeschi and Anne Tedeschi (Baltimore, 1992).

Ginzburg, Carlo, *The Night Battles: Witchcraft and Agrarian Cults in The Sixteenth and Seventeenth Centuries*, trans. John A. Tedeschi and Anne Tedeschi (London, 1983).

Ginzburg, Carlo and Poni, Carlo, 'The Name and the Game: Unequal Exchange and the Historiographical Marketplace', in *Microhistory and the Lost Peoples of Europe*, eds. Edward Muir and Guido Ruggiero, trans. Erin Branch (Baltimore, 1991), 1–10.

Goldstein, Jan, *Hysteria Complicated by Ecstasy: The Case of Nanette Leroux* (Princeton, 2011).

Griffiths, Elizabeth and Overton, Mark, *Farming to Halves: The Hidden History of Share-farming in England from Medieval to Modern Times* (Basingstoke, 2009).

Groebner, Valentin, *Defaced: The Visual Culture of Violence in the Late Middle Ages* (London, 2004).

Guillorel, Éva, Hopkin, David M., and Pooley, William G., eds, *Rhythms of Revolt: European Traditions and Memories of Social Conflict in Oral Culture* (London, 2018).

Handler, Richard and Linnekin, Jocelyn, 'Tradition, Genuine or Spurious', *Journal of American Folklore*, 97, no. 385 (September 1984), 273–90.

Harker, David, 'Cecil Sharp in Somerset: Some Conclusions', *Folk Music Journal*, ii (1972), 220–40.

Harris, Ruth, *Lourdes: Body and Spirit in the Secular Age* (New York, 1999).

Harris, Ruth, 'Possession on the Borders: The "Mal de Morzine" in Nineteenth-Century France', *Journal of Modern History*, lxix (1997), 451–78.

Harris, Ruth, *The Man on Devil's Island: Alfred Dreyfus and the Affair That Divided France* (London, 2011).

Harris-Lopez, Trudier, 'Genre', in *Eight Words for the Study of Expressive Culture*, ed. Burt Feintuch (Urbana, 2003), 99–120.

Haywood, Ian, *The Making of History: A Study of the Literary Forgeries of James Macpherson and Thomas Chatterton in Relation to Eighteenth-Century Ideas of History and Fiction* (London, 1986).

Heiniger-Casteret, Patricia, 'Une Collecte chez Jean-François Bladé', in *La Voix occitane* (Bordeaux, 2009), 599–614.

Heyberger, Laurent, *Santé et développement économique en France au XIXe siècle: essai d'histoire anthropométrique* (Paris, 2003).

Heywood, Colin, *Growing up in France: From the Ancien Régime to the Third Republic* (Cambridge, 2007).

Hobsbawm, E.J. and Ranger, Terence, eds, *The Invention of Tradition* (Cambridge, 1983).

Hochschild, Arlie Russell, *The Managed Heart: Commercialization of Human Feeling* (Berkeley, 1983).

Holbek, Bengt, *Interpretation of Fairy Tales: Danish Folklore in a European Perspective* (Helsinki, 1987).

Hopkin, David M., 'Intimacies and Intimations: Storytelling between Servants and Masters in Nineteenth-Century France', *Journal of Social History*, 51, no. 3 (February 2018).

Hopkin, David M., 'Legends and the Peasant History of Emancipation in France and Beyond', in *Storied and Supernatural Places: Studies in Spatial and Social Dimensions of Folklore and Sagas*, eds. Ülo Valk and Daniel Sävborg (Tartu, 2018).

Hopkin, David M., 'Les Religieux et la culture vernaculaire en Europe au XIXe siècle: François Cadic dans son contexte', in *François Cadic—un collecteur vannetais, 'recteur' des Bretons de Paris*, ed. Fanch Postic (Morbihan, 2011).

Hopkin, David M., 'Paul Sébillot et Les Légendes Locales: Des Sources Pour Une Histoire "Démocratique"?', in *Paul Sébillot (1843–1918): Un Républicain promoteur des traditions populaires*, ed. Fanch Postic (Brest, 2011).

Hopkin, David M., *Soldier and Peasant in French Popular Culture, 1766–1870* (Royal History Society, 2003).

Hopkin, David M., 'The Ecotype: Or a Modest Proposal to Reconnect Cultural and Social History', in *Exploring Cultural History: Essays in Honour of Peter Burke*, eds. Melissa Calaresu, Joan Pau Rubiés, and Filippo de Vivo (London, 2010), 31–54.

Hopkin, David M., *Voices of the People in Nineteenth-Century France* (Cambridge, 2012).

Hull, Isabel V., 'Review: The Body as Historical Experience: Review of Recent Works by Barbara Duden', *Central European History*, xxiix (1995), 73–9.

Hult, Marte H., *Framing a National Narrative: The Legend Collections of Peter Christen Asbjørnsen* (Detroit, 2003).

Hunt, Lynn Avery, *Measuring Time, Making History* (Budapest, 2008).

Hutton, Ronald, *The Witch: A History of Fear, from Ancient Times to the Present* (New Haven, 2017).

Illich, Ivan, 'A Plea for Body History (Twelve Years after Medical Nemesis)', *Bulletin of Science, Technology and Society*, vi (1986), 19–22.

Isambert, François-André and Terrenoire, Jean-Paul, *Atlas de la pratique religieuse des catholiques en France* (Paris, 1980).

Jacoby, Karl, *Crimes against Nature: Squatters, Poachers, Thieves, and the Hidden History of American Conservation* (Berkeley, 2001).

Jonas, Raymond, *France and the Cult of the Sacred Heart: An Epic Tale for Modern Times* (Berkeley, 2000).

Jones, Mari C., *Jersey Norman French: A Linguistic Study of an Obsolescent Dialect* (Oxford, 2001).

Jones, Mari C. and Singh, Ishtla, *Exploring Language Change* (London, 2005).

Jones, Peter, *Liberty and Locality in Revolutionary France: Six Villages Compared, 1760–1820* (Cambridge, 2003).

Jones, Peter, *Politics and Rural Society: The Southern Massif Central, c. 1750–1880* (Cambridge, 1985).

Julliard, Étienne, *La Vie rurale dans la plaine de Basse-Alsace, Essai de géographie sociale* (Paris, 1953).

Kirshenblatt-Gimblett, Barbara, 'Folklore's Crisis', *Journal of American Folklore*, 111, no. 441 (Summer 1998), 281–327.

Kuter, Lois, 'Breton vs. French: Language and the Opposition of Political, Economic, Social, and Cultural Values', in *Investigating Obsolescence: Studies in Language Contraction and Death*, ed. Nancy C. Dorian (Cambridge, 1989), 75–89.

Lakoff, George and Johnson, Mark, *Metaphors We Live By* (Chicago, 1980).

Lapalus, Sylvie, *La Mort du vieux: Une histoire du parricide au XIXe siècle* (Paris, 2004).

Laqueur, Thomas, *Making Sex: Body and Gender from the Greeks to Freud* (Cambridge, 1990).

Latry, Guy, 'Deux voyageurs de l'an VI dans les Landes de Gascogne', in *Les Landes de Bordeaux: Moeurs et usages de leurs habitants, suivi de Voyage dans le département des Landes*, ed. Guy Latry (Pau, 2004), 7–27.

Latry, Guy, 'Introduction', in *Contes des Landes*, ed. Françoise Morvan (Bordeaux, 2011), 13–28.

Latry, Guy, 'Miroirs voilés: la photographie dans l'oeuvre d'Arnaudin', in *Félix Arnaudin: imagier de la Grande Lande*, ed. Jacques Sargos (Bordeaux, 1993), 145–51.

Latry, Guy, 'Représenter dans l'ecriture: Collecte et transcription chez les folkloristes à travers un exemple gascon', *Cahiers de Littérature Orale*, lii (2002), 116–32.

Latry, Guy, 'Une Enquête de Félix Arnaudin dans le Bazadais', *Cahiers du Bazadais* (1987), 29–41.

Laurent, Donatien, *Aux Sources du Barzaz-Breiz: La Mémoire d'un peuple* (Douarnenez, 1989).

Le Breton, David, *Anthropologie du corps et modernité* (6th edn, Paris, 2011).

Le Goff, Jacques and Truong, Nicolas, *Une Histoire du corps au moyen âge* (Paris, 2009).

Leder, Drew, *The Absent Body* (Chicago, 1990).

Lefebvre, Georges, *The Great Fear of 1789: Rural Panic in Revolutionary France*, trans. Joan White (New York, 1973).

Lehning, James R., *Peasant and French: Cultural Contact in Rural France during the Nineteenth Century* (Cambridge, 1995).

Lehning, James R., *The Peasants of Marlhes: Economic Development and Family Organization in Nineteenth-Century France* (Chapel Hill, 1980).

Lescarret, Jean-Pierre, *La Vie dans la Grande-Lande au temps des bergers et des loups* (Pau, 2008).

Leshauris, Pierre, 'La Révolution de Sabres (1863)', *Bulletin de la Société de Borda* (1979), 385–410.

Lomax, Alan, *Folk Song Style and Culture* (Washington, DC, 1968).

Loux, Françoise and Richard, Philippe, *Sagesses du corps: La Santé et la maladie dans les proverbes* (Paris, 1978).

Lyons, Martyn, *Readers and Society in Nineteenth-Century France: Workers, Women, Peasants* (Basingstoke, 2001).

Magraw, Roger, 'Rural Anticlericalism in Nineteenth-Century France', in *Disciplines of Faith: Studies in Religion, Politics, and Patriarchy*, eds. Jim Samuel Obelkevich, Lyndal Roper, and Ralph Samuel (London, 1987).

Mangin, E., 'La Situation religieuse des Landes au milieu du IIème Empire', *Bulletin de la Société de Borda* (1950), 68–73.

Maria-Caballeros, José, 'Sharecropping as an Efficient System: Further Answers to an Old Puzzle', in *Sharecropping and Sharecroppers*, ed. T.J. Byres (London, 1983), 107–18.

Massé, Pierre, 'Survivances des droits féodaux dans l'ouest (1793–1902)', *Annales Historiques de La Révolution Française* (1965), 270–98.

Matteson, Kieko, *Forests in Revolutionary France: Conservation, Community, and Conflict, 1669–1848* (Cambridge, 2015).

Matthews-Grieco, Sara, 'Corps et sexualité dans l'Europe d'ancien régime', in *Histoire du Corps*, eds. Alain Corbin, Jean-Jacques Courtine, and Georges Vigarello (3 vols, Paris, 2005–6), i, 167–234.

Mayer, Arno, *The Persistence of the Old Regime: Europe to the Great War* (New York, 1981).

Maynes, Jo, *Taking the Hard Road: Life Course in French and German Workers' Autobiographies in the Era of Industrialization* (Chapel Hill, 1995).

McMillan, James, 'Religion and Gender in Modern France: Some Reflections', in *Religion, Society, and Politics in France since 1789*, eds. Frank Tallett and Nicholas Atkin (London, 1991), 55–66.

McNeill, Lynne S., *Folklore Rules: A Fun, Quick, and Useful Introduction to the Field of Academic Folklore Studies* (Colorado, 2013).

McPhee, Peter, *Revolution and Environment in Southern France, 1780–1830: Peasants, Lords, and Murder in the Corbières* (Oxford, 1999).

McPhee, Peter, '"The Misguided Greed of Peasants"? Popular Attitudes to the Environment in the Revolution of 1789', *French Historical Studies*, 24, no. 2 (20 March 2001), 247–69.

Medick, Hans and Sabean, David Warren, eds, *Interest and Emotion: Essays on the Study of Family and Kinship* (Cambridge, 1984).

Meurger, Michel, 'L'homme loup et son témoin. Construction d'une factualité lycanthropique', in Jean de Nynauld, *De la Lycanthropie, transformation et extase des sorciers (1615)*, eds. Maxime Préaud and Nicole Jacques-Chaquin (Paris, 1990), 143–79.

Mieder, Wolfgang, *The Wisdom of Many: Essays on the Proverb* (New York, 1981).

Milroy, James and Milroy, Lesley, 'Linguistic Change, Social Network and Speaker Innovation', *Journal of Linguistics*, xxi (1985), 339–84.

Mol, Annemarie, *The Body Multiple: Ontology in Medical Practice* (Durham, NC, 2003).

Monjaret, Anne, 'De l'épingle à l'aiguille: L'éducation des jeunes filles au fil des contes', *L'Homme*, 173 (1 March 2005).

Morvan, Françoise, *François-Marie Luzel: Enquête sur une expérience de collecte folklorique en Bretagne* (Dinan, 1999).

Moulin, Annie, *Peasantry and Society in France since 1789* (Cambridge, 1991).

Mulliez, Jacques, 'Du Blé, "mal nécessaire". Réflexions sur les progrès de l'agriculture de 1750 à 1850', *Revue d'Histoire Moderne et Contemporaine*, xxvi (1979), 3–47.

Noiriel, Gerard, *Les Ouvriers dans la société française* (Paris, 2002).

Noyes, Dorothy, 'Humble Theory', *Journal of Folklore Research*, 45, no. 1 (2008).

Ó Giolláin, Diarmuid, *Locating Irish Folklore: Tradition, Modernity, Identity* (Sterling, VA, 2000).

O'Neill, Brian Juan, 'Social Conflict in the Galician Folktale', *Cahiers de Littérature Orale*, xiv (1984), 13–49.

Oates, Caroline, 'Metamorphosis and Lycanthropy in Franche-Comté, 1521–1643', in *Fragments for a History of the Human Body*, eds. Michel Tazi Feher, Ramona Naddaff, and Nadia Tazi (3 vols, New York, 1989), i, 305–63.

Pearce, R., 'Sharecropping: Towards a Marxist View', in *Sharecropping and Sharecroppers*, ed. T.J. Byres (London, 1983), 42–70.

Peer, Shanny, *France on Display: Peasants, Provincials, and Folklore in the 1937 Paris World's Fair* (Albany, 1998).

Pellegrin, Nicole, 'Corps du commun, usages communs du corps', in *Histoire du Corps*, eds. Alain Corbin, Jean-Jacques Courtine, and Georges Vigarello (3 vols, Paris, 2005–6), i, 109–65.

Péristiany, Jean G., ed., *Honour and Shame: The Values of Mediterranean Society* (Chicago, 1966).

Plack, Noelle L., 'Agrarian Individualism, Collective Practices and the French Revolution: The Law of 10 June 1793 and the Partition of Common Land in the Department of the Gard', *European History Quarterly*, 35, no. 1 (1 January 2005).

Plack, Noelle L., 'Environmental Issues during the French Revolution: Peasants, Politics and Village Common Land', *Australian Journal of French Studies*, 47, no. 3 (2010).

Planhol, Xavier de, *Géographie historique de la France* (Paris, 1988).

Pocius, Gerald, 'Art', in *Eight Words for the Study of Expressive Culture*, ed. Burt Feintuch (Urbana, 2003), 42–68.

Pooley, William G., 'Can The "Peasant" Speak? Witchcraft and Silence in Guillaume Cazaux's "The Mass of Saint Sécaire"', *Western Folklore*, lxxi (2012), 93–118.

Pooley, William G., 'Independent Women and Independent Body Parts: What the Tales and Legends of Nannette Lévesque Can Contribute to French Rural Family History', *Folklore*, cxxi (2010), 190–212.

Pooley, William G., 'Native to the Past: History, Anthropology, and Folklore in Past and Present', *Past and Present*, 239, no. 1 (May 2018), e1–e15.

Pooley, William G., 'The Singing Postman: The Mobility of Traditional Culture in Nine-teenth-Century France', *Cultural and Social History*, xiii (2016), 43–62.

Porter, Roy, *Flesh in the Age of Reason* (London, 2004).

Porter, Roy, 'History of the Body Reconsidered', in *New Perspectives on Historical Writing*, ed. Peter Burke (2nd edn, London, 2001), 233–60.

Porter, Roy, 'The History of the Body', in *New Perspectives on Historical Writing*, ed. Peter Burke (London, 1991), 206–32.

Porter, Roy and Vigarello, Georges, 'Corps, santé et maladies', in *Histoire du Corps*, eds. Alain Corbin, Jean-Jacques Courtine, and Georges Vigarello (3 vols, Paris, 2005–6), i, 335–72.

Postic, Fanch, 'Le Beau ou le vrai ou la difficile naissance en Bretagne et en France d'une science nouvelle: la littérature orale (1866–1868)', *Estudos de Literatura Oral*, iii (1997), 97–123.

Rearick, Charles, *Beyond the Enlightenment; Historians and Folklore in Nineteenth Century France* (Bloomington, 1974).

Reeves, James, ed., *The Idiom of the People: English Traditional Verse* (London, 1958).

Ribéreau-Gayon, Marie-Dominique, 'Perceptions sensorielles et représentations des Landes de Gascogne', in *Le Littoral gascon et son arrière-pays* (Arcachon, 1993), 145–60.

Robb, Graham, *The Discovery of France: A Historical Geography from the Revolution to the First World War* (New York: Norton, 2007).

Roodenburg, Herman, *The Eloquence of the Body: Perspectives on Gesture in the Dutch Republic* (Zwolle, 2004).

Roper, Jonathan, 'England—the Land without Folklore?', in *Folklore and Nationalism in Europe during the Long Nineteenth Century*, eds. Timothy Baycroft and David Hopkin (Leiden, 2012), 227–54.

Roper, Lyndal, *Oedipus and the Devil: Witchcraft, Sexuality, and Religion in Early Modern Europe* (London, 1994).

Rosenwein, Barbara, 'Controlling Paradigms', in *Anger's Past: The Social Uses of an Emotion in the Middle Ages*, ed. Barbara Rosenwein (Ithaca, 1998), 233–47.

Rublack, Ulinka, 'Fluxes: the Early Modern Body and the Emotions', *History Workshop Journal*, liii (2002), 1–16.

Sahlins, Peter, *Forest Rites: The War of the Demoiselles in Nineteenth-Century France* (Cambridge, MA, 1994).

Samarin, William, 'Language of Silence', *Practical Anthropology*, xii (1965), 115–19.

Sargos, Roger, *Contribution à l'histoire du boisement des Landes de Gascogne* (Bordeaux, 1949).

Sargos, Jacques, 'Félix', in *Félix Arnaudin: imagier de la Grande Lande*, ed. Jacques Sargos (Bordeaux, 1993), 15–29.

Sargos, Jacques, *Histoire de la forêt landaise: du désert à l'âge d'or* (Bordeaux, 1997).

Schwarzbaum, Haim, *The Mishle Shu'alim (fox Fables) of Rabbi Berechiah Ha-Nakdan: A Study in Comparative Folklore and Fable Lore* (Kiron, 1979).

Scott, James C., *Domination and the Arts of Resistance: Hidden Transcripts* (New Haven, 1990).

Scott, James C., *Weapons of the Weak: Everyday Forms of Peasant Resistance* (New Haven, 1985).

Segalen, Martine, *Love and Power in the Peasant Family: Rural France in the Nineteenth Century* (Chicago, 1983).

Sennett, Richard and Cobb, Jonathan, *The Hidden Injuries of Class* (new edn, New York, 1993).

Sewell, William, 'The Concept(s) of Culture', in *Beyond the Cultural Turn*, eds. Richard Biernacki, Victoria Bonnell, and Lynn Hunt (Berkeley, 1999).

Singer, Barnett, *Village Notables in Nineteenth-Century France: Priests, Mayors, School-masters* (New York, 1983).

Smith, Jay M., *Monsters of the Gévaudan: The Making of a Beast* (Cambridge, MA, 2011).

Soboul, Albert, 'Survivances "féodales" dans la société rurale du XIXe siècle', *Annales*, 23, no. 5 (1968), 965–86.

Sohn, Anne-Marie, *Du Premier baiser à l'alcôve: La sexualité des Français au quotidien, 1850–1950* (Paris, 1996).

Sohn, Anne-Marie, 'The Golden Age of Male Adultery: The Third Republic', *Journal of Social History*, 28, no. 3 (1 April 1995), 469–90.

Specklin, Robert, 'Les Progrès techniques', in *Histoire de la France rurale*, eds. Georges Duby and Gabriel Wallon (new edn, 4 vols, Paris, 1992), iii, 167–201.

Stark, Laura, *The Magical Self: Body, Society and the Supernatural in Early-Modern Finland* (Helsinki, 2006).

Stoler, Ann Laura, *Along the Archival Grain: Epistemic Anxieties and Colonial Common Sense* (Princeton, 2008).

Stone, Lawrence, *The Family, Sex and Marriage in England, 1500–1800* (New York, 1977).

Tangherline, Timothy R., *Danish Folktales, Legends, and Other Stories* (Copenhagen, 2014).

Tangherlini, Timothy R., *Interpreting Legend: Danish Storytellers and Their Repertoires* (New York, 1994).

Tangherlini, Timothy R., '"It Happened Not Too Far from Here...": A Survey of Legend Theory and Characterization', *Western Folklore*, il (1990), 371–90.

Taussig, Michael, 'Culture of Terror—Space of Death: Roger Casement's Putumayo Report and the Explanation of Torture', *Comparative Studies in Society and History*, xxvi (1984), 467–97.

Temple, Samuel, 'The Natures of Nation: Negotiating Modernity in the Landes de Gascogne', *French Historical Studies*, xxxii (2009), 419–46.

Tenèze, Marie-Louise, 'Aperçu sur les contes d'animaux les plus fréquemment attestés dans le répertoire français', in *Lectures and Reports: Fourth International Congress for Folk-Narrative Research in Athens*, ed. Geōrgios A. Megas (Athens, 1965), 569–75.

Thompson, Stith, *Motif-Index of Folk-Literature; a Classification of Narrative Elements in Folktales, Ballads, Myths, Fables, Mediaeval Romances, Exempla, Fabliaux, Jest-Books, and Local Legends* (5 vols, Copenhagen, 1955).

Thuillier, Guy, *L'imaginaire quotidien au XIXe siècle* (Paris, 1985).

Thuillier, Guy, 'Pour une histoire de l'hygiène corporelle: Un exemple régional: le Nivernais', *Revue d'Histoire Économique et Sociale*, xlviee (1968), 232–53.

Tilly, Charles, 'Did the Cake of Custom Break?', in *Consciousness and Class Experience in Nineteenth-Century Europe*, ed. John Merriman (New York, 1979), 17–44.

Toelken, Barre, *Morning Dew and Roses: Nuance, Metaphor, and Meaning in Folksongs* (Urbana, 1995).

Toelken, Barre, *The Dynamics of Folklore* (new edn, Logan, 1996).

Traimond, Bertrand, 'Le Feu est dans la lande ou l'incendie comme fait social', *Revue Forestière Française*, xxxiie (1980), 333–43.

Uther, Hans-Jörg, 'Indexing Folktales: A Critical Survey', *Journal of Folklore Research*, xxxiv (1997), 209–20.

Uther, Hans-Jörg, 'The Fox in World Literature: Reflections on a "Fictional Animal"', *Asian Folklore Studies*, lxv (2006), 133–60.

Uther, Hans-Jörg, *The Types of International Folktales: A Classification and Bibliography, Based on the System of Antti Aarne and Stith Thompson* (Helsinki, 2004).

Verdier, Yvonne, *Façons de dire, façons de faire* (Paris, 1979).

Vigarello, Georges, 'The Upward Training of the Body from the Age of Chivalry to Courtly Civility', in *Fragments for a History of the Human Body*, eds. Michel Tazi Feher, Ramona Naddaff, and Nadia Tazi (3 vols, New York, 1989), ii, 148–97.

Vigarello, Georges and Holt, Richard, 'Le Corps travaillé: gymnastes et sportifs au XIXe siècle', in *Histoire du Corps*, eds. Alain Corbin, Jean-Jacques Courtine, and Georges Vigarello (3 vols, Paris, 2005–6), ii, 313–77.

Weber, Eugen, 'Fairies and Hard Facts: The Reality of Folktales', *Journal of the History of Ideas*, xlii (1981), 93–113.

Weber, Eugen, *Peasants into Frenchmen: The Modernization of Rural France, 1870–1914* (Stanford, 1976).

Whited, Tamara L., *Forests and Peasant Politics in Modern France* (New Haven, 2001).

Whorf, Benjamin Lee, *Language, Thought, and Reality: Selected Writings of Benjamin Lee Whorf* (Boston, MA, 1956).

Wilkins-Jones, Clive, 'One of the Hard Old Breed: A Life of Peter Henry Emerson', in *Life and Landscape: P.H. Emerson: Art and Photography in East Anglia, 1885–1900*, eds. Neil McWilliam and Veronica Sekules (Norwich, 1986), 2–6.

Williams, Alfred, *Folk-Songs of the Upper Thames: With an Essay on Folk-Song Activity in the Upper Thames Neighbourhood* (Detroit, 1968).

Zonabend, Françoise, 'Pourquoi nommer?', in *L'Identité: Seminaire interdisciplinaire*, ed. Claude Lévi-Strauss (Paris, 1977), 257–79.

Unpublished Theses

Traimond, Bernard, 'La Sociabilité Rurale Landaise: Histoire et Structure, XVIIIème–XXème Siècle', Doctorat de 3ème Cycle en Anthropologie Sociale et Historique, École des Hautes Études en Sciences Sociales (1982).

Visual Sources

'Fonds Arnaudin', Musée de l'Aquitaine.

Websites

Association d'étude, de promotion et d'enseignement des musiques traditionnelles des pays de France: 'Arnaudin: Chants populaires de la Grande-Lande 2', https://web.archive.org/web/20130712040203/http://www.aepem.com/Arnaudin2.php.

Galli-Dupis, Florence, 'Les Fonds Félix Arnaudin (1844–1921), collecteur et photographe des "Choses de l'ancienne Grande Lande"', www.garae.fr/spip.php?article206.

Regal, Brian, 'Where Have All the Werewolves Gone?', *Fortean Times* (2010), http://www.forteantimes.com/features/articles/3061/where_have_all_the_werewolves_gone.html.

Index

Note: For the benefit of digital users, indexed terms that span two pages (e.g., 52–53) may, on occasion, appear on only one of those pages.

Aarne, Anti 22–3
Aarne-Thompson-Uther tale-type catalogue
    ATU 103C ('The Donkey, the Wolf and the
        Lion') 148 n31, 150
    ATU 123 ('The Wolf and the Seven Young
        Kids') 149–50
    ATU 155 ('Ingratitude is the World's
        Reward') 152
    ATU 333 ('Little Red Riding Hood') 22–3, 58–9
    ATU 716 ('The Halfchick Tale') 149–50
    ATU 752A ('Christ and St Peter in the Barn')
        134–5
    ATU 753 ('Christ and the Smith') 134–5
    ATU 1182 ('The Level Bushel') 134–5
About, Edmond 76, 81, 84n.199
    novel, Maître Pierre 11–12, 58–9
Abu-Lughod, Lila 28, 146n.21
Académie Celtique 33–4
acquaintances, networks of 60–1
Aesop's Fables 26, 143, 146–7; see also animal
    tales
ageing 65
agro-pastoralism 66–7
agro-sylvopastoralism 15–16
alcohol; see drunkenness.
Aldhuy, Julien 12n.63
American Civil War 14, 84–5
Andries, Lise 94n.22, 98n.46, 99n.48, 101–2,
    101n.64
anger
    involuntary social response 6–7
    liver believed to be seat of 71–2
    'right to feel' 157–8
    strategy to overcome oppression 157–8
    viciousness, audacity, and 71
animal tales 58–9, 143n.1, 145–50, 158–63,
    162n.1, 165–7
animal tales
    as allusions to historical events and
        problems 145–6
    emphasized social cohesion 150
Anjou, the 94, 100–1
anthropologists, linguistic 65

anti-clericalism 102–3, 137–8
antimodernism 44
Anzieu, Didier 101
archaeological finds 41–2
Archives Départementales des Landes 38
Arengosse 80–1
Ariège, the 16, 110
Ariès, Philippe 6–7
Arjuzanx 15–16, 80–1
Arnaudin, Simon (known as Félix) 21–6
    avoided racial discussions 35–6
    chose not to rely on marginal figures 58
    collected folklore in everyday situations 46
    death of 37–8
    desire to preserve what he saw as a
        disappearing world 61–2
    dialect dictionary 46
    dialect notes 67
    dictionary notes 87
    difficulty collecting religious folklore 136–7
    dishonest or self-deluding 76
    emphasized elderly patois speakers 50–1, 53
    ethnographic interest in women's
        work 67–8
    felt like an outcast within his own class 31–2
    fieldwork in Souis 44–5
    fieldwork techniques similar to laboratory
        control 44–5
    folklore collection 9–10, 16, 161–2
    In the Days of the Stilts 38
    influenced by right-wing thinkers 36–7
    interest in folk songs 40
    key elements of self-image 29–30
    majority of informants were younger than
        himself 53
    many of his singers and storytellers born
        outside the moorlands 61–2
    mortality a recurring theme in diary 31
    nostalgia for a disappearing existence 27–8
    obsession with purity of local dialect 69–70
    obsessive nature of 45–6
    overemphasized ideas of static
        communities 61–2

Arnaudin, Simon (known as Félix) (*cont.*)
  paradoxes to his hunt for perfect
    informants 62–3
  participant in oral cultures of the Landes
    57–8
  played down influence of print culture and
    mobility 58–9
  politics fit poorly to ideas of left and right
    36–7
  preferred female informants 53–4
  pruned his singers and storytellers based on
    clear criteria 51, 53
  Remnants of the Old Moorlands 38
  resistance to other folklorists 35–6
  romanticized the occupations of his
    informants 58–9
  saw forestation as key factor in decline of rural
    traditions 33–4
  selective vision of conduits along which
    traditions travel 58–9
  sense of authenticity 62–3
  series of notebooks on 'Fairs' 47
  sought out the oldest informants 53
  staged photographs of all-female spinning
    bees to illustrate books 53–4
  strict ideas about purity of dialect and
    patois 66–7
  suspicious of verbose informants 62–3
  tried to play down role of certain types in his
    fieldwork 55–6
  typical folklorist 47–8
  understanding of links between singing,
    dancing, and sex 138–9
  vision of the pre-modern 'dreamscape of
    unlimited space' 28–9
  worried about death of Gascon patois 69
Arnaudin, Ariste 29, 31
Arnaudin, Barthélémy 29, 43, 57, 67–8
Arnaudin, Michaël 31–2
arsonists 14–15
Asbjørnsen, Peter Christen 33–4
authenticity 22
  of folklore, debate over 27–8
Auvergne 102–3
Azadovskii, Mark Konstantinovich 159n.84

Bacon, Marie-Thérèse 29
Bakhtin, Mikhail 22n.122, 75
Baladès, Claire 52
Baladès, Marie (known as Marichoun) 56–7, 60
ballads 21, 127–8
baptisms, ringing church bells after 134
Bardet, Jean-Philippe 108n.9, n11

Bardou, Pierre 44n.113
Barranx, Serge 36
Barrès, Maurice 36–7
Barrière, Jeanne (known as Cérise) 52
Barthélémy, Jean 37n.60, 45
Bascons, village of 94
Bauman, Richard 20n.107, 125n.3
Bazadais, the 39
Bearman, Chris J. 20n.112, 45n.119, 49n.1
Beauce, the 102–3
Beauquier, Charles 101n.61
Beaurepaire-Froment, Paul 34–5, 37–8
Beauvau 100–1
beggars, semi-professional and professional 58
Beiner, Guy 18–19, 60n.58, 89n.3
beliefs
  shapeshifters 94
  sorcery 94–5
  supernatural 106
  werewolves 164–5
  witchcraft 96–7
Belmont, Nicole 34, 34n.34
Bendix, Regina 22n.123
Beresford, Matthew 97n.39
Bernède, Jean 46
Bertrande, Dorine 49
Bhaduri, Amit 144n.8
'Bibliothèque bleue' (popular pamphlets) 58–9
biomechanical experience 80
bio-power 165–6
black clothing 110, 167
Bladé, Jean-François 27–8, 113, 146–8, 152
Blanc, E. 15n.82
blasphemy 99–100
Blécourt, Willem de 93n.19
Bloch, Marc 60
Blok, Anton 107n.1
bodies
  epoch-specific 1–2
  exploited 143
  monstrous 89
  sexuality, and rites of passage, popular
    traditions around 1
bodily autonomy, conflicts over 165–6
bodily cultures 165–6
bodily expectations, modifications of 161–2
bodily experiences 64–5
bodily identities 125–6
bodily integrity 99–100, 161
bodily morality, judgemental 81–2
body parts
  and fluids 70
  metaphors for understanding 79–80

body size, references to 82
body, the
    as burden 78–9
    changing attitudes to 23
    changing culture of 16, 164
    compared to pine tree 84, 87, 162
    cultural flexibility of rural attitudes to 167
    folk traditions of 65
    historicizing the 161
    historiography of 87
    history of 3
    metaphorical boundaries of 93
    'modern' 5–7, 24–5, 64, 75, 164, 166
    opaque languages of 74
    pre-medical knowledge of 78
    references to religion when discussing 87
    sexual toponymy of 77
    spread of urban ideas about 166
Bois, Louis du 102–3
Boisgontier, Jacques 38, 41–2, 92n.13
Boissier, Albert 102nn.66,68
Bon, Antoinette 102n.71
Bordeaux 36, 56, 61–2, 84–5, 101–2
Boré, Tchitchique de 111–12
Boston 155–6
Bottigheimer, Ruth B. 27n.2
Boucher, Henry du 36
Boudon, Jacques-Olivier 17n.92
boundaries, symbolic significance 105
Bouniord, Jean 120
Bouniord, Justine 163
Bourg 95–6
bourgeois and Catholic moral codes 25–6
bourgeoisie 31–2, 57–8
Bouzats, Jean 92–3
Bouzats, Marichoun 25, 161
'Branch of the Pic de la Mirandole Family in the
    Landes' (article) 40
breasts, sexualization of 77–8
Breton, David le 4–5, 164n.5
Breton songs 27–8
Brittany 101–2, 134–5
Brouqueyre, Catherine (known as Liya de
    Bidau) 45
Broustra, Elisabeth 60–1
'Bulletin de la Société de Borda' (journal) 36
Burke, Peter 19n.101, 33–4
Burton, Richard 133n.50
Butler, Judith 19–20
Bynum, Caroline Walker 87n.227, 99n.50,
    100n.59, 101n.62

Cabanel, Patrick 22
Cailluyer, Jean 11, 144n.4

Callen 54–5
Callon, G. 108n.10
Camelat, Miquèu 69
Carnoy, Henri 29, 33–4, 99
Cataline (singer) 42–3
Catholic Church 102–3, 133
Catholic moral codes 25–6
Catholicism 94, 102–3, 105–6, 133, 166–7
    and scepticism, tensions between 103
    continued to pervade everyday life in the
        moorlands 135
    in the moorlands 134
Cazade, Jean 43, 56–7, 67
Cazalis 53
Cazaux, Guillaume 20n.111
Cénac-Moncaut, Justin 105, 116
Certeau, Michel de 31n.17
Cévennes, the 98–9
Cézallier 98–9
chaffres (nicknames) 52
Chaingy 98–9
Chalosse, the 39
Chamberlain, Alexander Francis 1
charivaris (local songs sung to shame sexual
    and marital transgressions) 113
Chasteigner, Alexis de 46n.123
chastity
    absent partners as a justification for 127
    and strict social codes 107
    emphasis on 107, 113
    silence and 125
    songs emphasizing 113
Chateaubriand, François René de 29–30
Cheesman, Tom 22n.126
children as an asset 117–18
Cholvy 137n.74
Christian imagery 136–7
Church and secular authorities, conflicts
    between 137–8
Church and State, conflict over 141–2
civilization 17, 165–6
class 22, 105, 144, 147–8
    and occupational identity 66
    social 57–8
Claverie, Elisabeth 17n.94, 75n.107
clientelism 14
clothing 65–6
    and sexuality, association between 78
    black 110, 167
    red 110
Clout, Hugh D. 12n.62
Cobb, Jonathan 155–6
Cocchiara, Giuseppe 33–4
Coffin, Tristram P. 109n.16

Coirault index of French traditional song
Coirault 102 ('When the Shepherdess Goes to the Fields') 130
Coirault 114 ('I Made Myself a Bunch of Flowers') 129
Coirault 206 ('How Is Your Flock, Shepherd?') 124
Coirault 206 ('The Herb of Love') 116
Coirault 320 ('I Have a Little Brother') 126
Coirault 320 ('The Fountain that Restores Virginity') 116
Coirault 407 ('A Kiss to Remember Me By') 113
Coirault 716 ('Take a Sweet Kiss from My Mouth') 113
Coirault 801 ('The Girl Who Had Strolled out Too Often') 113
Coirault 902 ('A! Mama, Are You Pleased?') 139–40
Coirault 1113 ('The Girls of La Rochelle') 129–30
Coirault 1115 ('Jan de la Réole Had Three Daughters') 127–8
Coirault 1502 ('My Father's Garden') 129
Coirault 1710 ('On the Bridge of Lyon') 127, 133–4
Coirault 1803 ('In the Town of Salles There Is') 129–30
Coirault 1829 ('On the Pretty Bridge of Avignon') 127
Coirault 1905 ('On the Banks of a Stream') 129
Coirault 2301.1 ('The Girls of La Réole') 128, 133–4
Coirault 2315 ('The Mother and Her Daughter') 128
Coirault 2325 ('Pregnant Although She Didn't Feel It') 108–9
Coirault 2417 ('I Got Up Early in the Morning, the Very Early Morning') 126–7
Coirault 3809 ('When the King Went Out') 131
Coirault 4517 ('On the Bridge of Toulouse, Saint John's Eve') 129, 138
Coirault 4521 ('My Father and Mother') 126–7
Coirault 4717 (Good Evening, Master of the House) 127–9
Coirault 4905 ('I Want to Choose') 122
Coirault 5405 ('Girls, Don't Love Men So Much') 123
Coirault 5703 ('My Father Is Marrying Me Off, Ho Ramonet') 130–1
Coirault 5704 ('The Old Man Who Would Only Sleep') 114–15
Coirault 5715 ('The Old Man Who Made His Wife Spin') 113–14
Coirault 5721 ('Not All of the Cows on the Moor Belong to the Same Farmer') 114
Coirault 6206 ('Do Not Go, Beautiful') 129
Coirault 6219 ('My Father and My Mother') 126–7
Coirault 6416 ('All Artisans Are Thieves') 105
Coirault 7211 ('I Got Up Early, Before the Sun Had Risen') 128
Coirault 8112 ('There's a Place in Heaven') 126–7
Coirault 8805 ('When Jesus-Christ Was Just a Child') 133–4
Coirault 12005 ('The Girl Who Wanted to Shave Her Cunt') 113–14
Coirault 12008 ('The Miller Cuckolded by the Monk') 113–14
Coirault, Patrice 25, 105n.81, 110
catalgoue 113–14, 116, 124, 140n.96
Coissac, Georges-Michel 96, 103, 103n.77
Coleman, William 6n.28
Colin, Michel 60–1, 67–8, 111–12
colonization, internal 11–12
colour red associated with sexuality and drinking 107
Commensacq, village of 66–7, 80–1, 94, 134, 136–8
Connerton, Paul 2n.4
contraception
attitude to 166–7
songs about 116
spread of 108
Cooper, Adrienne 145n.9
Cooper, Frederick 21n.120
Corbières, the 16, 145
Corbin, Alain 7, 17, 78n.131, 107, 141n.106, 145, 167n.13
Cormeau, Henri 96–7
corpulence, attitudes and references to 82–3, 87–8, 165–6
Corsica 150–1
Cosquin, Emmanuel 36n.51
Couloudou, Marie 81
Courréguelongue, Marie 122
courting, rural, revolution in 108
courtship, rejecting 127
Couture, Léonce 36
Cox-Jensen, Oscar 59n.48
Creuse 102–3
criminal trials, werewolf beliefs in 164–5
Crouzet, Henri 12
Cuisenier, Jean 102–3
cultural changes 161–2

cultural concerns 122
cultural contact, prejudice against 22
culture
    as process of making meaning 19–20
    fin-de-siècle 37
    of honour and shame 107
    of singing 125
    oral 18–19, 22, 53, 57, 148
    traditional, mobility and transmission of
        61–2

dancing and sex, symbolic relationship
        between 138–9
Darlanne, Marie 30–2, 43–4, 67–8, 132–3
Darnton, Robert 19–21, 66nn.11–12
Darwinism, relationship between traditions, race,
        and 35–6
Daugé, Césaire 7–8, 29–30, 46
Daugé, Maria 67–8
Daugey, Marie 114
daüne (Gascon word for a matriarch) 92–3
Dauphiné, the 101–2
Davanne, Alphonse 42n.99
Davis, Natalie Zemon 19n.99
Degert, Antoine 37n.61
Dégh, Linda 20n.110, 22n.126, 53n.22, 54n.27,
        56n.38, 61n.69, 89–90, 158n.83
Déguignet, Jean-Marie 17
Delarue, Georges 58n.46, 110
Delarue, Paul 22–3, 58–9, 100nn.54,56
democratic politics in the nineteenth century,
        spread of 16
demonologists 97–8
Desbordes, Robert 9n.52, 16n.83
devotion and anti-clericalism, micro-geography
        of 137–8
diabolism 99–100
dialect dictionary 41–2, 46
dialect, local, emotional palette of 71–2
dîme (feudal charge) 13–14
donkeys, loyalty of 147
Dordogne, the 145
Dorson, Richard Mercer 22n.125
Dourthe, Victor 35–6
'dream of uprightness' 78–81
Drouet, Dr 97n.36, 99
drunkenness 70–1, 75–6, 87–8, 115–16
Dubos, Marguerite (known as Maguide) 47
Dubos, Rose 53
Duby, Georges 17n.89
Ducourneau, Marilys 132n.48
Ducout, Marie (known as Caroline) 60
Duden, Barbara 72, 72n.58, 73–4, 75n.98
Dufourcet, Eugène 35

Dulas family, the 57
Dulau, Joseph 49
Dulucq, Marie 51–2, 140–1
Dumartin, Abbé 94n.20
Dumartin, Fillon 60
Dupart, Jeanne (known as Marianne
        Hailloune) 54–5
Dupin of Loc-Bielh, Marinéte 49
Dupin-Brigailles, Justine 123–4
Dupin-Brigailles, Marguerite 120
Dupouy, Étienne 51
Dupuch, Antoine 68
Dupuy, Francis 54–5, 153n.52, 154nn.57,60,
        158n.80
Duvic, Marie 53

ecological imbalances 12–13
economic and non-economic structures of
        subordination 144–5
economy, local, and landscape, changes to 12–13
economy, moral 160
ecotypes 22–3, 110
Efron, David 2n.4
Elias, Norbert 165–6
Ellis, Bill 90n.4
Ellis, John 20n.112
Emerson, Peter Henry 37n.57
emotional palette of local dialect 71–2
emotional pressures and social changes 155
environmental change, historians of 16
environmental changes in the moorlands 32
epoch-specific bodies 1–2
Escource, village of 92–3
ethnic groups 22
ethnographic photographs 42
evil eye, the 70
exhaustion, fatigue and tiredness 81–2
exploitation, metaphor for 84
exploitative labour conditions 161
exploited bodies 143

fairies 59n.48, 66n.12, 98–9
fairs
    annual 47
    series of notebooks on 47
fairytales 20n.112, 27n.2, 58n.45, 98n.46,
        146n.19, 159n.84
family
    institutions of 158
    planning 117–18
    religion, gender, and 101
Faré, Henri 14–15
fatness; see corpulence
Faure, Olivier 6n.29

Favret-Saada, Jeanne 94–7
Fédéroff, Yvette 110
Félibrige (organization for the promotion of
    Occitan language and culture) 36
fellatio and masturbation 5
female sexuality
    increasing pressure on 118
    repression of 25
feminine culture 25–6
feminine identity, rebellious 115
feminization of religion 133n.50
Festy, Octave 17n.95
feudalism 57–8
fieldwork methods 42
fin-de-siècle culture 37
First World War 6, 40, 43, 101–2
Flandrin, Jean 6–7
Foix, Vincent 35, 40–1, 44
folk memory, endurance of 21
folk songs, free sexuality of 165–6
folk tales 21, 145–6, 152
    Spanish 147n.24
folk tradition, -s 16, 106, 164, 167
folklore
    and 'fakelore', dichotomy between 22
    as a performance 18–21
    collections 2–3
    debate over authenticity of 27–8
    definition of 18
    forestation and 32
    idea of a national 33–4
    key methodology of 22–3
    oral 18, 59–60
    political imperative to record 33–4
    religious 134–7
    source for understanding rural cultural
        change 17
    sources 17–18
    sources and methods of 23
    studies in France, 'renaissance' in 34
    supernatural 94
'folkloric turn' 18–19
Folksongs of the Grande-Lande 45
food supply 12–13
forest fires, series of 14–15
forestation
    and folklore 32
    as key factor in social changes leading to
        decline of rural traditions 33
    mass 12–13
    of the moorlands 31–2
    project 166
Forth, Christopher E. 37n.59
Foster, George 6

Foucault, Michel 5, 7n.40, 77, 165–6
foxes; see also animal tales
    and sharecroppers 144
    'Fox and the Wolf', tale of 148
    Reynard the Fox 26
    Roman de Renart 26, 58–9, 143, 145–6
    tales about 26
France, Marie de 98–9
France, rural politics in 16
France, Vichy 36–7
Fraysse, Camille 94n.20, 101n.60
French countryside, politicization of 164
French Revolution 9, 41–2, 60
    devastation of communal woodlands
        during 10–11
    Revolutionary reforms 10–11
French rural civilization, apogee and crisis
    of 17
Fronsac, Pierre 52
Furet, François 59n.57

Gaidoz, Henri 34, 40–1
Gallagher, Catherine 2n.9
Gallicisms 85–6
Galli-Dupis, Florence 38n.66
Garbay, Antoine 147–8
Garbay, Jeanne (known as Néte de Penalh)
    50–1, 121–2
Garein, village of 137–8
Garner, Alice 13n.70
Gascon
    as threatened language 85–6
    decline of 64
    dialect, dictionary of 24–5
    dialects 86
    language of everyday life 67
    patois 40–1
Gascony, moorlands of 7, 27
Gastes 80–1
Gazette des Tribunaux 69nn.27–28
Gelin, Henri 99n.51
Gellibert, Jean 61–2
Gellibert, Jeanne 121–2
Geloux 51–2
gender 19–20
    complementarity 123
    imbalance 53–4
    religion, and family 101
Gennep, Arnold van 1, 7–8, 24, 101–2, 140
Gentes, Catherine 125–34, 137–42, 161,
    163–4
Gévaudan, the 98–9
Gill, Desmond 154
Ginzburg, Carlo 141–2, 159n.85

Gironde, the 9, 14–15, 136–7, 140–1
Glize, Marinette 47
goblins 98–9
Goethe, Johann-Wolfgang von 29–30
Goldstein, Jan 2n.6, 72n.58, 76n.116
gossip
  and jealousy 117, 123
  rise of 117
Goujon, Catherine 140–1
Goyard, Jean 95–6
graffiti, text messages, and social media,
    traditions of 21
'Grande-Lande', the 9, 39, 66–7
Great Fear of 1789 59–60
'Grimm of Gascony', the 27–8
Groebner, Valentin 70n.40
Guérin, Urbain 12n.66, 39n.72, 118n.63
Guibert, Louis 102n.71
Guillaumin, Émile 13–14, 144–145, 153n.56
Guillon, Charles 114n.40
Guillorel, Éva 21n.118
Guyenne 96–7, 102–3

Handler, Richard 21n.115
Harris, Ruth 1n.3, 19n.104, 37n.58
Harris-Lopez, Trudier 25n.134
Hartland, Edwin Sidney 34
Hazera, Jean 51
health and sickness, figurative language of 74
Heiniger-Casteret, Patricia 28n.6
Hélias, Pierre-Jakez 17
Hertz, Robert 96
Heyberger, Laurent 1n.3
Heywood, Colin 3
Hilaire 137n.74
Histoire du Corps 1–2
historiography of the body, narratives of 87
Hobsbawm, E.J. 20n.105
Hochschild, Arlie Russell 155n.69
Holbek, Bengt 146n.19
Holt, Richard 82–3
honour 6, 70–1, 107, 111–13, 131, 158
Hopkin, David M. 16, 17n.93, 18–20, 20n.109,
    21n.118, 23n.129, 37n.55, 42n.98, 44n.111,
    45–6, 57n.41, 62, 89n.3
horror, poverty of 97
'Hottentots' 8–9
household, the 26
  integrity of 164
  survival of 105
housing, conflicts relating to 153–4
Hult, Marte H. 33n.32
hunger 65–6, 82
Hunt, Lynn Avery 21n.120

Hutton, Ronald 97–8
hygiene, poor 6

identity
  bodily 125–6
  rebellious feminine 115
  regional 64
  shaped around poverty 163
illegitimate children, attitudes to 111–12
Illich, Ivan 2n.5
illness, early modern experiences and
    descriptions of 73–4
informants, linguistic 67–8
innuendo 77
interiorization 75, 87, 165–6
Ireland 33–4
Isambert, François-André 134n.56

jealousy 71–2, 121–4
Jeffery, Brian 110n.22
Johnson, Mark 65n.8
Joie, Anne 47, 62–3
joiners as embodiment of crudeness of manual
    labour 151–2
Joisten, Charles 96–8, 101–3
Jones, Mari C. 64n.3, 85–6
Jones, Peter 13n.71, 16, 16nn.85,87,
    21nn.113,120, 90n.6
Julia, Dominique 31n.17
Julliard, Étienne 21n.120
Jurman, hamlet of 92–3

Kirshenblatt-Gimblett, Barbara 21n.116
Kutern, Lois 69n.28

La Rochelle, wayward young girls of 133–4
La Tradition 35
Labeau, Denis 50–1, 56–7, 61–3
Labeyrie, Mariouquéte 118, 123–4, 163
Labile, Catherine 151–2
Labouheyre, village of 29, 39, 47, 56, 66–8,
    105–6, 148–9
  coin haul at 41–2
  mayor of 57
labour
  agricultural, grind of 7, 73–4, 78–80,
      159–60
  agricultural, tough and nutrition standards
      poor 83
  and exploitation 84–5
  changing demands of 108
  conditions, exploitative 161
  conflicts over 165–6
  demands and exhaustion of 87

labour (*cont.*)
  'emotional' 155–6
  manual, crudeness of 151–2
  modern urban wage 21–2
  movements of the early twentieth century 147
  sex, identity, and 80–1
  wage, new forms of 154
labourers
  Labourers agricultural, more undernourished
    than rest of French population 82
  Arnaudin preferred to present his informants
    as 57–8, 62, 67–8
  bodily experiences of 78–9
  Gascon the language of everyday life for 67
  manual, distrust of 36–7
  mobility of 80–1
  rural 1–2, 9–10, 56–7
labouring classes, rural, bodily culture of 65–6
Labrouche, Paul 36, 42n.100
Lacave family, the 57
Lafon, E. 15n.82
Lagoffun, Léonie 151–2
Laguë, Jean 51–2, 62–3
Lakoff, George 65n.8
Lalanne, Marie 56
Lamaison, Pierre 17n.94, 75n.107
Lamartine, Alphonse de 29–30
Lambert, Louis 110n.20
Landes de Gascogne 9, 13–15, 24, 29, 108,
    136–7, 144–5
landowners 84
  and sharecroppers, tensions between 16
language, -s
  change 84
  death 86
  of sexuality 77
  struggles between 66
Laporte, Talinote 67–8, 97
Laqueur, Thomas 2n.9
Larrouy, Pierre 61–2
Lassévils, Bernard 44–5
Latappy, Jeanne 61–2
Latrille, Augustine 53
Latry, Guy 3–4, 32, 35n.47, 36n.53, 38n.65, 39,
    41–2, 44–5, 44n.112, 46n.123, 53n.23,
    136n.71
Lavallée, Joseph 4n.14
Lavaud, Patrick 53n.25
Le Bras, Hervé 108n.9, n11
Le Goff, Jacques 7n.40
Le Sen, village of 137–8
Leder, Drew 3, 65nn.6,10
Lefebvre, Georges 59–60
Lehning, James 21–2

Lescarret, Jean 105
Lescarret, Jean-Baptiste 8n.46, 10–12, 29n.10,
    32n.26, 35–6, 38, 42–3
Lescarret, Jean-Pierre 4nn.15–16,21, 10n.55,
    11nn.57–58, 13–14n.75, 14n.76, 16n.86,
    52n.15, 54n.31, 67n.16
Lescarret, Magdelaine (known as Babelic)
    135–6, 163
Lescarret, Marichoun 89, 91–106
Leshauris, Pierre 135n.61, 145n.12
Lestruhaut, Marie 60–1
Letuaire, Pierre 95n.25
Lévesque, Nannette 58n.46, 99–100, 106
Limousin, the 80–1, 102–3
limping 138
linguistic anthropologists 65
linguistic changes 64
linguistic informants 67–8
linguistic regions 66–7
Linnekin, Jocelyn 21n.115
literacy 17, 59n.57, 60n.58, 166
Lit-et-Mixte, sharecroppers in 15–16
Little Red Riding Hood 22–3, 58–9
Lomax, Alan 109
Lombroso, Cesare 37
Lorraine (region) 16
Lorty, Marie 45
Loubère, Simon 134–5, 137–8
Loubeyre, Anne (known as Anna de
    Hourrègues) 60–1, 124
Loubeyre, Marie 60–1
Loux, Françoise 1
love-making
  attitudes to 163
  changing culture of 161
love
  permissive culture of 117
  shared culture of 109
Luglon, sharecroppers of 15–16
Luzel, François-Marie 36–7
lycanthropy; *see* werewolf
Lyons, Martyn 58–9

magic books 99–100
Magnes, Martin 57, 122
Magnes, Romain 55–6
Magraw, Roger 137nn.73,76
malnutrition 73–4
Marensin, the, region of 9, 39
Maria-Caballeros, José 144n.6
Marillier, Léon 34
Mariolan, Mariane de 57, 60, 90–3, 134–5,
    147, 163
marital bond, intensification of 123

marriage
  becoming both more fraught and more
    tender 123
  birth, and illegitimacy rates 108
  bond, intensification of 123
  sex before 118
Marsan, Pétronille (known as Filhoun) 60–1
Martinengo-Cesaresco, Evelyn Lilian 109n.13
Massé, Pierre 9n.51
Massif Central, the 101–2, 134–5
masturbation and fellatio 5
Matteson, Kieko 10n.56, 90n.6
Mauriac, François 84n.199
Mayenne, the 102–3
Mayer, Arno 21n.117
Maynes, Mary Jo 17n.92
McNeill, Lynne 18
McPhee, Peter 11n.57, 16n.87, 90n.6
MacPherson, James 27–8
McWilliam, Neil 37n.57
medical discourses 74
medicalization 7, 87, 165–6
Medick, Hans 108n.8
Mediterranean cultures 107
Mélusine (journal) 34
men and women, struggles between 66
Mensignac, Camille de 36, 94n.20, 100n.55
menstruation 139–40
metaphors
  for understanding body parts 79–80
  of local speech 156–7
  physical 65–6
Millien, Achille 34, 108–9
Milroy, James 69n.31
Milroy, Lesley 69n.31
Mios, village of 69
Miró, Juan 66n.13
misogynist songs and speech 87–8, 122
Mistral, Frédéric 36
mobility and transmission of traditional
    culture 61–2
'modern body' 5–7, 24–5, 64, 75, 164, 166
Mol, Annemarie 2n.6
Monge, hamlet of 148–9
Monicien, Jean 43, 67, 67n.20
Monjaret, Anne 164n.6
Mont-de-Marsan, town of 24, 29, 140–1
moorlands, the
  agro-sylvopastoralism of 15–16
  Catholicism in 134
  changing boundaries of everyday life in 89–90
  Christian imagery in 136–7
  dialect of 85–6
  environmental changes in 32

forestation of 31–2, 90
  sexual culture of 107–8
  sexual repression of 110
  sexually explicit songs of 111–12
  social tensions in 144–5
  songs that emphasized chastity not sung
    in 113
moral codes, bourgeois and Catholic 25–6
'moral economy' 160
moralism 117
moralistic community regulation 107
morality, bodily 81–2
Morvan, Françoise 38n.69
Moulin, Annie 13n.74
'moussuralhe' ('gentlemen') 67
Mulliez, Jacques 6n.31
Musset, Alfred de 29–30

Napoleon III 56–7
Napoleonic Wars 41–2
néo-dîme, references to 13–14
networks of close acquaintances 60–1
Nièvre, the 108–9
night visions 95–6
Nivernais, the 101–2
Noiriel, Gerard 154n.62
Normandy 102–3
Noyes, Dorothy 47n.136
nudity 78
nutrition, poor 6, 65
Nynauld, Jean de 97n.40

Oates, Caroline 98n.41
Occitan language and culture 36
occupational identity and class 66
Onillon, R. 94n.20
oral
  agreement 9–10, 155
  communication 58–9
  culture 18–19, 22, 53, 57, 148
  folklore 18, 59–60
  networks 59–60
  tales 35–6, 42, 58–9, 145–6, 150, 152
  tradition 27–8, 33, 35–6, 42, 58–9, 62–3,
    152, 158–60
Ortoli, Frédéric 150–1
'Ossian' poems 27–8
Otten, Charlotte 97n.40, 101n.63
Ozouf, Jacques 59n.57

Pabon, Jean 47
Parc Naturel Régional des Landes de
    Gascogne 38
'Pasteurian Revolution' 6

pastoralism 54–5
  and the pine, battle between 14–15
  conflict over 93
  marginal economy of 117–18
patois 35, 39–42, 47, 50–1, 64–7, 69–72, 84–6,
    162, 164–5
patriarchalism 123, 155
Pearce, R. 144n.5
'peasant' bodily culture 26
Pédéluc, Jean 81
Peer, Shanny 34n.37
Pellagra (fatal skin disease caused by
    malnutrition) 73–4
Pellegrin, Nicole 78–9, 87n.227
'Petites-Landes', the 39
Petit-Louricat hamlet of 51–2
Petronius 101
photographs, ethnographic 42
physical metaphors 65–6
Physiocrats 11–12
Picardy 99
piety 134, 163
  as defining characteristic 163
pine tree 10–11, 79
  human body compared to 84, 87, 162
  importance of 164
Pineau, Léon 100n.54, 102–3
Pissos 27, 66–7, 80–1
Plantié, Elisabeth (known as Babé) 40, 43,
    50–1, 61–2, 67–8, 111–12, 117, 125–6,
    130, 140, 147–52, 161–3
poaching 156–7
Polhemus, Ted 2n.4
politicization of the French countryside 163–4
politics and love-making, link between 108–9
Pomade, Marie 51n.8
Poni, Carlo 142n.108, 159n.85
Pontenx, village of 57
Pooley, William G. 19n.102, 20n.111, 21n.118,
    24n.133, 53n.24, 55n.36, 58n.46, 95n.24
Porter, Roy 1–2, 6, 64n.1, 70n.32, 72n.71
Postic, Fanch 34n.40, 42n.97, 89n.3, 103n.73
Poudens, Beroun 147
Poudens, Elisabeth 68
poverty 75
  and sexuality 117–18
  identity shaped around 163
  of horror 97
pre-marital sex 128
proletarianization 57–8, 147–8, 154–5, 159
proverbs 46
Pruzeau, Jeanne 140–1
Pyrenees, the 15–16, 134

Quercy, the 102–3
Queyrat, Louis 94n.20

Raba, Jeanne 140–1
Raba-Triscos family, the 140–1
Rabelais 75–7
Ranger, Terence 20n.105
Raymond, Anna 43
Raynaud, Catherine 60–1
Raynaud, Marie 60–1
Rearick, Charles 34, 34nn.35,38
rebellious feminine identity 115
Rebiste gascoune (journal) 36
red
  as cultural symbol 110
  associated with sexuality and drinking 107
  clothing, temptations of 110
Reeves, James 109n.17
regional identities 64
religion
  conflict 103
  feminization of 133n.50
  gender, and family 101
  religious folklore 134–7
Renwick, Roger de van 107n.4
'repercussion' 100
resin collectors' syndicate 144–5
'resistance, romance of' 28
Revel, Jacques 31n.17
'Revolution of Sabres' (riot) 135
Revolutionary assault on the commons 10–11
Revue de Gascogne (journal) 36, 40
Revue des Traditions populaires (journal) 34, 94
Reynard the Fox, tales of; see foxes.
Ribéreau-Gayon, Marie-Dominique 13n.70
Richard, Philippe 1
Richet 136–7
rites of passage, popular traditions around
    sexuality, bodies, and 1
Robb, Graham 9n.48
Rolland, Eugène 34
Roman de Renart; see foxes
Roodenburg, Herman 79n.144
Roper, Jonathan 34n.36
Roper, Lyndal 1n.3, 4–5
Roquefort 39
Rosenwein, Barbara 158n.79
Rossat, Arthur 41
Rouchaleou, Marie-Jeanne (known as
    Marguerite) 53
Rousseau, Jean-Jacques 29–30
rural attitudes to the body, cultural flexibility
    of 167

rural bodily culture 7
rural civilization, French, apogee and crisis
   of 17
rural cultures, collapse of 166
rural exodus 166
rural labouring classes, bodily culture of 65–6
rural politics in France 16
rural syndicalist movement 9, 15–16, 57–8, 160
rural tradition and urban modernity, false
   dichotomy between 21–2

Sabean, David Warren 108n.8
'Sabres, Revolution of' (riot) 135, 145
Sabres, village of 39, 51–2, 66–7, 80–1, 111–12,
   137–8
Sahlins, Peter 16n.85, 18–19
Saint-Étienne, town of 101–2
Saint-Sauveur, Jacques Grasset 76
Samarin, William 126n.4
Sand, George 29–30
Sargos, Jacques 3–4, 8n.45, 9n.50, 10–11, 10n.53,
   12n.62, 13–14, 13n.68, 14n.78, 15n.80,
   16n.86, 35n.43, 44nn.111,113, 55n.34,
   58n.44, 82n.185, 91–2, 151n.45, 154n.63
Sargos, Roger 9n.50, 10nn.53–54, 13n.68,
   17n.90, 137n.75
Sart, Joseph (known as Jules) 44, 57,
   117, 159
satanic dealings 99–100
Satyricon 101
Saubesty, Jean (known as 'the Boss') 40, 60–2,
   117, 148–52, 161–3
Sävborg, Daniel 89n.3
Savoie 101–2
Schweitzer, Charles 46n.127
Scott, James C. 28, 145–7, 151, 158n.78
   Weapons of the Weak 28
seamstress, -es
   and singing, connection between 140–1
   associated with sexual licence 139–40
   suspected of being fallen women 139–40
Sébillot, Paul 7–8, 34, 36–7, 37n.61, 40, 56–7,
   63n.78, 93n.16, 94–5, 136–7
Second Empire 14
Second Republic 14
secular authorities and the Church, conflicts
   between 137–8
secularization 7
Segalen, Martine 109n.18, 164n.7
Seignolle, Claude 96–7
Sekules, Veronica 37n.57
Sennett, Richard 155–6
servants as point of access into working-class
   culture 62

Sewell, William 19n.101, 20–1
sewing
   and limping 138
   considered incompatible with married
      life 140
   singing, and sex, cultural connections
      between 139–40
sex
   and dancing, symbolic relationship
      between 138–9
   and marriage, attitudes to 126–7
   before marriage 118
   extra-marital 25–6
   increasing liberalization of 25
   never a taboo of rural society 109
   pre-marital 128
   reticence about 133
   singing, and sewing, cultural connections
      between 139–40
sexual
   anatomy 77
   and marital transgressions 113
   assaults 77
   attacks, victims of 77
   behaviour 107, 117, 122
   culture 107–8, 110–11
   honour 70–1, 111–12
   identities 24–5
   identity, given 161
   knowledge 77
   liberation of the Third Republic 108
   licence 139–40
   meaning 77–8
   relations, carefree 111–12
   relationships 26
   repression 110
   revolution, urban, of the Third Republic 124
   revolution 107–8
   status 139–40
   toponymy of the body 77
sexuality 65, 76–7
   and clothing, association between 78
   and drinking, illicit topics of 125
   and poverty 117–18
   attitude to 166–7
   bodies, and rites of passage, popular traditions
      around 1
   female, increasing pressure on 118
   female, repression of 25
   of folk songs 165–6
   patterns of de-emphasizing 127
sexualization 87
   of the breasts 77–8
sexually explicit songs of the moorlands 111–12

shapeshifters 93, 95–8, 102–4, 167; *see also*
   werewolf
   belief in 94, 167
   metaphor linking bodily experiences and
     concerns of everyday life 164
   possibility of 167
   published narratives about 94–5
   religious explanations for aetiology of 99–100
sharecroppers 14, 16, 26, 57–8, 61–2, 67, 81–2,
     84, 117, 145
   and landowners, tensions between 16
   foxes and 144
sharecropping 9–10, 14–16
   and problems of rural social relations 155
   as personal relationship between father of
     household and landowner 155
   co-existed with new forms of wage labour 154
   dominated local agriculture 61–2
   'emotional labour' involved in 155–6
   expanding system of 13–14
   poverty placed no constraint on
     sexuality 117–18
   sources of conflict common to 153–4
   tool of proletarianization 57–8
   well suited to areas where class domination is
     extreme 144–5
shepherds 54–5
sickness and injury as forbidden topics 74
silence and chastity 125
Singer, Barnett 29n.12, 157n.76
Singh, Ishtla 64n.3
singing; *see* songs and singing
skin-ego 101
sleep paralysis 95–6
slenderness, new cult of 82–3
Smith, Victor 58n.46, 99–100
Soboul, Albert 9n.51, 13n.72
social boundaries 99–100
social changes 121–2, 155
   and emotional pressures 155
social class 57–8
social cohesion 150
social order 99–100
social reformers 101–2
Sohn, Anne-Marie 25n.136, 76–8, 107–8,
     117n.59, 120n.71, 124, 141–2
Sol, Eugène 97n.37
Solférino 56–7
songs and singing
   and culture, relationship between 109
   and dancing, traditional 134–5
   and seamstresses, connection between 140–1
   and storytellers 49
   Breton 27–8

concentrate on making love 109
   cultures, local 110–11
   daring or sexually explicit 111–14
   meeting point between individual feelings and
     desires 108–9
   present a communal consensus 125
   sewing, and sex, cultural connections
     between 139–40
   shared culture of 125
   sung to shame sexual and marital
     transgressions 113
sorcery, belief in 94–5; *see also* witches and
   witchcraft
Sore, village of 11, 14
Souis, fieldwork in 44–5
Sourbès, Pierre 145
Sournet, Pierre 138
Souvestre, Emile 36–7
Specklin, Robert 154n.59, 157n.73
speech, everyday, was misogynist 87–8
speech, local, metaphors of 156–7
standard of living, increase in 166
Stark, Laura 6–7, 71n.52
Stoler, Ann Laura 28
Stone, Lawrence 6–7
Storch, Johann 73–4
storytellers, singers and 49
subordination, economic and non-economic
     structures of 144–5
Summers, Montague (book, *The Werewolf*) 95–6
supernatural
   belief 106; *see also* beliefs
   figures 98–9
   folklore 94
   manifestation of 91
   narratives 70–1
syndicalist movement 9, 15–16, 57–8, 160

Taithe, Bertrand 37n.59
tales
   animal 58–9, 143n.1, 145–50, 158–63, 162n.1,
     165–7
   folk 21, 145–6, 152
   oral 35–6, 42, 58–9, 145–6, 150, 152
   Spanish 147n.24
Tangherlini, Timothy R. 53n.21, 54n.27, 106n.85
Temple, Samuel 9n.47
Tenèze, Marie-Louise 22–3, 58–9, 58n.46,
     100n.56, 145–6, 155
Terrenoire, Jean-Paul 134n.56
Third Republic 25, 107–8
   'Republic of Hygiene' 6
   sexual liberation of 108
   urban sexual revolution of 124

Thompson, Stith 22–3, 23n.130, 135n.59
Thore, Jean 39n.72, 76, 151
Thuillier, Guy 6, 166n.11
Toelken, Barre 18, 20–1, 107n.4, 109n.14,
    110n.21, 128n.19
Toulgouat, Pierre 14n.77
Toulon 103
Touraine, the 102–3
tradition, -s
    oral 27–8, 33, 35–6, 42, 58–9, 62–3, 152,
        158–60
    traceability of 22–3
Traimond, Bernard 15n.81, 16n.86, 54–5, 107–8
transport networks, spread of centralized 166
Trébucq, Sylvain 53n.25
Trensacq, village of 80–1, 137–8, 143
Truong, Nicolas 7n.40

urban ideas about the body, spread of 166
urban modernity and rural tradition, false
    dichotomy between 21–2
urban sexual revolution of the Third
    Republic 124
Uther, Hans-Jörg 22–3, 146n.18, 152n.50, 155,
    167n.15
'Uttenheim, the Werewolf of' 95–6, 164–5;
    see also werewolf

Valk, Ülo 89n.3
Vazsonyi, Andrew 89n.2
veillées (social gatherings) 58–60
Verdier, Yvonne 1, 2n.4, 87n.230, 139–40,
    139n.90, 140n.97
Verrier, Anatole-Joseph 94n.20
vices 81–2
Vichy France 36–7
Vidal, Dominique (known as Menicot) 147–8
Vidal, Henri 31–2, 43–4, 117–18, 143–9,
    151, 161–3
Vidal, Jean 57
Vigarello, Georges 70n.32, 79n.144, 82–3
Villemarqué, Théodore Claude Henri Hersart de
    la 27–8
Villenave 80–1
Vinson, Julien 34

violence 65, 75
    as fact of everyday life 6–7
    casual attitude to 75

Wallon, Gabriel 17n.89
Wallon, Simone 110
'web of dependency' 144–5
Weber, Eugen 2n.8, 3–4, 3nn.10,13, 6–7, 57n.40,
    63, 164n.7, 166n.10
werewolf 7, 89, 91; see also shapeshifters
    and threat to boundaries of the
        household 165–6
    banal and inoffensive 97
    book, The Werewolf by Montague
        Summers 95–6
    disgusting rather than terrifying 97
    had little to do with real wolves 97–8
    in criminal trials 164–5
    known by many names 98–9
    legend 25, 90–1
    lycanthropy 94–6, 103–4
    methods of transformation 99
    not what modern readers might expect 97
    of Uttenheim 95–6, 164–5
    story of 93, 164, 167
    tradition 93
Whited, Tamara L. 12n.61, 166n.9
Whorf, Benjamin Lee 65n.5
Wilkins-Jones, Clive 37n.57
Williams, Alfred 42n.102
witches and witchcraft 7, 94–5, 98–9, 105–6
    belief in 96–7
    legitimized by the French criminal justice
        system 95–6
    sorcery 94–5
women
    expressed resentment of untrustworthy,
        exploitative, and jealous men 122
    fallen 132, 139–40
words actively construct bodies 65
working practices 65
written and oral cultures, cultural contact
    between 22

Ygosse, village of 80–1